D0031866

The Meat Question

The Meat Question

Animals, Humans, and the Deep History of Food

Josh Berson

The MIT Press
Cambridge, Massachusetts
London, England

This book was set in Stone Serif and Stone Sans by Jen Jackowitz. Printed and bound in the United States of America.

Library of Congress Cataloging-in-Publication Data is available.

ISBN: 978-0-262-04289-5

10 9 8 7 6 5 4 3 2 1

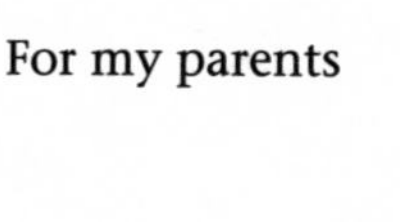

For my parents

Contents

Acknowledgments

This book was seven years in the making, and I have accumulated many debts. I have benefited from the support of staff and colleagues at the Max Planck Institute for the History of Science, the Rachel Carson Center for Environment and Society, the Max Planck Institute for Human Cognitive and Brain Sciences (CBS), the Hubbub initiative, and the Berggruen Institute. At CBS, Daniel Margulies and Natacha Mendes went out of their way to make me feel at home, as did Katja Heuer, Veronika Krieghof, and Arno Villringer. A number of people at Hubbub, notably Lynne Friedli, gave feedback on an early sketch for this book. At the Berggruen Institute, Nils Gilman, Jenny Bourne, Tobias Rees, and Dawn Nakagawa created the conditions for its completion. Andy Lakoff made possible my concurrent affiliation with USC.

Short-term fieldwork at the Wangka Maya Pilbara Aboriginal Language Centre, Port Hedland, in May 2010 influenced this book in ways neither my interlocutors nor I anticipated, and I am grateful to the staff and board members of Wangka Maya. Grace Koch put me in touch with the centre. Eleanora Deak facilitated my visit.

This project benefited from a 2015 workshop on "charismatic substances" that I helped organize, and I thank my co-organizer, Stefanie Gänger, and the participants. In the final years of research, Hilary Smith and Ben Wurgaft became key interlocutors. Hilary made time to read a big chunk of the manuscript and shared her own work on nutrition in China. Ben read the whole thing and offered detailed feedback. He also shared chapters from his book in progress on cultured meat.

Others who have influenced this book include Asif Agha, John Tresch, and Fernando Vidal. Shane Anderson, Geof Bowker, Marc DuBois, Hannah

Landecker, Hélène Mialet, João Rangel de Almeida, David Rocks, and John Stilgoe provided feedback of a less structured kind. Amanda Yiu and Rita Tishuk gave me places to stay. Suresh Ariaratnam encouraged me to think strategically about the book's reception. Beth Clevenger, Virginia Crossman, and Susan Clark made working with MIT Press a pleasure.

One evening in September 2014, Jessy Layne Tuddenham and I sat on the waterfront in Thessaloniki looking out at the Aegean and talking about meat. In the years since, I have returned to Jessy's questions that night about evolution and behavioral plasticity: If we are well adapted to eat meat, does that not mean we'd be better off if we did? Over the course of the writing of this book, Jessy served, unwittingly, as my model reader. When the text was complete but rough, she made time to read the whole thing, pushing me to clarify the argument and simplify the language. This in spite of the frank craziness she's put up with from me in consequence of this book. I am grateful for her help, but more than that, I am grateful simply to share a life with her.

Prologue: Breakfast at the End of Empire

In December 2015 I had lunch with an old friend. This was in Philadelphia. We went to a place that served vegan street food. There were kimchi tempeh tacos, sabich stuffed with tofu rather than egg, dandan noodles flavored with shiitake in place of pork. The place was packed. The prices, it need hardly be said, were not what they might have been in Tuxtla, or Baghdad, or Chengdu. Nonetheless, we emerged into the bright sun of an unseasonably warm late autumn day reeking of charcoal, hearts racing and faces flushed from chiles.

Ten days earlier, I'd picked up a financial news magazine left on a seat in a departure lounge and learned that October had marked the dawn of a new era for the Australian livestock industry: the live export of cattle by airplane. The test flight, a Boeing 747 that took off from Melbourne on October 20 carrying 150 head of cattle bound for Chongqing, came on the heels of a trade agreement between China and Australia that had cleared the way for a vigorous expansion of livestock exports. From 2012 to 2015, Australian beef exports to China grew sixfold in dollar terms, and China's demand for beef and other livestock products provided a key impetus for the trade agreement. Australian livestock exporters had long been pioneers in the shipment of live animals. The October 2015 Melbourne–Chongqing test flight represented a creative response to Chinese health regulations mandating that imported livestock be slaughtered within 90 kilometers (55 miles) of port of entry. The firm that arranged the flight described it thus:

> Angus and Hereford cattle were packed onto the aircraft's main deck—where you'd sit as an economy passenger—in crates of four or five. . . . The cows were given limited food and water before the trip to reduce the mess they'd make during shipment. What they did excrete during the 13-hour flight was soaked up by absorbent mats, which were destroyed at the destination, along with the crates.

These two scenes—lunch crush at the vegan street food bar, the Melbourne–Chongqing cattle run—stand as diametrically opposed points on a circle delimiting our theme. Meat is a large topic, so large that its character depends on where you are situated with respect to it. For many people, meat exemplifies privilege, and the power to have one's demand for meat satisfied—to have cattle fasted, crated, and flown 4,600 nautical miles—is economic power at its purest. For a smaller number of people, it is the power to refuse meat, indeed, to have animal-based dishes recast along animal-free lines, that exemplifies economic privilege. Animals raised for slaughter were once a key form of currency. Today they're an emblem of global capitalism.

The aim of this book is to unpack what I've come to call the Meat Question—*Should humans be eating meat, and if so who, and what kinds, and how much?*—in the most comprehensive way possible. The perspective we adopt is broad in the way suggested by the juxtaposition of vegan street food and live air freight. It is deep in that it encompasses the history of human meat eating and human relationships with other gregarious vertebrates over a span of more than 2 million years.

These relationships are fundamentally economic relationships, which is not to say that they are not at the same time political, ecological, emotional, and spiritual. In his landmark essay "The Original Affluent Society" (1972), the anthropologist Marshall Sahlins observes that at the end of the day, all economic relationships resolve to questions about what people eat and how they get it. As the anthropologist David Graeber shows in *Debt* (2011), you don't need cash, or even precisely defined units of credit, to have an economy. Historically, most economies have been founded not on currency but on debt, often denominated in human lives. Where currency has emerged, standards of commensuration for different debts have often been fluid and negotiable, with different kinds of transactions conducted with different tokens of exchange: firearms, bars of metal, bolts of cloth, strings of cowries, human beings, livestock. But the 5,000-year period that Graeber covers in *Debt* represents just the tail end of the nearly 2 million years since recognizably human animals first walked the Earth—and camped, and cared for their young, and went out in search of food. This is where the human economy begins, and this is where the story of the human relationship with meat begins too.

Carnivore Planet

Humans are eating more meat. Between 2010 and 2050, global demand for meat is projected to double. This comes on top of a historic surge in demand—between 1960 and 2010, per capita meat consumption in the developing world more than doubled, while in China, total meat consumption grew ninefold. In just the five years ending in 2015, Chinese beef imports grew tenfold as upwardly mobile consumer tastes shifted away from the historically favored, less expensive pork.

Much of this imported beef has come from Australia. Australian livestock producers, it is fair to say, are salivating at the prospects for growth afforded by new access to the Chinese market. But there is more to this story. In 2012, just as Australian cattle exports to China started to surge, the Australian government declared an end to a seventeen-year drought that had decimated the arid grasslands of Queensland and the southeast. The years since the Millennium Drought ended have seen rainfall below historic averages over a wider part of Queensland than during the second half of the drought. Cattle are grazers—ground feeders—but in the absence of grass, ranchers have taken measures to force their herds to behave like browsers, pulling down live mulga trees so that the cattle can get at the leaves. In 2014, Australian cattle ranchers culled—slaughtered—more than 9 million animals for want of adequate pasturage. In this context, market expansion looks less like a strategy of long-term growth than like a one-time fix for oversupply.

In every part of the world, producing meat on the scale necessary to meet current and forecast demand requires a huge commitment of resources. Let's start with land. Food production uses approximately 38 percent of the Earth's ice-free terrestrial surface area. Of that, 12 percent is given over to crops, 26 to pasturage. But 35 percent of the Earth's global crop yield goes to producing concentrated feedstocks for livestock. Upward of 75 percent of the Earth's agricultural land is devoted to raising animals for meat along with dairy products and eggs.

This proportion will increase as confined or "landless" production using concentrated feedstocks becomes the modal form of livestock production. By 2006 estimates, pure grazing systems accounted for just 8 percent of global meat production, confined feeding systems 45 percent, with the balance involving a mix of pasturage and confinement. The vast majority of growth in livestock production over the next twenty years will be in confined systems. Currently, in Europe and North America, just 40 percent of crop output goes directly to meeting human needs; in Africa, by comparison, it is 80 percent. So in those parts of the world with the most productive, most intensively managed agricultural surfaces, the majority of agricultural land is dedicated to livestock. No matter how carefully managed the livestock system, this represents a net loss for food production over using the same land to produce food that would go directly to meeting human needs. Taking feed, fertilizer, and fuel together, livestock production consumes 58 percent of the biomass that humans draw out of the biosphere annually.

What about water? Livestock accounts for nearly a third of the anthropogenic—of human origin—freshwater footprint. Ninety-eight percent of the water used in livestock production goes to feed production, so water costs depend on *feed conversion ratios*—how efficiently animals put on weight. These vary widely by species, breed, and living conditions. But even just considering protein conversion, where you'd think animals would have an advantage over plants, in terms of water costs, you'd be better off growing legumes than raising chickens. The water cost of feed production also depends on how you're supplying animals with nutrition—that is, how much pasturage and how much concentrated feedstock. It takes a lot more water to produce concentrated feedstocks than to keep pasture green, so again we see that *using cropland to support livestock yields a net loss in food production capacity.*

So far I've been talking about water footprint as if all types of water use were equivalent. In fact, water footprint encompasses three kinds of water uses: surface and groundwater consumed in the course of producing something ("blue" water), rainwater similarly consumed in the course of production, and "greywater" or runoff, water that carries by-products of production—pollutants—to the water table. More than 87 percent of livestock-related water is rainwater, so droughts like that in Queensland place huge marginal stress on aquifers.

Now let's consider greenhouse gas emissions. The most recent estimates from the Food and Agriculture Organization (FAO) integrate country-level data up to 2005. On the basis of the model produced from these data, the FAO estimates that livestock production accounts for 7.1 gigatons (Gt) of

CO_2-equivalent gas emissions (that is, a volume of gas equivalent in its contribution to climate change to 7.1 Gt carbon dioxide) annually. Two sources account for most of this burden: 45 percent comes from feed production, 39 percent from the methane produced by ruminants in the course of enteric fermentation. Livestock emissions include nearly half the global anthropogenic burden of methane, for nitrous oxide more than half. This 7.1 $GtCO_2$-equivalent represents 14.5 percent of global anthropogenic greenhouse gas emissions from all sources—*more than the total generated by all forms of transport,* including automobiles, marine freight vessels, and airplanes. If you take into account land use change—for example, the loss of carbon sinks from deforestation as land gets converted into crops and pasturage—the sum rises to 18 percent. Is this unreasonable? For reference, the food system as a whole—including not just agriculture but transport, processing, marketing, and preparation at the consumer end of the value chain—generates no more than 29 percent of global emissions. So livestock production accounts for more than half of all food-related emissions.

Livestock production carries other, less commonly mentioned costs. Chiefly, it is the main source of anthropogenic emissions of *reactive nitrogen species*—ammonia, nitrogen oxides, substances that are essential to plant growth but that at levels beyond those required to sustain biomass turnover contribute to eutrophication, leading to less resilient biomes. I could continue, but you get the point: in land, biomass, water, and deleterious by-products, animal-derived foods are expensive to produce.

They're not getting cheaper as fast as you might think. In the twenty years from 1985 to 2005, global crop yields per area harvested increased by about 20 percent. That's taking into account expansions in surface area under production, increased planting of multiple crops on the same surface in a single year, and a net shift of agricultural surface area from temperate zones to the tropics. Twenty percent sounds like progress until you hear that in the twenty years from 1965 to 1985, yields increased 56 percent (these figures do not take into account the longer-term costs, including soil exhaustion, aquifer depletion, and reactive nitrogen mobilization, of the intensive techniques of agriculture necessary to achieve these gains). In light of steeply declining marginal gains in agricultural productivity, even proponents of "sustainable intensification" have concluded that there is no way to meet human nutritional demands simply by closing yield gaps, that is, the gaps between the yields achievable using carefully selected cultivars and the most intensive techniques of land management and the yields commonly attained in parts of the world where these techniques are not widespread. *Demand-side mitigation*—getting people to change their eating habits—is the key to keeping up with demand. Mainly, that means reducing demand for meat and other animal-derived foods. And yet demand-side mitigation gets practically no attention in policy circles.

As things stand, worldwide demand for meat will grow at double the rate for rice and cereals over the next thirty years. When we ask how we're going to feed a world of 9.6 billion people, what we're asking is how we're going to feed a world of 9.6 billion carnivores—and what we're going to do with the waste.

Income and Evolution

More often than not, when you reel off a string of figures about global trends in animal consumption, you're met with a shrug. By this I mean not that people don't appreciate that these trends pose a problem, just that they're not surprised. This failure to be impressed takes two related forms.

With some audiences you hear: meat, more than any other kind of food, is *income elastic*. When people have more money, they eat more meat, and as incomes rise, so does demand for meat. For all that poverty and hunger remain pressing problems, incomes in the developing world have risen substantially over the past two generations. The same parts of the world that have seen dramatic growth in incomes have also seen dramatic urbanization, and urban populations tend to have higher incomes than rural populations. In light of these facts, how could you not expect meat consumption to shoot up? We see this phenomenon historically in the North Atlantic world, and we should expect it in China, Brazil, and everywhere else where growing numbers of people have enough money to purchase meat on a regular basis.

Geographer Vaclav Smil, an authority on energy flows in the meat economy, takes a longer view:

> There is absolutely no doubt that human evolution has been closely linked in many fundamental ways to the killing of animals and eating their meat. . . . We are, indubitably, an omnivorous species with a generally high degree of preference for meat consumption, and only environmental constraints and cultural

> constructs of preindustrial societies led to lower meat consumption, a shift that was reversed in all modern affluent societies.

Smil's formulation, with its appeal to evolution, exemplifies the other form that the failure to be impressed by trends in meat consumption takes: *Meat made us human.* Meat made us what we are, and, by implication, meat continues to be essential to human flourishing today. We cannot simply wish away 2 million years of evolution.

Chances are these two statements—affluence means meat, meat made us human—seem uncontroversial. On one level, the Meat Question is a question about what the economist Amartya Sen, in his essay *Poverty and Famines*, called *food entitlements*—who has access to what and by what means (for instance, cash income, family ownership of agricultural capital). When we talk about an urban world, a world where people depend on income for food entitlements, entitlements boil down to purchasing power. In a world where aggregate purchasing power is growing, and with it aggregate entitlements to high-quality food, it seems inevitable that meat consumption should grow too.

I'm going to argue that this view misrepresents both the role meat has played in humanity's history and the role it plays in the global economy today. Not only did meat not make us human in ways that should determine how we eat in the future, we should not even feel confident that income elasticity is mediating rising demand for meat today.

Setting aside what we think we know about evolution and income, it is not hard to see the appeal of income elasticity: it allows us to model household-level behavior with data about trends in income and diet at the regional or country level. Unfortunately for methodological ease, it turns out that when you ask people about their income and food choices, you don't consistently see evidence of income elasticity. In one survey commissioned by the London-based policy research institute Chatham House, in fact, a positive correlation between household income and meat consumption appeared more often in high-income countries than in emerging economies.

In chapter 8 we'll take a closer look at income elasticity. For now, I start by asking: If it's relatively straightforward to get data that call into question our null hypothesis about the drivers of demand for meat, why do we continue to take this hypothesis for granted?

To answer this question, we need to ask a further question: How do we know what we know about the role that, as Smil puts it, "the killing of animals and eating their meat" played in human evolution?

Man the Hunter

> Hunting is the master behavior pattern of the human species. It is the organizing activity which integrated the morphological, physiological, genetic, and intellectual aspects of the individual human organisms and of the population who compose our single species. Hunting is a way of life, not simply a "subsistence technique," which importantly involves commitments, correlates, and consequences spanning the entire biobehavioral continuum of the individual and of the entire species of which he is a member.

This is William Laughlin, from his contribution to the 1968 volume *Man the Hunter,* proceedings of an eponymous symposium held at the University of Chicago in 1966. More than any other event, "Man the Hunter" marks the emergence of human behavioral ecology—essentially, the study of how foragers, people who meet their nutritional needs by hunting and gathering, get by—as a distinct field of research. When I read comments such as Smil's, I often think of Laughlin's remarks. But the symposium's conveners, Richard Lee and Irven DeVore, did not share Laughlin's conviction. Participants, they write, had "agreed to use the term 'hunters' as a convenient shorthand, despite the fact that the majority of peoples considered subsisted primarily on sources *other than meat*—mainly wild plants and fish."

This is not a throwaway comment. Lee and DeVore spend the first half of their introduction to the 1968 proceedings defending their characterization of their object of inquiry as Man the Hunter in increasingly sheepish tones:

> The hunting of mammals has been considered the characteristic feature of the subsistence of early man. . . . Modern hunters, however, depend for most of their subsistence on sources other than meat, mainly vegetable foods, fish, and shell fish. Only in the arctic and subarctic areas where vegetable foods are unavailable do we find the textbook examples of mammal hunters. Over the rest of the world, hunting appears to provide only 20 to 40 per cent of the diet.

They go on to say that while some of the archaeologist contributors hold that fishing and the use of plant seeds represent late innovations in human history, "Our own view is that vegetable foods in the form of nuts, berries, and roots were always available to early man and were easily exploited by even the simplest of technologies." These foods, they suggest, might have been the province of "early woman." Still, "hunting is so universal and is so consistently a male activity that it must have been a basic part of the early cultural adaptation, even if it provided only a modest proportion of the food supplies."

This is a rather more equivocal picture than we might expect. As more ethnographic evidence came in, the outlook for Man the Hunter dimmed further. Here is archaeologist Richard Gould, writing about the Ngatjatjara whom he and his wife had observed in the Western Desert of Australia in the wet seasons of 1966–1967 and 1969–1970:

> The diet is primarily vegetarian. Women and girls forage for a total of seven staple plant species . . . and thus provide the bulk of the diet. . . . At least 90 percent of the time females provide about 95 percent of the food available to the group as a whole. . . . In a sense, it is the dependable efforts of the women in gathering that free the men for more chancy hunting activities. In terms of the amounts of food obtained, we could easily refer to the Western Desert people as gatherers-and-hunters, since the bulk of their diet on most occasions consists of plant foods. Yet from the point of view of time expended, hunting ranks as a major subsistence activity.

Other ethnographers had contrasting experiences. Annette Hamilton wrote of her three-month stay with a foraging community farther south in the Western Desert:

> Men's hunting activities in the range areas at certain times of the year, especially immediately after rain when the game scatters to distant ephemeral waters, are often unsuccessful. If people relied entirely on vegetable foods at these times they would be in a sorry state, especially since varieties of vegetable foods do not occur all together, having instead a seasonal ripening pattern. If women gathered vegetable foods only, to the neglect of animal foods, people would be living on only one or two kinds of vegetable goods for weeks at a time. Women in the eastern Western Desert saw themselves as going out primarily *for meat*. The vegetable foods they gathered were an important supplement, rather than an alternative, to the animal foods.

But Hamilton notes that the situation she observed was exceptional in that "European-introduced factors" had disrupted the daily rhythm of foraging.

Hamilton's qualifying remarks remind us that none of the communities that behavioral ecologists observe today can be said to offer a straightforward proxy for how humans got food 50,000 years ago, let alone over the 2-million-year arc of human evolution. Lee and DeVore confess that "Man the Hunter" got off to a rocky start when their effort to formulate "evolutionary" criteria for hunters—"those populations with strictly Pleistocene economies: no metal, firearms, dogs, or contact with non-hunting cultures"—ended up excluding every ethnographically attested community of foragers in the world.

This question of the validity and limits of ethnographic analogies will trouble us throughout the book. The question is both technical and political—technical in that it is difficult to know how to account for differences in environment and culture between contemporary foragers and those of times past. By and large, foragers today represent relict communities that have been pushed to the margins of their prior range by herding, farming, and industrial societies. Industrial societies have expanded, often aggressively and with contempt for foragers' territorial claims, into environments that had supported foraging economies at population densities dramatically lower than what agrarian and urban societies consider appropriate. Colonizers and their livestock occupy the most productive land and take control of the best groundwater sources, often imposing unprecedented stress on the biome as a whole and leaving foragers with less of a subsistence base than they'd had before. Left without a way to get by, foragers are drawn to the new settlements dotting their country, where they assume the role of an underclass, trading labor, professions of faith in the newcomers' gods, and submission to tutelage in the ways of civilization for flour, sugar, raised meat, tobacco, and firearms. You see this pattern everywhere food-producing societies have entered places previously occupied by foragers. As a rule, colonization and dispossession have been accompanied by active efforts on the part of the colonizers to exterminate their predecessors in culture if not in blood. The methods are theme and variation. In Australia, as late as the 1970s, Indigenous children were removed from their homes and given to settler families for adoption. In Canada and the United States, Indigenous children were forcibly enrolled in residential schools where they were subjected to systematic sexual torture and punished for speaking their own languages.

In many cases—testament to humbling reserves of courage and wit—foraging peoples have achieved a kind of limited autonomy in which they've returned to the land in modified fashion, incorporating economic strategies borrowed from colonizers. But these communities continue to suffer some of the highest rates of preventable illness, substance abuse, and suicide in the world.

The foraging bands Gould and Hamilton describe represent the product of this history, spending part of the year camped in the bush, part of the year living on missions and cattle stations. Something similar could be said of most of the communities described in *Man the Hunter* and the literature it spawned. These are people foraging on land that is, by their own standards or those of their grandparents, marginal. Intergenerational transmission of knowledge about what things are good to eat and how to secure them has been disrupted, in some cases interrupted and learned relatively late in life, in others reconstructed on the basis of oral accounts without benefit of firsthand guidance. At the same time, these modern foragers avail themselves of all the things that Lee and DeVore would like to rule out: metal implements, flour rations. How, if it all, should we take their behavior as models for that of people living 15,000, 50,000, or 200,000 years ago?

This is the technical problem of ethnographic analogy. The political problem is that simply by proposing to take contemporary foragers as models of anything, you risk repeating the colonial erasure of their identity as individuals and communities with a specific history and specific claims to have their needs recognized in the broader political community in which they find themselves assigned marginal roles. In treating people as archetypes, we risk forgetting that they are people, with drives and aspirations not reducible to the need to eat.

Affluence

Among the commentators at "Man the Hunter" was the anthropologist Marshall Sahlins. I have alluded to his landmark essay "The Original Affluent Society." The essay appears as the opening chapter of Sahlins's 1972 book *Stone Age Economics*, but the 1972 version represents an elaboration of the commentary he gave at "Man the Hunter."

Sahlins was writing against a widespread assumption that life before the advent of farming and herding was life lived forever on the brink of starvation. In fact, from what poor evidence we have, including observations of contemporary foragers dealing with all the disadvantages already described, the gathering and hunting life was a good one. We tend to take for granted what Sahlins calls a "Galbraithean" route to affluence: "Man's wants are great, not to say infinite, whereas his means are limited, although improvable." The communities at the center of the Man the Hunter conversation, by contrast, have adopted a "Zen road" to the good life: "Human material wants are finite and few, and technical means unchanging but on the whole adequate." The Zen approach offers the more reliable path to freedom from want—so long as you're willing to accept a comparatively astringent way of life.

Accept, of course, is not quite the word, for it is not as if Pleistocene people were confronted with a choice among divergent subsistence strategies. By contrast, it is clear that in the remote parts of Canada and Australia today, choosing to live in the bush and get one's living by foraging has become an act of political defiance. Sahlins makes no bones about the fact that his formulation is polemic. This he considered a necessary corrective to the slanderous accounts of forager economy that dominated the literature at the time. But simply by introducing the possibility of what earlier we referred to as demand-side mitigation, Sahlins expands the design space of affluence in such a way as to invert the historical trajectory outlined by Smil in the passage quoted above. Affluence, Sahlins suggests, is not something that has been achieved in modern societies. It is, rather, something that has been lost under market capitalism.

This is strong stuff, but let's push it to its logical conclusion: *meat*—here the polemic is mine—*far from being the quintessential food of affluence, has become an exemplary food of precariousness.* To show that this is not simply polemic, that there's an empirical case to be made for treating rising meat consumption as a symptom of rising economic instability, will take the rest of the book. Here, I start by looking at the field data that Sahlins used to support his case.

These data came from a study of provisioning and nutrition in the Yolngu population of Arnhem Land, the peninsula that juts out into the Timor Sea from the northern end of the Northern Territory. The study in question was conducted in the course of the 1948 American–Australian Scientific Expedition to Arnhem Land, sometimes called the last of the great colonial field science expeditions. The part of the study that Sahlins relies on consists of short-term (a week or two) observations of time use and energetic yield in two Yolngu foraging camps. These show that the people in question spent on average four or five hours a day getting food, with a per capita yield of more than 2,100 calories a day, plenty of protein and calcium, and, at one site but not the other, adequate iron and vitamin C. On every foraging "bout" that the field workers observed, they got the impression that their respondents were not really straining themselves: when they'd collected enough food, they quit for the day. The work just did not seem terribly onerous.

These data are suggestive. But let's focus for a minute on a different part of the study, where the expedition's nutritionist, Margaret McArthur, looked at food behavior in a string of settlements on the coast and neighboring islands of eastern Arnhem Land. In this area, the Yolngu had been "encouraged," as McArthur puts it, "not against their will it would appear, to abandon their former nomadic life" in favor of tending communal vegetable gardens, with supplemental flour rations provided by church missions and the state. It was August 1948, the second half of the dry-cool season, when McArthur surveyed the feeding stations on Groote Eylandt and neighboring parts of Arnhem Land. Let's get a sense of what life there was like:

> At all settlements rations are distributed three times daily just before meal-time. At Umbakumba the natives are fed for the five and a half working days and when supplies are plentiful rations are also distributed during the week-end. At Angoroko and Oenpelli rations are given for the five working days, and those who attend church on Sunday are also fed. On Saturday they are encouraged to collect their own food from the surrounding country. At Yirrkala the natives who are working are fed for the whole period of their employment; the remainder may stay at the mission, but they have to find their own food.

For the most part, the communal gardens were given over to calorie-dense underground storage organs, specifically cassava (manioc) and sweet potato. At Umbakumba, 25 percent of the yield by mass was reserved for fruits and vegetables, principally watermelon, though "bananas, lettuce, cabbages, tomatoes, beans, turnips, swedes [rutabaga], onions, carrots and papaws" appeared in smaller quantities. Protein came from caught fish, turtles, and turtle eggs and, at certain times of the year, chicken eggs from layers kept on site. "At Angoroko," McArthur writes, "the following meal pattern is adhered to for the greater part of the year":

> Breakfast: Ground-wheat porridge, sweetened with golden syrup or honey; damper [a wheat-flour soda bread baked in the ashes of an open fire]; tea and sugar.
>
> Dinner: Wheat porridge or rice; fresh vegetables or golden syrup or honey; damper; tea and sugar.
>
> Supper: Damper and fish; tea and sugar.

"If there is not enough fish for everybody, the men and the girls' dormitory are given priority," while the women and children make do with starches. Indeed, fish entitlements had declined just prior to the expedition's visit to Angoroko when it was deemed too expensive to send the station truck the 4 miles (6.4 km) to the beach to retrieve the day's catch, limiting the station's Indigenous fishermen to what they could haul home on foot.

The pattern repeats. At Yirrkala, cyclone damage had hurt the productivity of the gardens, so there were not enough fruits and vegetables, apart from cassava, to go around, and the Indigenous population was subsisting on hardtack and meat stew distributed by the administration. At Oenpelli, McArthur found no garden that season and a similar bare-bones ration: flour, rice, beef, and buffalo. The beef came from a herd of cattle kept at the station, the buffalo from the surrounding marsh country. The meat consumption, at over 500 grams (one pound) a day per capita, was considerably higher than what Gould observed farther west twenty years later.

"All stations," McArthur notes, "have goat herds for milk. The surplus left after the requirements of the Europeans at the stations have been met is given to the native children. At Angoroko and Yirrkala there was no surplus."

So much for the workweek. On the weekends, Indigenous people were left to fend for themselves. Their success depended in part on where the stations they'd been settled were located. Umbakumba and Yirrkala, locals told McArthur, had never been particularly rich food environments—not places people would camp, certainly during the less productive dry season. At Angoroko and Oenpelli, by contrast, McArthur observes that concentrating so many people in one place permanently has imposed unsustainable stress on what had been productive environments for foraging. "With the passage of time," she writes, "the supply of native foods which the aborigines can obtain during the week-end is diminishing," to the point that some households set aside part of the flour ration they receive during the week to get them through the weekend. When people did go out foraging, their objective varied: fish and shellfish, wallabies, kangaroo at Oenpelli, and, above all, "vegetable foods." McArthur does not provide much detail on foraged plant foods, though fleshy *Solanum* fruits were probably common, and at Oenpelli, women daily went to a nearby water source to dig out lilies for their underground rhizomes.

This was the dry season, but Arnhem Land is not the desert. Historically, Yolngu country supported year-round standing populations at densities considerably higher than were typical of the arid country to the south and west, perhaps as much as one hundred times higher. This had been a country of abundance.

By contrast, life on the feeding stations, despite the hens, goats, cattle, trucks, and firearms, was a life of scraping by and hoarding rations for personal use. It was a life in which foragers' ultimate fallback strategy, shifting camp, was denied them by design.

There is something uniquely compelling about hearing what people distant from you ate for breakfast. It is when you see meals reduced to lists of foods that you start to realize how intimate eating is, how vulnerable people become when an ethnographer appears, clipboard in hand, to write down everything they eat. McArthur was not the only one making these lists. Around the time of the Arnhem Land expedition, the Australian government commissioned a series of household food budget surveys of Indigenous communities in Australia and New Guinea, then an Australian colony. The results (see chapter 6) make for gripping reading. They also offer clues about what to look for when we try to get beyond country-level data about how people eat in urbanizing parts of the emerging world today.

The Paleolithic Diet

But but but. What about Paleo diets? If the ethnographic evidence from foragers living in environments that resemble those where humans have lived for most of our history as a species suggests meat played a limited role in the human diet prior to the emergence of agriculture, then what is the basis for arguments that we are conditioned by evolution to thrive on a diet rich in meat?

In 1985 an article appeared in the *New England Journal of Medicine* under the heading "Paleolithic Nutrition: A Consideration of Its Nature and Current Implications." Its authors, the radiologist S. Boyd Eaton and the anthropologist Melvin Konner, were professors at Emory University in Atlanta. "Paleolithic Nutrition" represents what historians call an *index text,* a text that comes to serve as a point of origin and, at least implicitly, a point of reference, for a discourse or network of mutually implicated texts and motifs. In the case of paleolithic nutrition, the discourse in question has long since outgrown the walled gardens of peer-reviewed technical journals, but that is where it originated. Sometimes you can learn something by going back to the source.

First, a terminological point. Earlier, we saw that Lee and DeVore refer to *Pleistocene* hunters. In "Paleolithic Nutrition," Eaton and Konner refer to *Paleolithic* humans. *Pleistocene* is a stratigraphic term: it refers to the period in the Earth's climate history that precedes the Holocene, the warmer period, dating to approximately 11,650 years ago, that follows the end of the Last Glacial Maximum. *Paleolithic* refers to a technological register, observable in widely varying forms in the stone artifacts that co-occur with human remains at archaeological sites from 2.6 million years ago until about 15,000 years ago in Africa and Eurasia. In some places, including Australia, Paleolithic artifact assemblages appear well into the Holocene. The significance of the timing of transitions in artifact horizons for the cognitive faculties of the makers has been an object of controversy, since what you observe, archaeologically, of a community's technology depends on what kinds of materials were available in the place where that community lived. *Organic materials do not preserve the way mineral materials do.* The implications of this fact will occupy us at length in chapters 1 to 3. The question here is: When we talk about what people ate and how they got it way, way back, what are we talking about? The climate, physiography, flora and fauna that characterized their environment (Pleistocene)? Or the implements they used to exploit that environment (Paleolithic)? These are not the same. Nor, for that matter, are the modes of exploitation afforded by the tools visible in the archaeological record at a 2 million, 200,000, and 20,000 years ago. Humans in the strict phylogenetic sense enter the picture at least 200,000 years ago, but the diet and way of life of these earliest *Homo sapiens* would have been alien to those who weathered the cool-arid periods that preceded the onset of the Holocene.

That said, it is not hard to identify the people Eaton and Konner take as models of human nutrition in its evolutionary climax state: the humans who appeared in Europe around 40,000 years ago and provided the template for what archaeologists of Eurasia, at the time Eaton and Konner were writing, imagined as behaviorally "modern" humans. As we'll see in chapter 3, the story today looks different and less Europe centered. Nonetheless, the basic premise of Eaton and Konner's work—look for a comparative baseline for contemporary nutrition and its health implications—sounds plausible. The authors acknowledge the wide variance in the proportion of meat attested in the diets of historically observed foragers and settle on a reference figure of 35 percent. At 3,000 kilocalories a day for an active lifestyle in the subarctic conditions of the Pleistocene glaciation, this means just shy of 800 grams (1.75 pounds) a day of lean meat and close to 200 grams (0.5 pounds) of animal protein.

"Paleolithic Nutrition" incorporates a number of unwarranted assumptions, above all that human diet was more or less fixed until the advent of agriculture. Despite differences between contemporary foragers and their Pleistocene predecessors, Eaton and Konner write, "The range and content of foods they consume *are similar to those that our ancestors ate for up to 4 million years.*" In part I we'll see just how unwarranted this assumption is. But it's worth noting that compared to what came after, "Paleolithic Nutrition" is modest in its claims, especially with regard to meat. Compare, for instance, "Plant–Animal Subsistence Ratios and Macronutrient Energy Estimations in Worldwide Hunter-Gatherer Diets" (2000), whose lead author, Loren Cordain, more than any other nutrition scientist, has become associated with the Paleo movement. Cordain and colleagues conclude that in nearly three-quarters of foraging societies worldwide, at least half the diet by mass and close to two-thirds by energy came from animal products, with protein ratios pushing up against levels likely to cause hyperaminoacidemia and "rabbit starvation" (organ failure under an energetically adequate diet as the body reaches the limit of its capacity to convert amino acids to glucose).

Where do the data for these conclusions come from? Cordain and colleagues rely on an "ethnographic atlas" compiled by anthropologist George Murdock, editor of the journal *Ethnology,* and published in installments in the journal and in a tabular form designed for punch card sorting in 1967. Of the 862 societies included in the 1967 summary, 229 are listed, in the columns labeled "Subsistence Economy," as deriving none of their subsistence from agriculture or herding. These form the basis for "plant–animal subsistence ratios" and a number of other estimates of forager dietary ratios.

As anyone who has looked at the history of ethnographic atlases will tell you, the data that go into them tend to be of poor quality. Often they're based on short-term observations conducted at a limited number of sites by individuals with little access to local languages. All of these limitations apply to Murdock's *Ethnographic Atlas.* Then there's the fact that overwhelmingly, these reports were compiled by men. As we've seen, foraging is gendered in ways that it takes a mixed-gender team of fieldworkers to understand. Added to this is the fact that not only have ethnographers traditionally construed (and misconstrued) hunting as a male activity, meat itself has long been identified with masculinity. This was certainly the case in the era when the reports included in Murdock's *Atlas* were prepared (mainly 1860–1910). For the observers cited in Cordain's key source of ethnographic data, meat was simply more salient than plant-derived foods.

Am I saying the Paleolithic diet is bunk? Not exactly, since its key findings, going back to Eaton and Konner's 1985 article, are that people in times past consumed fewer refined carbohydrates and the meat they consumed was considerably leaner on the whole. If calling nutritional guidance that amounts to "Eat less processed food and less fatty meat" Paleolithic makes it more compelling for you, be my guest. But there are good reasons for not maxing out on animal protein, not least the stress it imposes on the gut microbiome and, by extension, the integrity of the distal gut (see chapter 2). These tend not to get much play in Paleo circles, where the stress falls on vitality in the near term to the exclusion of health over the long haul.

Carrying Capacity

Another reason not to max out on animal protein is that meat production at the levels necessary to satisfy projected demand imposes unsustainable stress on the Earth's biosphere. This brings us to the question of *carrying capacity,* or, as population biologist Joel Cohen put it in the title of his authoritative book on the theme, *How many people can the Earth support?*

The title is a bit misleading, because Cohen is not interested in coming up with a single figure for the Earth's human carrying capacity. Rather, his aim is to show the trade-offs and assumptions entailed in any particular estimate: What is total fertility like? What are the birth and death rates like? Do we want a world of fewer people who live longer lives, or do we want to maximize the number of people who have an opportunity to live at the expense of individual longevity? Above all, what kind of quality of life, and in particular what kind of diet, do we want people to have?

Cohen describes the questions he offers, about trade-offs between fertility and longevity and between population and quality of life, as questions of values. But there is another way to look at it: Is humanity to be an *r*-selected or a *K*-selected species? The terms "*r*-selected" and "*K*-selected" come from a version of the *logistic equation,* a differential equation that models the role of rate of reproduction (*r*) and carrying capacity (*K*) in the moment-to-moment change in the total population of some reproducing thing of interest, be it bacteria or human beings. The logistic equation describes a familiar S-shaped curve. Early on, the growth of the population is governed mainly by how fast it can reproduce, and it quickly reaches an inflection point, the first bend in the *S*, and shoots up. Further on in time, the *S* reaches its second inflection point and levels out—this is where growth of the population has become dominated by carrying capacity, the *K* term, rather than by reproductive capacity. As a rule, *r*- and *K*-strategies are not "choices" in the sense of being expressions of values worked out through discussion; they are simply adaptations to different environmental circumstances. Unstable environments where there's a high risk that an organism will die before it reaches reproductive maturity demand an *r*-strategy—high reproductive rate, low parental investment. Stable environments where individuals tend to survive into maturity demand a *K*-strategy—low reproductive rate, high parental investment.

What is interesting in the human case is that our reproductive strategy and life history are highly plastic. It is an open question whether humanity could really design its demographic niche. But in *Balancing on a Planet,* a book that reads like a sequel to *How Many People Can the Earth Support?* anthropologist David Cleveland argues that in fact, what is required for humanity to thrive in the coming generations is that we undertake a conscious shift from an *r*-strategy to a *K*-strategy.

What is even more interesting is that in a certain sense humans are already both *r*- and *K*-selected, combining high total fertility relative to other primates with high levels of investment in offspring. This, in fact, was the key innovation in human life history, visible in the paleontological record long before *H. sapiens* appears, that both necessitated and enabled the broadening of diet that we'll review in chapters 1 and 2. In essence, it was *other-directedness,* including a willingness to provide food and fosterage for children other than one's own, that provided the selective pressure for the shift to omnivory that proponents of the Paleo diet like to emphasize.

Ironically, it has become unacceptable to make the case for food system reform in other-directed terms. Michael Pollan offers a consensus view when he refers to the environmental crisis as "a crisis of lifestyle," of everyday consumer choices. Could things be otherwise? Is self-regard not human nature? Actually, Pollan's view reflects a rather recent understanding of liberal society. We don't have to go further back than 1950 to see a very different argument for food system reform. In *The Nutritional Improvement of Life*, nutritional biochemist Henry Sherman, writing in the wake of the establishment of the UN Food and Agriculture Organization, tries to convince Americans to eat less meat. He divides foods into ten categories according to what they contribute to human nutrition: grain products; legumes and nuts; potatoes and sweet potatoes; green and yellow vegetables; citrus fruits and tomatoes; other fruits and vegetables; milk and its products apart from butter; meat, fish, poultry, and eggs; fats; and sugar. Then he argues that we could toss out the last three and achieve "optimal intake of protein" nonetheless—in fact, we'd be healthier.

But health in the narrow sense is just part of Sherman's aim. He's more concerned with what "competition for foods of the meat–fish–poultry–eggs group" does to us psychologically, especially when those foods are inequitably distributed among classes and nations.

Sherman was writing for an audience that had, during World War II, grown comfortable with central planning, and his technocratic optimism rings naive today. But the fact that large-scale demand-side mitigation—efforts to shift people's preferences *for the benefit of distant others*—seems practically out of the question today speaks to a constriction in our public conversation about food.

Violence

Above all, this constriction is about our attitude toward political violence.

Up to this point, I've been speaking as if human interests were the only ones we need to take into account. To some readers, this will seem reasonable. Others will have been wondering, *What about the animals' perspective?*

Indeed. Simply to review the literature on trends in the human use of animal-derived foods is to find oneself complicit in a strange game of deanimation. Animals are "production units," their merits assessed in terms of disease resistance, climate hardiness, and tolerance of crowding. In comparisons of the productivity of animal production systems involving varying forms and degrees of confinement, the welfare of the animals in question is never costed, save as it can be operationalized in terms of production units lost to disease and other inconveniences of crowding. Animal suffering simply does not figure—literally, it does not get put in numbers—in technical discussions about livestock intensification.

Writing about life on the kill floor of an American slaughterhouse, the political scientist Timothy Pachirat describes a "politics of sight." When you no longer have day-to-day contact with animals, they cease to be present for you as moral actors. Then it becomes possible to load them into crates lined with absorbent matting, load the crates into a pressurized tube, and send the tube to the other side of the planet where the animals will be offloaded and slaughtered. We shudder to imagine the scene on board—what it would smell like, what it would sound like. But then, we're imagining what it would be like for *us,* were we to materialize at one end of the cabin, crates of cattle receding from view. We are less likely to try to imagine what it would feel like from the animals' perspective. Part of the reason is that so few of us these days have close-up experience observing other-than-human animals, save perhaps dogs and cats, in distress and pain—or even joy.

Most arguments for animal liberation begin with the proposition that the right way to think about the political relationship between other-than-human animals and humans is by analogy with the relationships of dominance and subjection that have existed between different groups of humans. Just as, over the past two hundred years, liberal society has come to recognize women, the unpropertied, and the colonized as subjects with interests and perspectives of their own, so must it do with the animals on whose labor and bodies our economy stands.

In emphasizing our kinship with other kinds of animals (in sentience, in the capacity to experience pain, in the drive to live), these views lose sight of other dimensions of the animal–human relationship. If, as I proposed, meat has become a food of precariousness, then humans forced by circumstance to rely on meat and animals raised for meat occupy coordinate roles in a single system of violence. To say that both experience pain tells us nothing about the economic and political relationships that keep them both in positions of subordination. Liberation for livestock, if we desired such a thing, would entail liberation for all those humans who have not benefited from the vision of affluence that has come to dominate our world. Whether the converse holds true—that justice for humans entails justice for the animals we eat—is a question we'll take up at the end of the book.

Part I, "Did Meat Make Us Human?" addresses the role of meat in human evolution, biological and cultural, from the first appearances of the genus

Homo some 2.8 million years ago up to the rise of livestock-based states in Iron Age eastern Eurasia sometime after 3,000 years ago. Chapters 1 and 2 cover the Pliocene and Pleistocene, when growing climatic volatility selected, in humans, for unprecedented versatility in diet and life history. Chapter 3 brings ethnographic evidence into dialogue with archaeological evidence to ask what, if anything, happened sometime after 70,000 years ago to produce the distinctively human pattern of cooperative subsistence, with its strong reliance on our capacities to infer others' intentions and formulate abstract templates for relationships that recur across our social world. Chapter 4 looks at how these capacities led, under certain conditions of climate, demographic pressure, and ways of thinking about animals, to domestication. A bridge between parts I and II discusses how the challenge of historical exposition differs for the periods covered in the book's two parts and outlines my strategy for part II.

Part II, "Must Affluence Mean Meat?" picks up the story in the modern era. Chapter 5 addresses the role of meat in colonization, with case studies from Australia and the Americas. Chapter 6 returns us to the dietary surveys already alluded to. Together with other forms of evidence—ration schedules, specifications for emergency food supplements—these provide us with an intimate view of how meat transformed the lives of marginalized peoples at the dawn of the era of global affluence. An intermezzo offers background on the history of nutrition science germane to the discussion in chapter 6 and that in chapters 7 and 8. Chapter 7 brings the story up to the present. Live export represents just one element in a complex infrastructural network in which cyclic changes in concentrations of biomass and energy in one part of the world—for instance, cattle rangeland in Australia—become coupled to corresponding pulses in biomass and energy elsewhere—emerging cities in China, say. Chapter 8 continues the present-day story. We return to the question of income elasticity, asking what makes it difficult to get information about the everyday provisioning strategies that link income and meat consumption. Zooming in on provisioning strategies among the urban poor leads us naturally to street food, bringing the conversation full circle. The epilogue takes up the theme of the coordinate forms of violence implicated in the meat economy and what, if anything, we might do about them. On a planet of improvable but ultimately limited resources, all of us, human and animal, in different but coordinate ways, have a stake in the Meat Question.

I Did Meat Make Us Human?

1 Humans

A Day at the Beach

Imagine a day at the beach. You arrive early in the morning, just as the sun is easing up over the horizon and the sky above the water is gray with mist. You are not alone. With you are your partner, if you have one, friends, or siblings; children, parents, and grandparents; perhaps a dog or two. When you arrive, the beach is empty—no other human beings and no animals, such as dogs, that you would recognize as markers of human presence. For the moment, this is a remarkably clean beach too: no cigarette butts, no beer cans, no discarded beach chairs or forgotten pails and shovels. The sole indication that humans have been here recently is a pair of tracks left by a wheeled vehicle sporting large lugged tires. Overhead, a handful of gulls wheel, and the wet sand at the edge of the water is littered with the shells of mussels and clams, the debris of their breakfast. Overnight, the tide has washed brown algae up on the beach in long mats, and these give off a faint brackish scent, not unpleasant, as they dry in the morning sun. The tide is just past ebb, and as you crest the dunes, you look down to see a glistening expanse of wet sand extending way, way out to where it meets a glassy sea, the boundary discernible only in the ankle-high breakers coasting in from the swell offshore.

Apart from the squealing of the gulls, the only sound comes from the distant crash of the surf and the rustling of dune grass in the breeze—and, now, from the shouts of the children, tumbling down the seaward slope of the dunes, the barking of the dogs chasing after them, and the scuff of high-tenacity nylon against cotton and skin as you make your own gingerly way down, loaded with supplies.

You have a reputation in your family as the one who would rather do laundry in the sink every night than pack a spare shirt, but it's important to keep the kids stimulated and your aging parents comfortable, and you have come prepared for every contingency, with towels, extra layers, and change of clothes, snacks salty and sweet, water, coffee you got up at three in the morning to brew, three kinds of tea to cold brew in one of the many drinking vessels on hand, a portable solar grill and a cooler full of things to put on it, an umbrella, seagrass mats or beach towels or blankets for those who prefer not to sit directly on the sand, sunscreen, topical insect repellant, antiseptic gel, a couple of Frisbee-type projectiles, a bodyboard the kids will fight over, pails with crenellated bottoms for building sandcastles, shovels, a wad of disintegrating polyethylene bags you keep under the sink to clean up after the dogs, a couple of paperbacks, a notebook and pencil, and, of course, digital media. All of this, save the cooler, umbrella, and bodyboard, fill a couple of nylon backpacks, much used and much loved, fraying at the edges but perfectly adequate to the task of hauling your material support system from car to beach.

You establish a beachhead, shoo the kids toward the water, get your parents set up with coffee and a bite of breakfast, and sit back to watch the day unfold. Soon the mist has burned off and the sun makes its appearance in the sky. Other groups start to appear up and down the beach, some demographically similar to yours, others just a single couple with a pair of older kids. You strike up a conversation, share your snacks. The kids play with kids from other groups. Down the beach you see a young woman sitting at the edge of the water, hands clasped around her knees, staring out at the ocean; apparently she is here alone. A beach patrol drives by, leaving a fresh set of tracks high up toward the dunes. The gulls wheel closer, eyes sharp for discarded pieces of food. The mats of algae reek. Around ten you call the kids in to have something to eat, transforming your campsite into a cheerful midden—a debris mound formed of bits of fruit, nuts, crackers, and maybe meat ground into the sand. By eleven, the soothing hush of surf and wind punctuated by the cries of gulls and children is broken as a nearby group shares its ultimate beach day playlist with the community. At noon, the teenagers start to appear, traveling in packs, nervously checking their surroundings for people they know, failing to notice when their ice cream wrappers bounce off the lip of the oil drums set out as trash containers and skitter across the beach.

Sometime in the afternoon, when the heat of the day is on the wane, the surfers reappear to claim the boards that, you now see, had been pitched discreetly at the edge of the dunes since before you arrived. Around four, you break out the solar grill. Other parties have the same idea, and by five, the air is suffused with the scents of grilled meat and fish, not to say beer, as the sun makes its leisurely way toward the horizon and the mood changes, the vigorous activity and bright talk of daylight giving way to a more subdued tone, movements made languid by the cumulative effects of sun and sea and the anticipation of food. Conversation slows too and grows more abstract, tending less toward the practicalities of keeping everyone fed and protected from the elements and more toward reminiscence and fantasy and the evaluation of the behavior of people not present.

By six the kids are cranking down and you get ready to leave, gathering your things and packing them up, a bit regretful not to be able to stay into the evening—looking out over the beach, dotted with camps of varying size and complexity, you imagine campfires, and the unique thrill of standing at the edge of a dark surf, the unnerving immensity of the sea. Cinching a compression strap on your pack, you notice that one of the friction tensioners has come off, and a carabiner that had been clipped to one of the daisy chains has disappeared. As you crest the dunes, bound for the car, you look back, hoisting your pack over one shoulder, to see the tide coming in, the children's sand labyrinths eroded into a network of canyons, then these too washed away and finally submerged.

Now imagine that you return the following morning. Again, the beach is deserted. This time, though, you have three hours of uninterrupted solitude in which to make sense of the scene before you. The trade-off is that your memory of the previous day's events has been wiped clean. You have a solid grasp of how people act at a beach—the repertoire of common behaviors, including the games people play and the kinds of foods they eat, along with the tools they use to accomplish these behaviors—but you have no knowledge of what actually transpired the day before. This time, looking out from the top of the dunes, you see ample signs of recent habitation: tipped-over umbrellas and food wrappers, fire pits marked by tinder submerged in ash tips, abandoned toys and containers. Alongside these signs are those you saw the day before: tire tracks, bivalve shells left by the gulls, mats of algae drying on the sand still damp from the receding tide.

Your task is to say what happened yesterday—not just, "People were here, eating, playing, and relaxing," but *who* was here, their ages, genders, status and social relationships, what kind of physical condition they were in, whether the activities they engaged in were casual or deliberate, light or strenuous, mundane or ritualized, productive or playful, the sizes of the different parties and the degree to which they interacted, cooperated, and competed for real estate and other scarce resources, the order of precession—who came first, who came later—and, of course, what they ate. Now let's make the task more difficult: you return not after a day but after a year. In the interim, the geological forces of sun, wind, salt, and sea have been at work on the material debris. Aluminum cans and plastic shovels are still more or less intact, though seagrass mats may be returning to the earth. Ants and gulls have long since carried away anything edible, but by close inspection of the wrappers, vessels, and cooking sites that remain, and what you know of what people eat at the beach, you can formulate hypotheses about what people ate that day and how they prepared it.

Now harder still: not one year but a hundred. You know that in that time, the beach has periodically been occupied a number of times, but your task is specifically to reconstruct that day a hundred years ago and distinguish the signal of that occupation from those of subsequent occupations, animal and human. You don't know much about the beach-going habits of the people from that time, and you're aware that the physiography, climate, flora and fauna have changed considerably. This time, however, you have the whole day to conduct your investigation, and you've brought a team of detail-oriented assistants to systematically sweep the beach to a depth of one meter, along with sophisticated remote sensing apparatus to probe deeper. Remember, you're not here just to say something about the material debris left by the people and their companion animals a hundred years ago. You want to say something about their *behavior*, that is, how they moved, what they did, how they got along, what they ate, their *cognition,* that is, how they thought, how they saw, heard, smelled, tasted, and made sense of the world around them, what kind of planning they undertook for the future and what they could infer about others' internal states on the basis of observable behavior, and, ultimately, their *physiology*: What were they capable of physically? What nutrients were essential to their survival? To their flourishing? Did they shiver when the sun went down, and was that shivering uncomfortable in the way it would be for you? Your real goal is to use the people who sat, stood, played, and ate on this beach on that day a hundred years ago as type specimens, exemplars of the behavior, cognition, and physiology of everyone who was alive at that time.

If this sounds absurd, imagine if the time lapse were not 100 years but 2 million. This is the task of paleoanthropology.

The comparison is a little unfair because in our thought experiment, I've limited you to two kinds of evidence: *artifact assemblages*—patterns of debris composed of durable things made by, or hypothesized to have been made by, humans—and *middens*, debris from the preparation and consumption of food. Other signs of human presence—footprints and vehicle tracks, site modifications such as scooped-out places for sitting and sandcastles, and the sounds and smells arising from human activity—preserve poorly even on the one-day horizon. Animal excreta preserve rather well and offer, as you might imagine, a unique perspective on what the animals that deposited them were eating, including evidence about meal composition, food storage (if a single fecal cast includes foods that are not coseasonal), and gender (via traces of sex steroids). Coprolites—fossilized fecal casts—can even serve as sources of the depositors' DNA. But verifying that fecal casts come from humans as opposed to other animals, whether contemporaneous or subsequent occupants of the same site, has proved tricky. Even in the case of our beach excavation, you'd need some other way of knowing that humans had brought dogs to the beach with them and that the dogs, but not the humans, had defecated in the open to do something useful with any coprolites you turned up.

So, artifact assemblages and middens. These are key types of evidence in paleoanthropology. But for early hominins—humans in the evolutionary broad sense—there are two more: sediment cores and skeletal remains.

Sediment cores first. The earth's atmosphere and biosphere are dominated by a small number of elements—nitrogen, oxygen, carbon, and others—and these occur in multiple stable isotopes that differ by the presence or absence of additional neutrons—so, nitrogen-14 and -15, oxygen-16, -17, and -18, carbon-12 and -13. The atmospheric background ratios of these stable isotopes vary very slowly. The metabolic activity of plants and animals produces more rapid localized divergences in stable isotope concentrations from the background ratios. We can use these divergences to infer things about the local history of the biosphere.

In the case of atmospheric oxygen, localized divergences in ^{18}O:^{16}O ratios appear in foraminifera, seafloor microorganisms preserved in layers of sediment deposited on the ocean floor. Since ^{18}O is heavier, it evaporates more slowly from the surface of the sea and precipitates faster as the air cools. By examining fluctuations in ^{18}O concentrations in fossilized foraminifera, you can observe both surface cooling and warming trends and trends in climate volatility over the past 5 million years. Deep sea sediment cores provide a useful proxy for continental and global changes in climate over periods of 41,000 to 100,000 years. These *marine isotope stages*, numbered from 1 (the last 14,000 years) to 104 (starting 2.6 million years ago), provide a useful rubric for relating archaeological data to broad trends in climate. Seafloor sediment also preserves atmospheric particulate, a measure of aridity, since dust from surface soils is more likely to enter the atmosphere when the air and surface are dry.

^{13}C:^{12}C ratios in paleosols, preserved specimens of surface soil from the deep past, provide evidence about changes in the composition of plant biomass. Carbon-13 concentrations tend to be higher in C4 plants, grasses adapted to hot, often arid environments with no forest canopy. (C4 plants are so-called because they use a photosynthetic pathway where the first intermediate product of carbon dioxide fixation is the four-carbon oxaloacetic acid, as opposed to the three-carbon phosphoglyceric acid produced in the photosynthetic pathway found in the vast majority of terrestrial flora.) Rising ^{13}C concentrations in successive paleosols have been cited as evidence of a transition from forest to savanna.

Next, skeletal remains. These provide evidence about body shape and, less securely, modes of locomotion, for instance, walking and running. Some researchers have used changes in the pelvic dimensions of female hominins as markers of increased brain size, which necessitates a female pelvis capable of passing large-headed babies. Stable isotope ratios in hominin bone collagen provide clues to diet (elevated ^{13}C indicating consumption of C4 plants or of herbivores that consumed them, elevated ^{15}N of animal foods). Faunal skeletal remains preserve signs of deliberate postmortem modification—biting, cutting, scraping—which have been interpreted as evidence, alternately, that hominins were eating the flesh of the animals in question or were scavenging the bones of animals eaten by carnivores to get at the marrow.

Ethnographic Analogies

Before we start to bring all this evidence to bear on the question of what the prototypical human diet looked like, I introduce two further, indirect kinds of evidence. What makes these indirect is that they draw not on debris from the times and places of early human habitation but on comparisons with the behavior of humans and other primates we can observe today. Let's go back to the beach, which has now been sectioned off into a grid, each cell 1 meter square. You're standing on the dunes watching your team methodically sift the contents of those 1-square-meter cells, wondering how you're going to make sense of what you find. Any particular configuration of debris could be made to fit a wide range of hypotheses about the events of a hundred years ago, and you have scant evidence to guide you in the selection of one hypothesis over another. Suddenly your eye is caught by movement on the horizon: a surfer paddling out into the swell. Following her as she glides in, you become aware that the beach is not in fact deserted: a knot of surfers is camped down a ways, shortboards forming a defensive palisade around their beat-up camper bus, smoke rising from a discreet white gas stove. Observing them, you feel admiration and wonder mixed with envy: these people are leading a pure life, meeting their needs with a minimum of effort and devoting the rest of their time to play, their firm, barely clothed bodies a testament to a life lived in direct contact with nature. Why is your own life not this way? Watching them eat lunch, laughing and mock-fighting, it dawns on you that their life, with its relatively simple technology and social structure and slower tempo, might represent a useful model for the lives of the people whose debris you've been excavating. Could surfers not represent a relict population for whom the beach served as a refugium—a safe habitat—as the rest of the world grew more complicated? Of course, contemporary surfers do not live exactly the same as people a hundred years ago—for one thing, surfers today interact with nonsurfers, and inevitably their way of life has been contaminated by influence from the nonsurfer world. But surely observing them would tell you something about how to interpret the stuff you're digging up.

The point of this exercise is to start thinking about the limits of *ethnographic analogy,* the use of present-day foragers as models of Pleistocene humans and proto-humans. Again, the comparison is not entirely fair, but if you detect something pointed in my description, you're right: ethnographic analogy is colored by conjecture—it cannot be otherwise—along with a difficult-to-parse mix of emotional responses. Archaism is charismatic, and from the vantage point of agricultural and industrial societies, nothing appears so archaic as a world in which people do not produce their food but simply find it. In fact, *find* does not do justice to foragers' resource management strategies, but it suggests the perceived gulf in worldview between foragers and those who observe them. This is not to say that ethnographic analogy has no place in reasoning about the history of human subsistence; it does, as we'll see.

Next, consider a second type of comparative evidence: primate models. Other-than-human primates, chimpanzees in particular, have long been made to stand in for an elusive last common ancestor (LCA) that lived some 8 million years ago. The use of chimpanzees as stand-ins for the LCA presupposes that the chimpanzee clade has been remarkably conservative in evolutionary terms, a presupposition that is not motivated by any evidence. With the recent description of *Ardipithecus ramidus,* a hominid that lived some 4.0 to 4.4 million years ago (Ma) and exhibits a range of skeletal features that diverge sharply from those of present-day chimpanzees, the chimpanzee model seems untenable. This matters because arguments that "meat made us human" often draw a contrast between human omnivory and the herbivory of other primates, even though chimpanzees are known to hunt colobus monkeys. Again, it is not that primate data have nothing to tell us about the evolution of human behavior. But for our purposes, these data represent a distraction in most cases. The exception, as we'll see in the next chapter, is in discussions of what human physiology today might tell us about the selective pressures on human evolution.

It's important to keep these two kinds of comparative evidence distinct because they serve distinct purposes. Ethnographic analogy, for all its problems, is not simply a coded way of treating foragers as something other than fully human. I do not want to give the impression I'm playing down behavioral ecology's racist past, which is as appalling in its crudeness as in its ugliness. But done sensitively, forager studies can serve to bolster demands for political recognition from groups marginalized for their reliance on foraging. Evidence from contemporary foragers is germane to discussions of the repertoire of physiological and cultural adaptations characteristic of humans of the past 50,000 to 100,000 (ka) years. By contrast, primate comparisons are germane to discussions of primate, including human, history over a span of 2 to 3 million years. As we'll see below, these are rather different discussions.

How Do We Know How Old Things Are?

Let's pause to think about what 2 million years means. If we conservatively say it takes twenty-five years for a human being to grow from birth to the point when she or he is a full participant in the productive and reproductive life of the community—if we call twenty-five years a generation—then something on the order of *80,000 to 100,000* generations separates us from the earliest hominins. Of those 100,000 generations, recorded history accounts for no more than the last 200. So the first question we should ask is, *When we find evidence of hominin occupations from way, way back, how do we know how old it is?*

The answer is that we have lots of ways, but which ones are applicable depends on what kinds of debris you're dealing with and a rough order-of-magnitude estimate for how old they are. Some of these methods are radiometric. Carbon dating is valid up to 55 ka at the most, but other radioactive decay series allow dating of human remains and mineral contexts to much greater time depths. U-series dating uses uranium decay series to date minerals precipitated from water to time depths of 200 to 500 ka depending on the species of uranium sampled. In some cases, U-series dating can be applied directly to bones and teeth if the uptake and leaching of uranium and its decay products can be properly accounted for. Optical stimulation luminescence (OSL) refers to a family of techniques that rely on the fact that minerals occur in crystal lattices, and these lattices have defects that serve as traps for electrons emitted by ambient radiation. When electrons are released from the traps, mineral samples emit luminescence. Heating and exposure to sunlight serve as reset events, emptying the traps. By shining a laser on a sample of quartz or feldspar and measuring the emitted luminescence, you can see how much radiation has accrued in the sample since it was last exposed to a reset event, a useful proxy for deposition time at time depths up to 200 ka.

For earlier times, the key to dating debris is to date the stratigraphic context in which the debris is found, for instance, by measuring argon decay or, in sedimentary contexts, alignment of the deposition process with the polarity of the earth's magnetic field at the time of deposition. Deposition is subject to a wide range of confounds, some of which I'll mention below.

An Early Hominin Chronology

To ask *What made them/makes us human?* and *What did they eat?* we need to have a clear fix on who *they* were. So let's set out a couple definitions.

The *Plio-Pleistocene* is a span of geological time comprising two consecutive stratigraphic periods, the Pliocene and the Pleistocene, the first running roughly 5 Ma to 2.6 Ma, the second running up to the start of the Holocene some 11,700 years ago. The Pleistocene and Holocene together are referred to as the *Quaternary,* the fourth period of the Cenozoic era. The Plio-Pleistocene is the time when hominins emerged as a distinct form of life. It is also a time of marked climatic variability, something we'll return to.

The *hominins* are a *clade,* a phylogenetic lineage, comprising modern humans, *Homo sapiens sapiens,* together with extinct species of the genus *Homo* and the extinct genera *Australopithecus* and *Paranthropus*. *Homo* itself has been dated, on the basis of crania and jaw bones that differ from contemporaneous skeletal remains attributed to australopithecines, to as early as 2.8 Ma. Even at dates of 2.8 to 2.6 Ma, *Homo* had a cranial capacity at least 30 percent greater than that of coeval *Australopithecus afarensis,* though body mass and daily energy expenditure are estimated to have been just 10 percent larger. Cranial capacity, it should be noted, is not the same as brain mass or even brain volume except at the coarsest grain of resolution; like a coastline with many small inlets, the cerebral cortex is characterized by fractal dimension, a high degree of involution that renders its surface area, mass, and inflated volume (imagine pumping helium into a cortex-shaped balloon) considerably greater than what can be registered by cranial capacity. This fractal dimension has tended to increase, over phylogenetic time, alongside cranial capacity, so cranial morphology provides but a weak guide to central nervous system complexity.

The evidence for this chronology comes from a small number of skeletal remains recovered from a small number of assemblages at Olduvai Gorge, Tanzania, and a handful of other sites extending west into present-day Kenya and north into Ethiopia. *Small number* is something I cannot emphasize enough. In statistical terms, assertions about the physiology, life history, and even body plan of early members of the human clade are severely underpowered—that is, the number of examples we have from which to form a judgment of an effect, a statistically significant difference, of a particular size (for instance, a 30 percent difference in cranial volume) are too small for us be very confident about the effect size. At one time, paleontologists favored a finely graded chronology of distinct species within *Homo*. Recent interpretations of the skeletal evidence have been more cautious, acknowledging that taxonomic boundaries, even at the genus level, say, between *Australopithecus* and *Homo,* are fluid.

By 1.8 Ma, however, skeletal and artifact assemblages from a number of sites indicate the emergence of hominins with a new kind of life history. The populations exemplified by these specimens, collectively known as *Homo erectus,* represent not a revolution in life history so much as a coalescence and amplification of features observed separately over the preceding half million to million years. Skeletal and dental remains with juvenile and adolescent features allow us to tentatively reconstruct this new life history. How do you identify a child's skeleton? Size and stature help. You can also look to see if the epiphysea of long bones, including the humerus and tibia, have fused, indicating the conclusion of limb growth, and if molars have erupted. On the basis of these kinds of evidence, paleoanthropologists have ascribed to *H. erectus* the germ of a distinctly human life history. What makes this life history distinctly human is how it combines elements of the *r*- and *K*-selection patterns described in the prologue: higher birth rate and total lifetime fertility combined with slower development over the course of infancy and early life and greater metaparental investment in the development of individual offspring. I write *metaparental* because a key part of the reproductive strategy that facilitated higher investment alongside shorter interbirth intervals was the emergence of *alloparenting,* parental-type investment in children other than one's own, in particular *grandmothering.* Compared with both other primates and with eutherians—placental mammals—more broadly, humans are remarkably *altricial,* that is, biologically immature, at birth. Young humans experience a prolonged infancy, a period of dependence on others for everything from feeding to locomotion to protection from cold and predators. Humans are also exceptional for the degree to which they rely on *culture*—cumulative, socially transmitted patterns of behavior that must be learned anew by each new member of the community. In humans, dependence extends into a prolonged adolescence. This is not just a time of renewed skeletal growth but a period of the acquisition and refinement of socially transmitted sensorimotor skills essential to subsistence and reproduction.

A corollary of prolonged infancy and adolescence is *developmental phenotypic plasticity,* that is, the individual's potential to grow in divergent ways depending on selective pressures, typically periods of food scarcity or other kinds of *environmental risk* operating within the time span of maturation. Developmental plasticity has been observed in divergences in body size of up to 24 percent among the skeletons of mature *H. erectus* individuals from different times and places. Phenotypic plasticity is not just a morphological and physiological phenomenon. It extends to behavior too. This can mean lifelong divergences in behavior that depend on early experience (think of tolerance of heat and cold). But usually when we talk about behavioral plasticity, we have in mind *versatility*: an individual or community's capacity to select among a repertoire of alternate behavior patterns depending on circumstances—for instance, adjusting one's diet from season to season or year to year.

Overall, the pattern observable in debris assemblages attributed to *H. erectus* is of slowed life history—prolonged development and prolonged postreproductive life, facilitated by and facilitating a novel form of *cooperative breeding* and cooperative provisioning. Cooperation, combined with improved diet, was the key to humans' greater reproductive success, measured in terms of the proportion of individuals who survived into adulthood, after 1.8 Ma. Encephalization—increased brain size relative to body size—is evident much earlier, and *H. erectus* exhibits a further expansion of cranial volume of roughly 25 percent over earlier species of *Homo*. The greater cognition made possible by a more complex central nervous system is evident in this period not just in tools (described next), increased dietary breadth, and the (somewhat speculative) evidence for cooperative breeding, but in the species' extended range and capacity for migration. By 1.6 Ma, *H. erectus* is found widely across Africa and Asia. The dramatic further encephalization characteristic of the later history of *Homo,* along with the suite of physiological and behavioral adaptations described next, was made possible by cooperation in production and reproduction.

Equifinality

One of the things I hinted at in our thought experiment about the beach was that debris is subject to *equifinality*. That is, a given assemblage may represent the debris of a wide range of phenomena as they unfolded at the time of deposition. If we observe a pattern of broken-chevron coruscations extending across the sand in two parallel tracks, we might be able to say with confidence, "A truck passed by yesterday," but after a week, we'd observe just a pair of vague indentations, and after a year, nothing—at one year, or even one week, from the proposed time of deposition, the scenario in which a truck passed by and the scenario in which no truck passed by are equifinal.

So the relationship between artifacts as they were at the time of deposition and what we observe some time later is labile. We can say more: it is not just durable artifacts, or the remains of living things, or traces of occupation events such as cooking fires, that are subject to equifinality; *it is the entire constellation of events that gives rise to a debris assemblage.* Indeed, it is a mistake even to speak of a labile relationship between artifacts "at the time of deposition" and what we observe sometime later. At a time depth of 2 million years, deposition itself is poorly bounded in time. Deposition does not happen all at once, and it is subject to a maddening array of confounds that make sport of the fantasy of reading a tidy history of occupation in the sequence of assemblages as they present to us with progressively deeper excavation. Those who came before, whether beachgoers or early hominins, did not take care to discard their material and bodily spoor in patterns conducive to interpretation, nor did they choose the moment at which they discarded something or died with an eye toward illuminating some feature of their behavior. Nor did they take care not to interfere with the debris that earlier occupants discarded.

So one thing equifinality means is that debris assemblages are coarsely grained in the time domain, that is, they have poor *temporal resolution* relative to the events we ask them to stand in for. They have poor spatial resolution too. Back to the People of the Beach. Let's say we can be sure that the people in question, those who used this beach a hundred years ago, represented a well-bounded *community.* What is a community? For our purposes, a community is a demographic time slice of a population. Depending on the kinds of questions we're asking, it might be three generations or it might be ten. Communities are bound together by some kind of *social structure,* a repertoire of typed social relationships governing things like food sharing, the care of children and adolescents, resolving disputes, and defending the community against outside threats. In humans, social structure also touches on the exercise of more specialized expertise, among other things for the manufacture of complex tools, the interpretation of meteorological and cosmological phenomena, and the treatment of injuries and ill health. Even where social structure takes on a life of its own, all these things—day-to-day life—demand a pattern of recurring interaction. This, in turn, entails that communities must have some kind of spatial coherence. The question is: *What is the relationship of the spatial coherence characteristic of a particular assemblage to that of the community whose debris it represents?*

When we come across a concentrated assemblage of tools and other debris, it is tempting to imagine that whatever the debris itself might tell us, the spatially concentrated character of its deposition indicates something new in the subsistence habits of the creatures that left them: a tendency to organize subsistence around a *home base,* with trips to procure food and raw materials for artifacts starting and ending in the same place. The appeal of home-base models owes something to the fact that it's simply easier to collect evidence where it's densely distributed and something to the fact that we tend to use others, in particular those far removed from us in time and way of life, as screens, projecting our own habits, in this case domesticity, on them. But think back to the beach: if we took for granted that the beach represented the home base of the people whose debris we're excavating, how much would we miss about the ritualized nature of the beach excursion? Whether an assemblage represents a home base, a tool cache, a ceremonial site, or some other kind of land use is something that needs to be read, cautiously, off the site itself. This demands a more capacious vision of how hominins have fashioned *niches* in the places they've lived.

Stone Tools

Equifinality applies to artifacts too. The archaeological record is biased toward materials that preserve well, namely, stone, and against organic materials: bone, antler, shell, grass, and the integumentary tissues of animals.

The earliest evidence of the use of stone implements by hominins comes from a site at West Turkana, Kenya, that has been dated to 3.3 Ma—500 ka before the earliest attested *Homo* skeletal remains. The next comes from Gona, Ethiopia, dated to 2.6 Ma. It is another 100 ka before evidence of stone tools begins to crop up regularly in the archaeological record, with confirmed instances distributed across East Africa: in the Afar Depression in what is now Ethiopia, in the Turkana Basin, Kenya, and at Olduvai Gorge,

Tanzania. Stone artifact assemblages from a slightly later period, 2.0 to 1.8 Ma, have been found at sites in South Africa and Algeria, before 1.8 Ma in Dmanisi, Georgia, and by 1.66 Ma in the Nihewan basin, China, and at two sites in Java.

A caveat: it is not clear that the earliest stone artifacts should all be attributed to *Homo,* nor can we say for sure that the increasingly widespread distribution of the artifact complex first observed in East Africa represents the migration of populations, as opposed to the transfer of a *technology,* that is, a socially transmitted repertoire of behaviors for manipulating the material world, to a population that was already there. Either hypothesis augurs for the growing cognitive and social sophistication of the makers before 2 Ma.

A second caveat: the relationship between the appearance of artifacts in the archaeological record and the appearance of the embodied skill necessary to produce them is not straightforward. The skill must of course predate the artifact, but by how long is difficult to say.

A third caveat: *the artifacts we find today may not have been the tools but the by-products of tool manufacture.* The clearest evidence of deliberate manufacture of tools from the period in question comes in the form of *cores* and *flakes,* where flakes can actually be fitted back into a core found nearby or where flakes exhibit signs of repeated *débitage,* the chipping off of smaller fragments to form a sharp edge capable, say, of cutting tendons or scraping bones. One implication of débitage manufacture is that a given core may serve as the basis for flake production many times, but of course we see it only in the form it had at the time it was discarded. There are ways around this *final artifact fallacy,* including experimental replication of tool manufacture and microscopic observation of débitage trauma. We'll see other instances where accidents of the deposition process obtrude into debris analysis.

The type of débitage observed in these earliest stone artifact assemblages exemplifies what are known as Oldowan industries, so-called after Olduvai Gorge, Tanzania. Starting around 1.7 Ma, a more sophisticated tool complex begins to appear, the Acheulean, after Saint-Acheul, near Amiens, France, characterized by more precise control over débitage. Acheulean industries continue as late as 300 ka. But even Oldowan assemblages, comprising stone artifacts and faunal skeletal remains, offer evidence of marked innovations in subsistence strategy. The question, as ever, is how to interpret this evidence.

Faunal Assemblages

At some Oldowan sites in East and South Africa, skeletal remains of animals other than hominins suggest that hominins were using stone flakes—scrapers and choppers—to derive food from animal carcasses and skeletons. This was not hunting or even butchery. In most cases, it was more likely a form of scavenging in which hominins took possession of the skeletal remains of animals that had been killed and consumed by great cats. Here again, equifinality rears its head. Not only do bones not preserve the way stone does, not all kinds of bones preserve at the same rate. Bone *taphonomy*—decomposition and degradation—varies, among other things, with bone density and diameter. If consumers of faunal skeletons, hominin or otherwise, were crushing bones to extract marrow, the resulting fragments would degrade faster and be more likely to disappear from the record. A preponderance of limbs in faunal deposits associated with early humans suggests that hominins were collecting what was left after the cats had eaten most of the muscle and breaking the bones to get at the marrow.

Some limb bones exhibit not only carnivore tooth marks and signs of scraping and crushing with stone tools but cut marks that suggest hominins were getting muscle meat that the carnivores had missed. A handful of researchers have interpreted these cut marks as signs that "meat made us human" from the start. But the evidence comes from a small set of assemblages, mostly from a single site at Olduvai, and there's no reason to consider these sites more exemplary than others.

Nor is there evidence to suggest that the manufacture of stone tools arose mainly to facilitate access to marrow and meat, as opposed, say, to C4 grasses and underground storage organs. Clearly, before 2 Ma, hominins had emerged who could subsist on a broader range of foods, perhaps alternating among different subsistence bases according to seasonal or annual availability. Clearly, this emergent dietary versatility encompassed animal bodies, including marrow, periosteum, and muscle and connective tissue. It seems likely that dietary versatility was driven not just by increasing variability in climate but by the increased energetic demands of bodies and life histories oriented toward cooperation. That is, by the time of *H. erectus,* hominin diet was not just distinctly versatile; it was distinctly improved.

Meat formed part of this improvement. Whether it was an essential part depends what you mean by "essential." If by "essential" you mean, *Were there instances when a community's survival depended, transiently, on its members' ability to access and digest animal bodies?* then the answer is yes. If by "essential" you mean, *Did absence of meat in the diet impair individuals' growth and health, including the development and maintenance of neurological function?* the answer is *probably not at this stage*. If that were the case, we'd expect to see a clearer signal in evidence from tools and teeth (see the next section). This distinction, between "essential as a fallback in times of environmental stress (essential at the community level)" and "essential for proper development and health (essential at the individual level)," is something to keep in mind as we move into a more detailed discussion of the physiological adaptations implicated in dietary versatility.

Teeth and Versatility

Before we discuss dietary improvement, there is one more line of evidence to consider: teeth.

Like bones, teeth are subject to taphonomic processes, but because they tend to be more highly mineralized than bones, they preserve better. Dental evidence of diet can be divided into two categories, adaptive and use related. Adaptive evidence includes allometry (comparative size) and comparative morphology or shape—you're looking for signs that the genetically coded size and shape of teeth, or the relative sizes of molars and incisors, vary from one population to another over space and time, with implications for the types of food different populations ate. That is, you're betting that tooth form is *functionally adaptive*. Functional morphology offers a loose outer envelope on behavior. It tells you something about what an individual or population *was capable of eating* or *sometimes ate* or *had to be able to eat,* not what that individual or population regularly ate. If nothing else, functional morphology allows us to offer more informed speculation about the *fallback foods* a population relied on in times of scarcity. The relationship of molar to incisor size and the shapes of molar cusps and incisor occlusal (biting) surfaces suggest the types of trauma that teeth could inflict on food and, in turn, the fracture properties of the foods in question. Some foods, for instance, nuts, seeds, bones, and underground storage organs (tubers, bulbs, rhizomes), are hard but brittle—they resist initial fracture, but once you get a toehold, fractures tend to spread quickly. These foods demand a mortar-and-pestle type of chewing. Others, including grasses and meat, are fibrous and ductile: superficial lacerations may come quickly, but actually cutting through requires a repetitive sawing-shearing type of mastication.

In contrast to functional morphology, *dental microwear* tells you not what an animal could eat but what it did eat in the weeks leading up to its death. Different types of chewing leave different abrasive signatures on the surface of tooth enamel: crushing yields a topologically complex pitted surface, whereas shearing yields a pattern of fine striations that indicate the direction of shearing force. New abrasions succeed existing ones every time the animal eats, so that the window in which a given microwear signature is valid is measurable in days. Here is one instance where ephemerality helps us, since if diet varies day to day or season to season, you should expect to see a corresponding variation in the patterns of use wear characteristic of the foods eaten at different times. Of course, there's always the possibility that mortality is correlated with diet or season, especially if one of the observed dietary patterns represents high reliance on fallback foods. If anything, you'd expect dental microwear samples to be biased in favor of fallback or refuge diets, since mortality tends to increase in times of environmental stress.

What do these data tell us? Peter Ungar, a specialist in early hominin dentition, puts it flatly: "The most obvious conclusion we can draw from a review of the fossil evidence for diet in African early *Homo* is that there is not much of it, and what we do have is not very compelling." Let's not end on a downer: *H. erectus* was capable of relying on a broader variety of foods than predecessors and contemporaries. This broader diet included tissues of ungulates and other animals that inhabited the increasingly dry and unforested environment characteristic of eastern and southern Africa during the transition from the Pliocene to the Pleistocene—the marrow, muscle, and connective tissues of the long bones of ungulate limbs, certainly, and other tissues (nerves, fat deposits, organs) possibly.

It also likely included xeric (dry-climate) plants. Many researchers have been enamored of the idea that underground storage organs played a key role in providing the additional energy needed to support early humans' enlarged central nervous system and more cooperative, more migratory way of life after 2 Ma. If *H. erectus* made extensive use of digging sticks made of wood and bone and panniers made of grass, these might not show up in the archaeological record the way stone tools do. But as with all single-explanatory-factor hypotheses, it seems unlikely that humans in this period specialized in underground storage organs, that is, relied on them consistently in all seasons and climates. For one thing, even if digging and gathering tools disappeared, you'd still expect to find mortar and pestle—at this stage, humans were eating all their food raw, and uncooked roots pose a challenge to the most robust jaws. For another, dental morphology and microwear don't provide evidence of consistent crushing mastication.

The best we can say is that after 1.9 Ma, meat started to play a more prominent recurring role in protohuman diet, but by no means a dominant role. The innovations in physiology and behavior we've discussed up to this point were not made possible by meat. But they did facilitate a greater opportunistic reliance on meat. That, in turn, improved *H. erectus*'s survival just as any versatility would. The capacity to survive partly on meat also conferred more specific advantages. These would cause meat eating to be drawn into an evolutionary feedback loop, as we'll see in the next chapter.

2 Hunting

Improved Diet

In the previous chapter, I referred to the *improvement* of diet. Now it's time to make this term more precise.

When we talk about the quality of a diet, there are a number of different things we might have in mind. In some cases "high quality" means the opposite in paleoanthropological and contemporary contexts. In the first part of this book, discussion of nutritional quality uses paleoanthropological standards. What nutritional quality means today is something we'll consider later.

At the most basic level, a higher-quality diet is one that affords greater access to food energy—"calories"—at lower cost of incorporation into the body. By *cost* here, I mean energetic cost—calories consumed per calories expended in digestion or, to put it another way, the mass of material you need to ingest to attain a particular net energetic benefit. Nutritional quality, in this usage, is about *bioavailability.* Bioavailability is measured from the point of ingestion. It excludes costs, energetic or otherwise, associated with getting food from the world to your mouth. So a higher-quality diet may actually be energetically costlier overall if it entails, say, a more vigorous form of foraging or a more elaborate method of preparation that includes repetitive pounding and grinding. Cooking is one way to improve the bioavailability of foods. For humans, meat tends to be more bioavailable than plant foods. One of the questions we're trying to address here is, *In what period in the history of human physiology did meat become a practical high-quality food?*

Already we can see how nutritional quality in the paleoanthropological and contemporary senses diverge. Often today when we talk about a higher-quality diet, we have in mind one that is *less* bioavailable—less processed, lower in glycemic load, something that our bodies need to do more work to digest. The reversal in polarity of the association between bioavailability and nutritional quality is a very recent phenomenon, a product of the global *nutrition transition* alluded to in the prologue. When nutrition physiologists today refer to a contemporary nutrition transition, they're actually referring to the third such transition in human history. The second unfolded with the emergence of agriculture starting some 12,000 years ago. The first was the more gradual and uneven transition to a higher-quality diet after 1.5 Ma.

Beyond energetic availability, diets vary in the extent to which they meet the needs of the individual or community in question. These needs include sufficient quantities of the different kinds of macronutrient—carbohydrates, proteins, and fats—to support the growth and maintenance of the body's tissues and signaling systems. Macronutrient ratios are one area where modern humans exhibit exceptional physiological versatility in that humans can tolerate, indeed, thrive on, diets with a remarkable range of macronutrient ratios, including those that consist largely of carbohydrates from fruit and those that consist almost exclusively of protein and fats from animal sources. Indeed, it is misguided to speak as if there were a single set of optimal macronutrient ratios. Optimal for what? To support thriving under what environmental circumstances and behavioral regime? At what stage of life? Macronutrient needs differ according to the degree to which metabolism is oriented toward growth (childhood and adolescence) or maintenance (adulthood), and they vary over the course of childhood and adolescence according to which organ systems are experiencing rapid growth at that time. When we speak of optimal diets, we also need to specify the time horizon over which thriving is to be measured. A diet that affords a high metabolic throughput and consistent mood and energy level today but puts you at risk for inflammatory disease twenty years from now supports thriving on one time horizon but not another. A diet that imposes a significant environmental burden may be optimal for you but not for future generations.

Physiological versatility would be nothing without behavioral versatility. Here that means broad taste. Broad taste, of course, is something individuals can cultivate, but palatability does face limits. In particular, it is linked to the recurring combination of contrastive textures and tastes that make food biomechanically tractable—easier to swallow—and signal the presence of complementary macronutrient components and key micronutrients. Even under conditions of profound food availability stress, people find it difficult to get down a bowl of starch in the absence of condiments or *relishes.* Often it is in the relishes that we see meat and other high-value animal source foods.

Human thriving depends not just on versatility but on adaptations to the mix of resources available in a particular setting. Examples of this phenomenon, *metabolic niche construction,* include adult lactase persistence in populations where fresh dairy products have long played a key role in the diet, more copies of the gene for salivary amylase in the genome of individuals from populations that subsist on rices and cereals, and the recently described adaptation among Eastern Inuit to high intake of omega-3 polyunsaturated fatty acids. Later, we consider the newly salient fact that it is not just the human genome in the strict sense—that is, the autosomal and mitochondrial genomes present in human somatic cells—that matters for metabolic adaptation but the metagenome of the microbiota that colonize our intestinal tract.

There is more we could say about nutritional quality. Not all instances of a given macronutrient class are nutritionally and metabolically equivalent—different amino acids have distinct roles in tissue construction and endocrine and neural signaling, and short-chain and long-chain fatty acids follow distinct pathways to catalysis and storage. To a certain degree, the familiar macronutrients classes represent artifacts of the historical development of nutrition science rather than a considered functional typology of the elements of bodily growth and maintenance. But we have a basis to proceed.

Sometime after 1.9 Ma, hominins emerged who looked substantially more like us in skeletal plan and life history. They were also more like us in that they appear to have done well with a variety of diets, they used a cumulative repertoire of tools transmitted by social learning to enhance their capacity to secure food, and animal tissues played an increased role in their diets. Within another 200 to 400 ka, a new tool industry, the Acheulean, would emerge that demanded enhanced faculties of communication, cooperation, reading of others' intentions, fine motor control, working memory, episodic memory, and imagination. The Acheulean tool kit also suggests a more active way of life involving extensive walking and running. All these things are energetically costly and demanded an improved diet.

Was this improved diet meat based?

Enter Hunting

Superimposed on variation from site to site, we see broad commonalities in the pattern of life attributable to humans over a period of a million years, from about 1.5 Ma to 500 ka. At the species level, we can think of the people—by the end of this period, it certainly makes sense to call them people—of this million-year interval as a spongy network of closely related kinds of beings. Over the course of this period, we see but a modest *secular trend* or directional change over time in skeletal morphology and technology.

The Acheulean industries that coalesced by 1.5 Ma differ from the Oldowan in a number of ways. For one, patterns of débitage on worked flakes exhibit the makers' awareness of the effects of the sequencing of gestures—striking point A and then neighboring point B will produce a different outcome from striking B and then A. This suggests in turn a nascent *syntactic facility*, a key dimension not just of manufacture but of language. Assemblages come to be dominated by a new genre of lithic artifact, the *biface hand ax*, characterized by one long axis and independent bilateral symmetries in the two cross-sectional dimensions. Making bifaces demanded not just improved manual fine-motor control and hand-eye coordination but the ability to simultaneously manage a number of different dimensions of variance—breadth and symmetry in the two cross-sectional dimensions, asymmetry along the long axis—and, beyond that, *a capacity to hold an image of the desired finished form in your mind as you worked.* Once these new somatic and cognitive capacities become established in the lithic record, they appear to coast along with little cumulative development for nearly a million years.

Scavenging continues all through this period. As faculties of cooperation and coordinate activity developed in *H. erectus,* along with fine-edged tools better suited to butchery, it is possible that in certain seasons, an increased part of the diet came from the peripheral muscle of ungulates scavenged from carnivore kill sites by a band of humans descending as a group, with some members of the group dissasembling the carcasses, some providing defense against lingering carnivores, and some transporting meat and other resources back to camp. Is this hunting? The boundary between scavenging and hunting gets fuzzy if we imagine the human scavengers tracking the carnivores, waiting for them to make a kill, and then swooping in to chase them off. Is meat eating the *basis* of human subsistence at this stage? Again, that depends on where and when you look and what season this is and what the weather has been like over the past year. Later *H. erectus* may have been habitual scavengers and yet relied on plant foods for the bulk of their diet for the bulk of the year. Direct physical evidence of plant consumption, in the form of *phytoliths*, mineralized plant remains, stuck to teeth and tools, is clear for later periods but sparse at 1 Ma.

Sometime after 800 ka this all starts to change. Between 600 and 500 ka, a new species appears in the hominin record in eastern and southern Africa. *H. heidelbergensis* is conventionally accorded the place of last common ancestor of the two species recognized to have attained a "modern" level of cognition and social behavior, *H. neanderthalensis* and *H. sapiens*. But the term *last common ancestor* is misleading. DNA evidence suggests that humans living in Iberia at 430 ka belonged to a lineage that had diverged from that of *H. sapiens* more than 100 ka earlier. Yet *H. neanderthalensis* and *H. sapiens* were still capable of interbreeding nearly 400 ka later during their brief overlap in Europe. Again, we are dealing here not with a tree but with a spongy network or *metapopulation* whose various subpopulations overlapped in the basic physiological constraints on their diet and behavior.

Cranial capacity suggests *H. heidelbergensis* exhibited a further encephalization of 40 percent or more by gross volume over late *H. erectus*. By 300 ka, its descendants had achieved wide distribution across Africa and Eurasia, and we observe the coalescence of at least two distinct social–technical horizons: the Middle Paleolithic (MP) in western Eurasia, the Middle Stone Age (MSA) in Africa. In both Africa and in Eurasia, humans after 300 ka were practicing a form of foraging that we would have no trouble understanding as hunting.

Middle Paleolithic Eurasia

Some accounts date the onset of the Middle Paleolithic to as late as 240 ka, but the features by which it is known appear separately some time before. In addition to the distinctly robust Neanderthal skeletal morphology, these include the widespread, sustained use of fire; the manufacture of compound artifacts such as hafted spears; and a range of new techniques of lithic manufacture. The most striking of these is the *Levallois method*, which entails shaping a stone, the *nucleus* or *core*, in such a way that a flake may be removed from it with a single well-placed blow. The Levallois technique appears to have emerged multiple times in Africa and western Eurasia.

Bark resins and adhesives appear in the Eurasian archaeological record from around 200 ka, suggesting not just an expanded understanding of the ends to which fire could be put but a degree of imaginative planning that transcended the association of a given material or artifact form with a fixed set of affordances and uses. At least in some cases, manufacture now entailed assembling a variety of raw materials from different places and combining them in ways that imposed constraints on the sequence of activity—syntax again—and at the same time afforded the possibility of higher-order planning in the form of the modular partial preparation of subassemblies. The elaboration of such *operative chains* for manufactures is a clear sign that humans of this period occupied a new plateau in *planning*. This expanded cognitive–social horizon could not fail to shape their subsistence habits too.

Many observers of this period have been unequivocal that the leitmotiv of Middle Paleolithic subsistence was the cooperative hunting of large ungulates. Archaeologist Mary Stiner's view is exemplary: "It is safe to say that MP people were dedicated large game hunters" who could not otherwise have consistently met their energetic needs in the places where they lived. Eurasian humans were surviving, in some cases for upward of a hundred generations on end, in places where vegetation was not abundant year-round.

The evidence for Middle Paleolithic hunting includes stable nitrogen isotope ratios in bone collagen along with *faunal assemblages* in a wide range of contexts, from Iberia east across the northern Mediterranean to the Levant and north to the British Isles and northern continental Europe. These assemblages provide clear evidence of carcass transport from kill sites to camps. An extended sequence of assemblages at Schöningen, methodically excavated by Hartmut Thieme and colleagues and referred to, in their reports, as the Horse Butchery Site, has been particularly influential in shaping current opinion on the nature of Neanderthal subsistence. In a discipline defined by scarcity of data, it is easy to appreciate the appeal of the Horse Butchery Site, which has yielded the remains of upward of 15,000 mammals and 1,500 lithic implements, along with a handful of wood and bone artifacts. "The finds from the Horse Butchery Site," Thieme's group puts it drily, "brought the debate about hunting versus scavenging among late archaic hominins . . . to an abrupt end."

If you're wondering why the text has suddenly erupted in direct quotations, it's because I'm concerned to convey the spirit of recent debates about Paleolithic subsistence. For some time, Middle Paleolithic archaeology has been a little obsessed with establishing the *trophic status* of its protagonists—that is, where they stood in a hierarchy of energetic transformations with primary (autotrophic—photosynthetic and chemosynthetic) carbon and nitrogen fixation at one end and a hypothetical top predator at the other. How many hops were they removed from photosynthesis? How *high up* were they, how close to the apex of the food web?

So let's consider some of the difficulties of faunal assemblage analysis. Apart from simply documenting an accretion of animals with clear marks of defleshing and burning, zooarchaeologists are concerned to establish *kill profiles*—how many animals of what types and what ages. This tells you something about the predators' identity and strategy—obligate carnivores tend to pick off the young and the old, while humans tend to target animals in their prime. Archaeofauna census is anything but straightforward. To derive a count of specimens, you might identify a mandible from one, a femur from another, while taking care that they do not in fact belong to the same animal. In some cases, specimen counts will depend on who is doing the counting. But in all cases, small animals are more likely to be undercounted—not so much because bone fragments will go unnoticed but because, owing to decay, they won't be there to begin with. This tends to undercut the view of Neanderthals as large game specialists. At lower latitudes, you do see evidence of a much broader dietary strategy, including birds, turtles, and small mammals. Evidence of sustained use of shellfish and other littoral and marine resources does not appear until after 150 ka, but then again, the evidence might not preserve so well and some of the key sites may be underwater today.

What about nitrogen isotope analysis? Careful isotope studies suggest that even in colder environments, Neanderthals relied extensively on plant foods to meet their protein no less than their caloric needs. These have been joined by two new forms of evidence: phytoliths observed in the dental calculus and on the tools of MP humans and DNA recovered from phytoliths and oral microbiota. These suggest that in some times and places, Neanderthals kept a diet rich in fungi, pine nuts, and mosses with practically no meat. From a physiological perspective, dietary breadth makes sense. Exclusive reliance on the peripheral muscle of lean terrestrial mammals would incur a risk of protein toxicity, especially for pregnant women and young children. Ethnographic studies of Inuit diet indicate that circumpolar hunters limit consumption of meat in the prototypical sense in favor of fat and what carbohydrates are available—including the contents of ungulates' intestines.

Middle Stone Age Africa

Is the evidence any clearer for contemporaneous early *H. sapiens* in Africa? Yes, if by "clearer," we mean that the evidence of breadth, diversity, and secular variability in human subsistence strategy is less subject to the kinds of sampling biases that beset the study of Middle Paleolithic Eurasia. Let's pause to emphasize that breadth, diversity, and secular variability refer to distinct things. By *breadth*, I mean reliance on a broad range of resources within a particular community. Not every single thing that was known to be good to eat was eaten every day. The availability of resources varied seasonally, annually, and over longer periods within an individual lifetime. By *diversity*, I mean that the panel of things people relied on to meet their energetic and nutritional needs varied from place to place depending on what the local environment had to offer. By *secular variability*, I mean that subsistence strategy changed over longer spans of time. In particular, variability was driven by the increasing volatility of the cooling–warming cycles that characterize the Earth after 3 Ma. Breadth, diversity, and secular variability exemplify versatility on three distinct spatiotemporal horizons.

It is in Middle Paleolithic Africa that we meet *Homo sapiens*, "ourselves," for the first time. The clearest evidence for how *H. sapiens* lived in the 200 to 250 ka prior to the end of the Pleistocene comes from a panel of sites in South Africa that exhibit sustained or recurring occupation over many generations. As in Eurasia, the literature has been obsessed with hunting. Lithic assemblages dominated by prepared-core débitage and fine blades and marked by an absence of large hand axes appear as early as 280 ka. The most compelling evidence of innovation in tool design and fabrication technique comes from two chronologically distinct culture complexes identified at upward of thirty or more sites extending along the southern tip of the continent. These include open-air, rock-shelter, and cave settings. Some are right on the present-day coast, others more than 100 kilometers (60 miles) inland. The earlier of these culture complexes is named for a site at Still Bay and dates from 75 to 80 ka, with some sites showing ongoing or recurring occupation over a period of 8,000 years. Among other innovations, the Still Bay culture is associated with the use of heat treatment in the production of small implements that might have been used as darts or spear points. The second key culture complex is named for Howiesons Poort, roughly 65 to 60 ka. The Howiesons Poort industry is distinguished by its makers' fondness for adhesives ranging from ochre to plant gums. These they combined with a number of hafting techniques to produce what are unmistakably projectile weapons, including, possibly, the earliest attested arrows.

As in Eurasia, the cumulativity of these innovations is limited—apparently useful technologies sometimes disappear from the lithic record, perhaps reappearing elsewhere after a gap. Do these reappearances represent the continuation of traditions that for whatever reason have become archaeological invisible in the intervening period, or do they represent *homoplasy*, that is, convergent independent innovations? Difficult to say. When we turn to the evidence from faunal assemblages, we see something similar: modest evidence of increasing dietary breadth over time overlaid on a stronger signal of diversity and variability that is not directional.

One problem is how to measure breadth. Later we'll see that hunters don't always base decisions about what to hunt on ease of capture. But if you assume that a need to minimize risk plays some role in shaping hunting behavior, then a shift away from large, docile ungulates toward smaller, more mobile prey and an increased reliance on shellfish and other aquatic resources might look like an adaptive response to environmental stress, that is, situations where the easy prey is no longer available. Shellfish make regular appearances in anthropogenic assemblages on the southern coast of Africa from 164 ka, but quantifying their role in the diet is tricky: Does their accretion in middens over many generations make it easy to overestimate how regularly humans relied on them? Or are they subject to compaction, making it easy to underestimate their use? Or were shellfish simply not the kind of food you were expected to bring back to camp for final processing and distribution the way you might with meat and underground storage organs? It is easy to imagine scenarios in which shellfish and other aquatic foods were consumed the moment they were found, as you walked along the beach, or perhaps were collected and processed at an impromptu camp. Especially in times and places where humans not only used fire but could ignite it at will, this kind of one-off camp must have been ubiquitous: you're out foraging, you want a break, or you need to warm up or dry off, you've collected a substantial quantity of food but it's not the type of thing you're inclined to carry all the way back to camp. This scenario is common among foragers today. Signs of deferred consumption—carrying something back to camp before consuming it—are useful markers of the emergence of cooperative foraging in early *Homo*. But even at a much later date, not all consumption is deferred, and it is the things that never make it back to camp—shellfish, dates, berries—that might, had we but access to them, do the most to expand our view of what early humans were eating, including their sources of key micronutrients and fatty acids. As it is, renewed inspection of teeth and tools has begun to yield extensive evidence of plant consumption in southern Africa as in Europe and the Levant, including a variety of grasses but not, intriguingly, tubers, bulbs, or rhizomes.

A final word is in order about the communities we've been discussing: *they were very, very small*. Genomic estimates of *effective population size*, an approximation of the number of individuals in a community who reproduced in a generation, suggest that the Neanderthal population of Europe averaged no more than 5,000 during warmer periods and 2,500 during glaciations, with a peak of 10,000. As late as 20 ka, effective *H. sapiens* populations in Europe and eastern Asia fell as low as 1,200. Local extinctions must have been common, and the final disappearance of the Neanderthals at 41 to 39 ka likely was more a product of interbreeding and "genetic swamping" by newly arrived *H. sapiens* than of competition or rigid cleaving to a provisioning strategy that had ceased to be effective. Recently there's been great enthusiasm among cultural evolution theorists for the idea that low population density is itself maladaptive in that it limits the potential for both innovation and the cumulative transmission of existing technologies—that is, that we are forever running on a treadmill of cultural attrition, with small populations more susceptible to losses of technology. The problems with this theory are many. For what it's worth, it seems not to hold for humans of this era.

The Physiological Legacy of Dietary Versatility

There's a second way to approach the question of what made us what we are. We can ask, *What does our physiology say about our evolutionary history?*

No question, the fat, connective tissue, marrow, nervous tissue, and muscle of vertebrates have formed key parts of the diet in many times and places over the long arc of the human clade. Hunting has been central to human subsistence since the late Pleistocene. Does this make us obligate carnivores, or does it make us versatile? Was the key selective pressure in human evolution the need to reliably secure a higher-quality diet under variation in the mix of resources available in different times and places? Or was it a more specific need for animal tissues that drove innovation in tool design and the expansion of social networks and relationship repertoires?

If you take away nothing else from this book, remember this: *in history, the answer to either/or questions is always "both."* But the either/or formulation does give us something to push back against.

To recap, the basic insight from comparing human life history with the life histories of other primates is that humans grow slowly. Infancy represents a continuation of gestation. Morphologically we are born altricial, with incomplete development, something that stands out even more when you contrast it with human babies' social *precocity,* their adeptness at reading social signals and getting adults to entrain their actions and emotions to their own needs and moods. The elongated nature of human life history continues through childhood, adolescence, adulthood, and postreproductive life. At the same time, humans exhibit higher total fertility than other primates: we have more kids, and we have them faster. The resources to shepherd these kids through their prolonged dependency and adolescence come from cooperative breeding.

The physiological concomitants of human life history include encephalization (big brainedness), adiposity (fatness), and a distinctive energy-use profile. These form a network—they are mutually implicated in ways that suggest the causal arrows run in all directions.

Encephalization

Encephalization—the evolution of large brains—has been a recurring theme in our discussion. I've mentioned cranial capacities and alluded to indirect evidence for the appearance of novel cognitive faculties—planning, coordination, inferring others' intentions, imitative learning, syntax. Observations of contemporary other-than-human primates provide evidence of *cognitive buffering* of resource volatility—bigger-brained species show a greater capacity to smooth out seasonal variation in the availability of key foods. If you could identify the mechanisms behind this or show that buffering unfolds over longer periods, it would bolster arguments for an evolutionary feedback loop between dietary versatility and brain size. For now let's stick to anatomy and physiology. Two observations: first, we have big brains. Whether you look at all eutherian mammals or just primates, humans lie way off the regression line for the relationship between lean body mass and brain mass: our brains are disproportionately large for our bodies. Second, these big brains are energetically expensive, requiring, in adults, up to 25 percent of resting metabolic rate. Compare this with upper bounds of 10 percent in other primates and 5 percent in other-than-primate mammals.

Where do we get the energy to run our big brains? Over the past twenty-five years, this has been a key question in evolutionary anthropology. For many observers, our expensive brains represent exhibit A in the case for meat's role in human evolution. Meat, the argument goes, supported encephalization, and the quest for more meat drove further encephalization, which made possible the complex industries, fine motor skills, and ballistic faculties needed to bring down large mobile prey.

Up to this point, I've tried to avoid mention of disciplinary undercurrents in the literature—who cites whom, which phrases take on a life of their own. But here it's unavoidable, because encephalization is one case where there's a clear *index paper*, that is, a single source that has become a touchstone for an entire discourse. The paper in question is Aiello and Wheeler's "The Expensive-Tissue Hypothesis: The Brain and the Digestive System in Human and Primate Evolution," which appeared in *Current Anthropology* in 1995. Aiello and Wheeler hypothesized that there has been an evolutionary trade-off between two kinds of expensive—energetically demanding—tissue: cerebral white matter and splanchnic tissue or gut. Encephalization, the expensive tissue hypothesis goes, demanded a compensatory reduction in the size of the gut. This in turn demanded a higher-quality diet than that typical of other primates. This has often been taken to mean a meat-based diet, though it could also mean a diet with a higher proportion of cooked foods, whether of plant or animal origin (Aiello and Wheeler refer to "animal products, nuts, or underground tubers").

Aiello and Wheeler were careful to frame the expensive tissue hypothesis as a hypothesis, but you'd be amazed how often their paper has been cited as expert authority for the *fact* that reduced splanchnic mass testifies to the decisive role of meat eating in human evolution. In any event, a careful investigation, using 191 specimens from 100 mammal species, including 23 primates, has shown that the brain–gut trade-off does not hold as a general principle—not for mammals, not for primates. Nor does a brain–*X* trade-off hold for any other internal organ. A follow-up report left the door open to some other kind of tissue trade-off, say, between brain mass and muscle mass—in addition to being "overfat" (see below), humans are "undermuscled" relative to other primates. But no one has proposed a plausible mechanism for how access to meat or any other kind of food could serve as the selective pressure to drive this kind of trade-off. An energy budget *allocation trade-off*—a trade-off between energy shunted to brain activity and to other things (tissue maintenance, locomotion, reproduction)—is more plausible (see below).

Reduced gastrointestinal mass in humans may represent not a trade-off with brain mass but an *outcome* of improved diet, which may itself represent both an outcome of encephalization and an enabling factor in subsequent encephalization. As diet improved, selection pressure for a long gut would be relaxed, while pressure for metabolic efficiency would continue.

Dietary Quality Revisited

There's a further problem with the idea that meat offered the solution to the energetic demands of encephalization: it relies on an overly crude understanding of *expensive*. This becomes apparent as soon as you try to work out the physiological mechanism by which meat would offset cerebral nutritional demands. First, the brain can't do much with the energy in meat. The brain relies on glucose as its primary fuel. Like most other organs, under carbohydrate fasting, the brain shifts, over a period of days in adults or about twenty-four hours in infants, to ketones derived in the liver from long-chain fatty acids that get released into the blood from fat stores as blood insulin declines. But the energy in the lean meat of wild ungulates is mainly in the form of protein. The body has a limited capacity to convert amino acids into sugars. Protein does not represent a sustainable source of energy for the maintenance of nervous tissue.

Second, energy is not the sole expense. The brain is distinguished by the fact that it is 50 to 60 percent lipid by dry mass. This "structural" lipid mass plays a range of roles, among others insulating the long-distance signal propagation channels that underlie *functional connectivity,* the patterns of coactivation in different parts of the brain that subserve higher-order cognition, including attention, planning, and the inferring of others' intentions. Of this lipid mass, nearly a third consists of long-chain polyunsaturated fatty acids, chiefly the omega-6 arachidonic acid and the omega-3 docosahexaenoic acid, the DHA of nutrition supplement fame. In many human dietary niches, DHA is scarce. The body can synthesize it from alpha-linolenic acid (LNA), but this synthesis is widely understood to be "inefficient": no more than 4 percent of dietary LNA gets converted to DHA in men, no more than 9 percent in women. The mature brain is remarkably effective at conserving structural DHA in the face of calorie or lipid stress elsewhere in the body, but during the last trimester of gestation and the first couple years of life, babies need a reliable source of DHA, whether from maternal milk, other dietary sources, or via conversion from LNA.

The main direct dietary source of DHA is aquatic foods—phytoplankton manufacture the fatty acid, and it gets concentrated in animal bodies as you move up the trophic web, so that molluscs, crustaceans, and fish represent good sources. But clinical evidence indicates dietary LNA represents a more-than-adequate source of DHA for the growth and maintenance of the central nervous system. If anything, you'd imagine that increased access to aquatic resources might have relaxed selection pressure for the capacity to synthesize DHA. So there's no reason to imagine earlier hominins were *less* efficient at DHA synthesis than we.

Where are the terrestrial dietary sources of alpha-linolenic acid? It's highly concentrated in chloroplast membranes, so leafy green plants represent a strong source, as do mosses, the fatty tissue of herbivores that consume these things, and the usual range of oilseeds, including flax, hemp, and walnuts.

Meat may well have played a role in buffering the vagaries of access to a higher-quality diet in early humans. But it wasn't because it was essential to brain development.

Adiposity

When you compare human bodies to those of other primates, three things stand out immediately. Bipedalism is one. Big-brainedness is another. The third is adiposity or fatness.

Compared to other mammals, humans are astonishingly fat, especially at birth. Human neonates have more than three times the fat as a proportion of body mass as newborn sea lions, five times that of baboons, more than seven times that of caribou. And in contrast, say, to caribou, or sea lions, human newborn fat deposits consist predominantly of energy-storing "white" adipose tissue as opposed to the thermogenic "brown" tissue essential to maintaining a warm body in a cold environment. What do we do with all this fat?

One well-supported hypothesis is that fat stores serve to buffer energetic risks from infectious disease and food scarcity during infancy and that it is the metabolic demands of the brain that make such high adiposity adaptive—not the demands of brain growth but the basal metabolic activity needed to maintain existing nervous tissue. Measured as a proportion of either total energy expenditure or resting metabolic rate, the human brain is phenomenally expensive in childhood and adolescence, peaking at age five at over 40 percent of daily glucose expenditure and at least 65 percent of resting (that is, excluding physical activity) glucose expenditure. The relative energetic expense of brain metabolism also seems to be inversely correlated with the rate of body growth. Growth slows in childhood just as the brain is becoming energetically more demanding, then picks up again after age seven (in girls) or nine (in boys).

This suggests that physiological buffering and cognitive buffering, far from representing evolutionary alternatives, have worked together to broaden the human niche. Physiological buffering in the form of high adiposity, especially at birth and in childhood, serves to support cognitive buffering in the form of an enlarged central nervous system and the prolonged period of motor and social learning needed to put it to use. Cognitive buffering in the form of cooperative foraging and cooperative breeding makes it possible in turn to provide pregnant women and young children with an energy-denser diet to foster physiological buffering. Did this energy-denser diet include fat from the marrow canals of ungulate limb bones? Undoubtedly. Did it include lots of other things, many of plant origin? Yes.

Physical Activity

If humans exhibit high levels of cerebral and adipose mass, they also exhibit a low rate of energy expenditure. Actually, this is the case for all primates—the order exhibits a *grade shift* in total energy expenditure (TEE) relative to other placental mammals, with primates consistently showing TEEs roughly half those of other mammals scaled by body mass. By contrast, basal metabolic rate (BMR, sometimes RMR for resting metabolic rate), the energy expended on tissue maintenance at rest, exhibits no such grade shift. That is, BMR represents a higher proportion of TEE in primates, including humans, than other mammals, while physical activity, defined as the ratio of TEE/BMR, accounts for a smaller proportion. It's been hypothesized that this represents a marker of primates' large brains relative to body size. Indeed, humans show a high BMR for body mass relative to other primates.

Scaled by TEE, primates exhibit a rate of growth and reproduction in line with that of other mammals. That is, *the TEE grade shift tracks the shift in the primate order to a slower life history*. The selective pathway that led to the grade shift (perhaps an adaptation to seasonal food scarcity) remains unknown.

Most remarkable, TEE in humans seems to be constrained to a narrow adaptive band, with differences in physical activity level playing a marginal role. Within individuals, increasing physical activity (say, when you take up high-intensity interval training or endurance running) generates a transient spike in TEE. But gains in TEE plateau rapidly, with the body compensating via a *decline* in basal metabolic rate, suggesting that the protective effect of vascular exercise comes from limiting the metabolic activity dedicated to nonessential inflammation.

For all that energy expenditure seems like an obvious source of insight into the history of dietary adaptation, it is difficult to know what to make of these observations. One starting point is the fact that humans diverge sharply from other primates in both physical activity level and efficiency of terrestrial locomotion. Our long legs, elongated Achilles tendon, and rigid plantar arch make us effective walkers and runners, and longer limbs offer the added advantage of increasing surface area for heat dissipation during high-intensity activity. A number of observers have proposed a feedback loop between cursoriality—running—and dietary quality, mediated by a novel hunting strategy in which early humans ran ungulate prey to exhaustion.

One problem with the chase-hunting scenario is that it is not clear that gains in dietary quality could drive locomotor adaptions: with mammalian foraging returns on the order of 50 calories earned for every calorie expended on locomotion, selection pressure for more efficient locomotion would have been relatively relaxed. On the other hand, the diameter of the semicircular canals of the inner ears, the principal organs of graviception or balance, is enlarged in *H. erectus* relative to earlier hominins, suggesting selection for higher-frequency head movements. Whether this "higher-frequency" activity was walking (120 beats per minute, bpm), running (180 bpm), or something else, perhaps dancing, we cannot know.

The more interesting question may be not, *What does cursoriality imply about diet?* but, *What does cursoriality imply about the causes of encephalization?* Aerobic physical activity has been implicated in enhanced expression of brain-derived neurotrophic factor (BDNF) and other neurotrophins, along with insulin-derived growth factor 1 (IGF-1) and vascular endothelial growth factor (VEGF), all of which play critical roles in the signal pathways that stimulate neurogenesis and gliogenesis. Clinically, vascular exercise has been linked to improved memory, specifically spatial memory. But BDNF, IGF-1, and VEGF are also prominent in signaling pathways regulating oxygen transport and glucose and lipid metabolism. So it is possible that selection for heightened sensitivity to up-regulation of these signaling molecules in the *limbs* provided the initial ratchet for more rapid brain development. In other words, encephalization was partly a by-product of a more vigorous motor style. In evolution as in development, moving precedes thinking.

A Holobiont Perspective

Up until now, we've been talking as if, from a genetic perspective, what makes a species are potentialities encoded in the genome of the individual's "own" cells. But human cells make up just 10 percent of the cells in our bodies. The other 90 percent consist of the microbial communities that colonize our skin, orifices, and gastrointestinal tract. These compose the human *microbiome*. The microbiome forms an integral part of our bodies and has a key role in digestion and immune function. Growing recognition of the role of the microbiome in animal physiology has prompted reconsideration of what an organism is: not an autopoietic network of cells of a single germline but a *holobiont*, "a large interdependent and symbiotic community that evolves as a unit and cannot be understood by examining independent members alone."

In placental mammals, including, for the most part, humans, the *primary inoculation,* the moment when the body is first colonized by the microbial communities that will form the basis for its microbiome, occurs with passage through the birth canal. Secondary inoculation begins with suckling and continues over the course of the animal's life through the sharing of food and living space. The gut microbiome is also highly sensitive to diet, with the relative abundance of different kinds of microbiota responding to changes in diet within hours.

How can we sense this response? When you sample the gut microbiome, you can't limit your sample to organisms of a particular phylotype (for example, species, genus). But you can sequence the ribosomal RNA operon of the entire community. One region of the rRNA genome, known as 16S, has proved especially useful as a marker of taxonomic identity. By assessing the relative abundance of different 16S sequences in the rRNA of the entire microbial community, you can identify the relative abundance of different taxons with known functional significance.

Experimentally, this technique has been used to demonstrate remarkable plasticity in the human gut microbiome. In one study, participants asked to keep either a strict plant-based or a strict animal-based diet for five days showed rapid remodeling of the taxonomic profile of the gut microbiome. Those on the plant-based diet came to have microbiomes functionally similar to those of herbivores, while those on the animal-based diet acquired microbiomes functionally similar to those of carnivores. These taxonomic and functional differences were mirrored by changes in the relative abundance of microbial metabolites in the colon, specifically short-chain fatty acids associated with carbohydrate (for the plant-based diet) or amino acid (for the animal-based diet) fermentation.

The authors of this study hypothesize that rapid functional plasticity in the human gut microbiome "may reflect past selective pressures during human evolution," that is, seasonal and daily variability in the relative abundance of different kinds of foods. But really, we don't have a basis to assume that the human gut microbiome is uniquely versatile. Or rather, to the extent that the human gut microbiome exhibits distinctive versatility, it is a function of the fact that humans exhibit distinctive versatility in diet. So while gut microbiome versatility clearly *mediates* human dietary versatility, it is not so clear that it *enabled* it in an evolutionary sense.

Compared to other hominids—chimpanzees, bonobos, gorillas—humans exhibit drastically impoverished microbiome diversity, both alpha (diversity of phylotypes within the microbiome of an individual) and beta (across individuals). Long-term adaptation to animal consumption is observable in the elevated signal of *Bacteroides* species in humans relative to other primates. But you see a similar divergence in *Bacteroides* prevalence among different human populations, and this seems to track divergent levels of meat and saturated fat in the diet. You also see a loss of microbiome diversity between "traditional societies" ("communities exclusively eating local, nonindustrially produced foods") and contemporary urban societies. This includes a complete loss of *Treponema* species, abundant in the guts of foragers and small-scale agriculturalists and in those of other-than-human hominids. Treponemes have been implicated in the metabolism of complex carbohydrates.

To judge from gut microbiome signatures, if anything, it is "modern" urban populations, particularly in the United States, that exhibit specialization for animal consumption—not the foragers so often held up as models of a meat-based subsistence strategy.

The Roots of Versatility

Part of what makes meat salient is that it is easy to construct a scenario to illustrate the hypothesis that hunting made us what we are. As you read, the scenario is probably playing in your head like a movie: *EXT: A grassy plain abutting a lake, 1.5 Ma. A herd of gazelles is watering itself. Suddenly, their heads turn. CUT TO: A BAND OF HOMININ HUNTERS descending from a ridge, javelins raised.*

Scenarios stimulate the imagination and lend coherence to a mass of difficult-to-interpret evidence. The problem is that they are useful only for explaining events that unfold over a single *episode*—events we could watch as they happened. Subsistence and diet are not like this. They are not defined by a single foraging bout or a single meal. Rather, they consist in patterns that unfold over a range of temporal and spatial scales simultaneously—the day, the season, the year, 100,000 years, the camp, the biome, the continent, the planet. The patterns in operation at different scales interact in ways that make the total effect difficult to predict from its constituent parts. Some of these scales surpass the limits of episodic imagination.

Versatility is more difficult to imagine than specialization, which is why I've taken such pains. But having made the case, we're still faced with the question of causation. What inspired the shift toward versatility?

We need to be cautious here. Historians and anthropologists sometimes speak of a "functionalist fallacy"—an erroneous assumption that just because culture (socially propagated recurring behavior) mediates human adaptation to environment, its shape must be strongly determined by the demands of the environment where it took form. The dynamic landscape of behavior is high-dimensional, with many stable attractors—imagine basins in a landscape, places that it is easier to enter than to leave. It is easy to overfit a postulated adaptive pressure to a set of examples of observed behavior. A couple of times I've alluded to relaxed selection, instances where function became less of a constraint on the shape of some trait as it evolved, because the functional advantage conferred by change in one direction or another was not great enough to determine the direction of change. In these cases, behavior evolves by drift—for instance, biases in errors of learning and biases in how learners select models to learn from. Still. Over the long run, a divergence as marked as that between the dietary gamut of present-day humans and the dietary gamut of other present-day hominids—gorillas, chimpanzees—warrants some kind of adaptive motivation. Are there candidates?

Climate change, for one.

Way back, I mentioned the marine isotope stages, alternating intervals of warmer and cooler air at the surface of the earth. We infer marine isotope stage boundaries from changes in the concentration of oxygen-18 in fossilized foraminifera sampled in cores drilled from the floor of the sea. Warmer stages such as the present (MIS 1) feature lower concentrations of ^{18}O, which precipitates faster than ^{16}O as the air cools. The even-numbered stages represent times of expanded glacier cover in the northern hemisphere and cooling and drying elsewhere. MIS 2 was the Last Glacial Maximum. I also said the periodicity of the marine isotope stages has been 41 to 100 ka. Let's drill a little deeper.

What are the factors in long-term climate periodicity? Insolation, the solar radiation incident on the Earth, is one. Insolation varies according to characteristics of the earth's orbit, giving rise to *orbital forcing* of climate. Orbital forcing encompasses 2 degrees of cyclical change in the eccentricity of the earth's orbit with periods of 100 and 400 ka, cyclical variation in the obliquity of the earth's axis of rotation relative to its plane of orbit with a period of 41 ka, and two types of precession, or wobble, in the Earth's axis (imagine a spinning top slowing down) and in the orientation of the Earth's orbit (imagine a rod, fixed at one end, rotating about its fixed point—the rod here is the major axis of the Earth's orbit). In combination with periodic variation in the eccentricity of the Earth's orbit, these produce additional climatic cycles with periods of 19 and 23 ka.

Deep-sea cores show a cooling trend in surface temperature over the past 10 Ma. After 5 Ma, the cooling trend accelerates. In eastern Africa, one effect of cooling is increased aridity. The cool-dry intervals represent times of stress for terrestrial biota, producing a series of *turnovers*, times when phylotypes (species, genera, families) disappear and new ones appear at increased frequency. Around 2.8 Ma, the periodicity of climate change lengthens from circa 20 to 41 ka.

But even as marine isotope stages get longer, they also get more pronounced. That is, the amplitude of the swings in climate increases. Why global climate became more volatile after 2.8 Ma is not clear. Tectonic uplift in East Africa and on the Tibetan plateau was one factor. Between 1.2 Ma and 800 ka, the dominant periodicity of global climate cycles lengthens again, to 100 ka, and the amplitude of the swings increases further. In Africa, all through the Pleistocene, finer-grained intervals of regional high climate volatility on the order of 1 to 10 ka alternated with periods of smoother change in climate.

Over the time in which hominins evolved, the key trend in global climate has been toward greater volatility. It is periods of high volatility that correspond best with key events in hominin history, including the emergence of new species, behavioral innovation, and dispersals out of Africa.

Here again, the temporal scale of the phenomena in question poses a challenge to our imagination. It is easy to conjure up a scene of life in a particular climate, be it warm and wet or cool and dry, more difficult to imagine the alternation between the two. This is the interpretive challenge of paleoanthropology: to see the very deep forest for the fragments of bark we have to work with. There was no single human selective environment or a unitary Paleolithic niche. We evolved to thrive under a range of conditions and on a range of diets. After about 45 ka, human versatility experienced a new efflorescence, with implications for our relationships, predatory and otherwise, with other large vertebrates. This is the story we take up in the next chapter.

3 Modernity

Fire Sticks and Planning

Chapters 1 and 2 took a broad view of the category *human.* But in one sense, the broad view is the only view, because if humans are specialized for anything, it is versatility. We see this today: humans occupy a distinctly wide range of environments, human life history varies considerably from place to place and over time, and humans have constructed a uniquely broad array of dietary niches.

Up to this point I've had little to say about those dimensions of human behavior that most people, if you buttonholed them in the street, would probably tell you are the essence of what it means to be human. These include the pervasive use of *symbols,* palpable tokens that stand in for other things that are either not present or have no intrinsic palpable form. Symbols are the basis of language as we know it, but symbolic behavior represents just one stream in a broader river of *channeled syntactic expressive behavior* characterized by the use of recurring repertoires of palpable gestures—*vocabularies*—to refer to phenomena in the world at large. For the most part, these gestures are not symbolic in that they do not have meanings fixed by social convention the way words do. But they are no less expressive—think of music—and this expressiveness is distinctly human.

Something else that is distinctly human, if perhaps a little less salient than language and music, is our capacity for pattern recognition, causal inference, and long-range planning. These come into focus, for instance, when you ask why it is that humans are the only animals to practice *prescribed burning,* the use of fire as an instrument of landscape modification. Setting fire outside the context of the satisfaction of immediate needs (for warmth, light, food preparation, defense against predators, or to show others where camp has been established) entails a capacity to associate actions in the present with outcomes at some point in the future, beyond the horizon of what, continuing the discussion from the end of the last chapter, we might call *episode salience*: the time and space within which we can take in events as a scene or episode and rehearse them later in memory. How far beyond the limit of episode salience? Rebecca Bliege Bird, Douglas Bird, and colleagues spent more than ten years exploring subsistence strategies among the Martu, a Western Desert Indigenous Australian people who have, over the past thirty years, established a homeland at the northern edge of the Western Desert. Of the Martu perspective on prescribed burns, they write,

> Martu use a five-tiered seral classification of spinifex grasslands to characterize their landscapes. *Nyurnma* is the stage immediately following a burn, when there is no surface vegetation except surviving shrubs and trees. *Waru-waru* characterizes a community of new green shoots from the seed bank of diverse forbs and grasses, usually following a *nyurnma* within a few months, depending on precipitation. *Nyukura* is a community where fruiting plants have matured, and there is an abundance of resources for people and other herbivores. Herbs such as *Solanum diversiflorum* and other bush tomatoes, along with seed grasses such as woolybutt (*Eragrostis eriopoda*), are most abundant in *nyukura,* usually 1–4 years postfire. *Manguu* characterizes patches where spinifex has started to crowd out other grasses and forbs, a process that usually takes 5–10 years following a burn. *Manguu* has spinifex hummocks close enough to carry a fire. *Kunarka* is the final stage of spinifex growth, in which large hummocks of grass completely dominate the patch, and the hummocks are so old that they begin to die in the middle and form circular rings several meters across, a process that can take up to 20 years.

Twenty years, practically a generation. This is the essence of a uniquely human subsistence strategy. Keep in mind that twenty years is the *minimum* horizon of deferred expected returns over which the Martu operate when they practice prescribed burning. This is just the period of time for which they have words explicitly designated as terms of landscape classification. It is clear, from what Martu who were part of the homeland movement say about the landscape they encountered when they first established settlements in the desert, that they understand the effects of prescribed burning and its absence over periods of multiple generations.

Prescribed burning represents one example of *niche construction,* the phenomenon in which a community applies selective pressures to its environment even as the environment applies selective pressures to the community. We've alluded to this phenomenon in our discussion of dietary niches. It's useful to imagine niche construction as a braided rope, where the different strands represent different dimensions of the package of phenomena, physiological, behavioral, and environmental, that contribute to the life of the individual and community. Humans are hardly alone in practicing landscape modification. But they are alone in the degree to which they form precise representations of expected outcomes at points in time and space beyond the horizon of episode salience. We recognize associations between actions and outcomes even when the outcomes are so distant as to bear no direct trace of the action itself, and we formulate symbolic schemas for communicating and reflecting on these long-distance associations. The planning of deferred returns is a pervasive feature of human life, including agriculture. One of the reasons I've started with prescribed burns is to drive home the point that the type of planned long-range landscape modification we associate with farming and herding is not limited to societies that grow food. The Martu, for instance, view the responsibility to shape the land with fire in much the same terms as they do the responsibility to raise children and collectively provide for the community. Burning is a central part of *holding* or *carrying* the country. The word is the same as that for holding or carrying a child: "nurturing, feeding, giving it room to grow according to its own inevitable processes, fostering its autonomy and self-direction, and not controlling or managing it."

In this chapter we look at how behavior of a type exemplified by prescribed burning became prominent in humans and with what implications for what we eat. The types of behavior I have in mind are those that demand pattern recognition, causal inference, planning, coordination, and cooperation, facilitated by multiple orders of symbolic representation (for example, words for landscape succession, metaphorical linkage of landscape modification and child rearing) over horizons that exceed not just the episode but in some cases the lifetimes of the individuals doing the planning and cooperating. What role did a desire for meat play in either fostering a distinctively human pattern of behavior oriented around infraepisodic (that is, longer than the episode) cooperation or amplifying that pattern once it had been established? The Martu are hunters. Hunting is central to their self-image. While they make use of a wide range of plant foods (not to mention flour, sugar, tea, jam, and other staples of life on the Australian settlement frontier), when they talk about holding and caring for the land, they have in mind above all its animals, and when they talk about holding and caring for children, they mean providing meat. This is not the same as saying, "Meat made us modern." But human relationships with other vertebrates were central to the development of the interiority, reflexivity, and other-directedness that underlie practices such as prescribed burning.

In the previous two chapters, I alluded to collective provisioning and collective rearing without offering much in the way of specifics. Most of what we can say about the collective life of early hominins and archaic humans has an element of conjecture. On the basis of osteological evidence of altriciality and decelerated life history, we can speculate that community structure incorporated some form of institutionalized alloparenting. On the basis of cut marks and other features of faunal skeletal remains, we can speculate that the people who brought the fauna in question to these sites for butchering practiced some form of institutionalized redistribution of the fruits of foraging. As we draw closer to the present, traces of collective life become more numerous and less ambiguous. Osteological, faunal, and lithic materials are joined by new kinds of evidence, including artifacts made from bone, antler, shell, and other organic substances. These include beads, that is, artifacts whose sole purpose seems to have been ornamentation, ochre and other mineral pigments daubed on surfaces, and, at length, figurines, flutes and other musical instruments, petroglyphs (wall paintings), and burials. A picture begins to emerge of people who were cognitively, socially, and emotionally our equals. Catching ourselves in the mirror of history invites us to ask three questions: What was their relationship, subsistence and otherwise, to animals? To what degree do contemporary human–animal relations represent a continuation of patterns established over the last 100 ka of human evolution, and to what degree a divergence? And do the answers to the first two questions matter for how we act today and in the future?

The Problem with Modernity

Cognitively, socially, and emotionally our equals. What to call this new phenomenon? It's not simply about language or even symbolic behavior, nor is it just to do with the time horizon of coordinate action, spiritual life, or the impulse to make art. There is no one strand of behavior with a recognizable archaeological signature that could serve as a metonym, a covering term, for the things I've been gesturing at. What we're confronted with is a constellation of mutually implicated behavioral tendencies. As with niche construction, we can imagine a braided rope, but in this case, I'd also like to call attention to a trend: over time, the rope grows thicker, capable of bearing a heavier load. The load in question is the pattern of socially transmitted skill—embodied knowledge—that we call culture. Culture, in this sense, encompasses techniques of artifact manufacture, including both the recombinant sequencing or syntax of steps in the manufacturing process and the motor skills required to accomplish each step. It equally encompasses other repertoires of sensorimotor action, including language, music, foraging, and navigation, together with other kinds of knowledge that are not so obviously embodied, notably kinship systems and an awareness of what kinds of things are good to eat. All these things make up culture. But what should we call the rope that supports culture? What should we call the phenomenon that makes it possible for a community to sustain the transmission of a body of innovations over many generations, even to maintain it in dormant form when it cannot be put into practice and then to revive it later, as the Martu have done?

For a while, the preferred term of art among archaeologists was *behavioral modernity*. We sometimes refer to *H. sapiens* as "anatomically modern humans." I avoided this term when we first encountered *H. sapiens* in the previous chapter because it imposes a teleological filter on the archaeological record: if *H. sapiens* are modern, then every other kind of human must be archaic, a rough sketch for us. (Would the term "anatomically extant humans" be any less descriptive?) When we start talking about behavior, our tendency to imagine evolution as moving toward an optimum, a single attractor that happens to be us, is magnified. We like to tell stories in which we come out on top, stories in which, owing to our unique combination of pluck and grit, we pulled through where others failed. We like to tell stories of revolution: population bottlenecks, glacial maxima, stories of how we triumphed over adversity through technological innovation and went on to colonize the world while other pretenders to the human mantle went extinct.

This is not the kind of story I'm going to tell. In recent years, a number of archaeologists have started to feel queasy about the whole concept of behavioral modernity. The gist of their critique is this: behavioral modernity, as it was formulated in the 1980s, is circular. Promoters of the modernity view took the package of artifacts typical of assemblages from one time and place, Europe after 45 ka, and attributed to one kind of human, the *H. sapiens* then newly arrived in western Eurasia, and applied it as a filter to assemblages from other times and places. That is, they created a *trait list*. They neglected the time-averaged nature of the archaeological record, including the fact that first appearance dates indicate not the earliest date at which an artifact was manufactured or used but a date by when that type of artifact had become common enough that at least one exemplar could be expected to survive the rigors of deposition. They attributed the sources of modernity to the innate cognitive potential of *H. sapiens* without considering the role of context—for example, population density, or the availability of materials well suited to the manufacture of objects of *symbolic storage* such as beads.

Australia in particular has emerged as a problem case for behavioral modernity. Humans arrived in Sahul, the Pleistocene continent that incorporated present-day Australia and New Guinea, by around 50 ka. From what we can tell from the archaeological record, they did not arrive with the full package of traits ascribed to behaviorally modern humans. Instead, those traits emerge over time, along with others that seem plausibly diagnostic of expanded capacities for planning and socialization and that have received less attention in other parts of the world. Concerted landscape modification is evident in the Papua New Guinea highlands by 30 ka. By the same date, long-distance networks for the exchange of shell, ochre, and stone seem to have been in place in Australia, with some artifacts turning up more than 200 kilometers (125 miles) from the nearest site where the raw material could have been procured. Beads, pendants, and other objects of personal ornamentation appear as early as 42 ka but are not widespread until much later. At the same time, ochre appears widely in the archaeological record from at least 42 ka, including in many contexts where its role was clearly ceremonial or symbolic (as opposed to adhesive), notably burials. Alongside a large number of burials dating as far back as 40 ka, Lake Mungo in southeastern Australia has yielded some of the earliest known cremations, some before 25 ka. Signs of economic intensification, including shell middens, appear by 33 ka. Many of these traits have been observed at sites in South Africa at dates preceding the late dispersals of *H. sapiens* out of Africa and into Eurasia. Yet clearly the humans who arrived in Sahul between 65 and 50 ka could not have been lacking the innate faculties necessary to support the sophistication in planned landscape modification, symbol use, and socialization we associate with modern humans. (For one thing, the crossing from Sunda—present-day Southeast Asia—to Sahul required a journey over open water, which would entail a considerable capacity to imagine unseen outcomes.)

The incidence and archaeological visibility of the kinds of behaviors we associate with evolutionary modernity have been shaped by the environmental and demographic context in which different communities made their living. Late Pleistocene trends in the apparent cognitive sophistication of human communities in different parts of the world need to be viewed against the backdrop of regionally salient conditioning factors—climate, flora and fauna, migration—rather than as evidence of either differentiated innate faculties or diffusion following a one-time cognitive revolution.

Diet in the Upper Paleolithic

So if the trends observed, with different tempos and rhythms, in Africa, western and eastern Eurasia, and Sahul at least since MIS 3 (57 ka—the warmer period that preceded the Last Glacial Maximum) represent neither a revolution nor a steady increase in technological and social complexity, what do they represent? How do we get from the strategies of subsistence canvassed in the previous chapter to those exemplified by the Martu use of fire? Once again, *breadth* is a keyword for our discussion, this time joined by *intensification* and, possibly, a modest *decoupling* of subsistence base from environmental variation.

Let's take breadth first. *H. sapiens* appear outside Africa as early as MIS 5, with occupations in Israel at 119 ka and roughly contemporaneous if technologically different occupations in the Arabian peninsula. A separate dispersal into Southwest Asia formed the basis for the Upper Paleolithic industries observed across western Eurasia. Depending on which lines of evidence you favor, this second *H. sapiens* dispersal occurred either prior to 70 ka or between 60 and 50 ka and entailed the migration of populations from North, East, or southern Africa. Migration into central Europe is attested by 48 ka, after which a number of "transitional" lithic industries appear, purportedly exemplifying features of both the Middle Paleolithic and the Upper Paleolithic to come. Some of these features we encountered at a slightly earlier date in South Africa in the previous chapter. In general, blades get finer, with substantial evidence of retouching and the widespread appearance of *backed blades*, that is, blades where the maker has beveled the cutting edges on one face either to facilitate hafting or to provide a surface for safely handling the blade with the fingers. From time to time, Neanderthal skeletal remains crop up in assemblages assigned, on the basis of lithic stylistics, to transitional industries, much to the consternation of those who would prefer to view history as a clean succession of demographic horizons, each with its characteristic technological portmanteau. These "out-of-place" Neanderthals have been explained away as dating errors or the intrusion of lower strata of a settlement site that had been under recurring occupation into the *sapiens* strata. But it is more likely that certain places witnessed brief windows of overlap between the two kinds of humans in which subsistence techniques flowed back and forth. From around 42 ka, you start to see industries with unambiguous innovation not just in patterns of débitage but in categories of artifact, including some points that appear to have been intended as projectile tips.

What changes in diet accompany this shift in technology? Depends where you look and what you look at. Again, we'll focus on terrestrial fauna first, because that's what the bulk of the literature deals with. First, there are no obvious regional trends over the last 50 ka of the Pleistocene in the relative proportions of small and large game. Second, there are no clear trends in taxonomic diversity, that is, the number of different kinds of animals recovered from archaeofauna. But in some places you do see a trend in the relative proportions of the different kinds of small animals humans rely on, and this corresponds to a trend in the life history and locomotor behavior of the animals in question. Specifically, examining data from sites in Israel and Italy, archaeologist Mary Stiner and colleagues found that over time, people were relying less on things like tortoises and shellfish and more on lagomorphs (rabbits, hares) and birds.

Why is this interesting? In the previous chapter, I expressed skepticism about the precision of *prey rank* models that attempt to explain the relative abundance of different taxa in archaeofauna with reference to how difficult it would be to bring down different kinds of animals and how much energy or protein one could expect to earn. But it's not hard to see that catching a tortoise is a lot easier than catching a rabbit, and it requires less specialized technology (snares, projectiles). At the same time, tortoises and other sessile creatures, including shellfish, tend to have a rather slow life history. This makes them susceptible to overexploitation and a decline in productivity. In Israel and Italy, you can see the tortoises and limpets getting smaller in archaeofauna over time, suggesting increased reliance on less mature individuals. By contrast, faster-moving animals tend also to be faster to reproduce, at least in western Eurasia. So while rabbits and birds require more effort to catch, they turn out to be more resilient at the population level under intensive exploitation.

The authors propose that periods of growth in the relative proportions of mobile prey in archaeofauna offer a marker of demographic pulses, periods when population density was rising. So which came first, decline of sessile prey, innovation in technology and foraging style, or population pressure? As always, the answer is "both." Once you have the means to reliably capture and extract high-quality sources of protein, fatty acids, and trace minerals, be it from nuts or rabbits, you might find yourself enjoined to continue. Creating a reliable source of those nutrients that we can't buffer physiologically is a good way to ensure that more children make it through the early childhood developmental bottleneck when kids are most prone to malnutrition. Higher childhood survival rates in turn give rise to denser populations. Snares, being made from organic materials, do not preserve well in the archaeological record at these time depths. But ethnographic evidence, discussed below, provides corroboration for the view that "small, diverse, reliable" was the key to the demographic transitions that made possible the intensified cooperation and symbolic life alluded to above.

Farther west at approximately the same latitude, the story looks different. On the Atlantic coast of Iberia, in what is now Portugal, a number of carefully dated stratigraphic sequences have permitted reconstruction of changes in diet from the late Pleistocene through the early Holocene. This period encompasses the horizons of technology and subsistence strategy that we have been calling Middle and Upper Paleolithic, together with later assemblages designated, on the basis of changes in both lithic manufactures and settlement patterns, the Mesolithic. Over the course of this period, central and southern Iberia remained largely insulated from the climatic volatility that unfolded over the rest of Europe, making the peninsula something of a *refugium* for flora and fauna that could not tolerate the cold and continental seasonality of points north and inland. Charcoal and pollen provide evidence of finely graded successions of vegetation, with implications for changes in climate and seasonality. Pollen cores also provide a non-carbon-dependent way to date assemblages by associating particular strata of a site with known *pollen stages*. When these factors are taken together, the Atlantic coast of Iberia presents something of a natural experiment, a place where long sequences of continuous occupation at sites coastal and inland, in a relatively stable climate whose secular trends are well characterized, afford a view of the degree to which diet and subsistence strategy were shaped by factors other than climate and the relative abundance of different types of flora and fauna.

The results provide indirect evidence of the expanding time horizon of what in the previous chapter I called cognitive buffering. Perhaps now we could simply call it *planning*. Intensification and diversification of the diet *predate* the key climatic event in this period, the warming that marks the onset of the Holocene, with a growing emphasis on small (in this analysis, under 7 kilograms [15 pounds]) terrestrial mammals and, to a lesser degree, birds, fish, and reptiles, over the course of the late Upper Paleolithic and into the Mesolithic.

In Portugal, the balance of evidence suggests that *demographic pulses* (increases in population density) trailed the intensification of foraging and received a boost from the warming trend at the start of the Holocene. But these demographic pulses were made possible by the nutritional stability afforded by reliance, even through the cooling phases of the Pleistocene–Holocene transition, on a broader array of foods that must have included a number of plant foods alongside the animals preserved as skeletal debris. This increase in dietary breadth depended in turn on a community's capacity, first, to adjust its foraging strategy to respond to fluctuations in the availability of preferred foods—to identify consistent changes in the behavior, say, of rabbits or birds corresponding to seasonal, annual, and longer-term changes in climate—and second, to manufacture and deploy the complex instruments of capture necessary to make fast-moving prey a reliable resource. Dietary diversification bespeaks planning and cooperation over time frames significantly longer than the episodic frame we have in mind when we imagine large-game hunting.

What happens if we look beyond faunal assemblages? In chapters 1 and 2, we had good luck with dental microwear, and this turns out to be a useful source of evidence in the Upper Paleolithic too. One recent review of dental microwear from the western Eurasian Upper Paleolithic examined molars from twenty individuals unearthed at fourteen sites across France and central Europe. Each individual was associated with an assemblage dated to one of the three sequential technological horizons that have been characterized for the late Pleistocene in this part of the world, spanning the career of *H. sapiens* west of the Black Sea from shortly after arrival through the end of the Pleistocene, so roughly 42 to 13 ka. As in the dental microwear studies we discussed for *H. erectus*, we're concerned with two things: surface complexity (degree of pitting or, if you like, fractal dimension) and anisotropy (degree of striation—long parallel scratches) on the occlusal surface of the molar. Recall that surface complexity corresponds to consumption of hard or brittle foods and abrasives such as the silica in soil, anisotropy to fibrous foods and meat.

The strongest trend here is toward greater surface complexity in the final Upper Paleolithic. By the end of the Last Glacial Maximum, humans were relying more on plant foods and eating a greater variety of plants and animals than during the warmer period that preceded glaciation. By comparing molars from Paleolithic individuals to individuals from more recent times, the authors propose to offer greater precision: the early Upper Paleolithic teeth resemble teeth collected from Chumash sites (California coast, 5 to 4 ka), whereas the late Upper Paleolithic teeth resemble teeth collected from San sites (South Africa, 9 to 5 ka). What is the value in this? For the Chumash and San, we have ethnographic accounts of what people ate. Of course these data are problematic. A lot can change in 5,000 years (though probably not as much as in 30,000 years spanning a marine isotope stage boundary). In the case of the Chumash, the ethnographic data need to be handled with care for the reasons I offered in the prologue—essentially, field observer bias. Still, for what it's worth, the early Upper Paleolithic occlusive microwear resembles that induced by a rather specialized coastal diet with as much as two-thirds animal content (including fish and marine mammals). The late Upper Paleolithic microwear, by contrast, resembles that induced by a diet adapted to the rigors of desert foraging, one that maximizes diversity to ensure a reliable flow of nutrients and includes up to 80 percent plant matter.

The results get more interesting when you expand the sample to include Middle Paleolithic Neanderthal molars and extend the analysis of variance to include *biome type*—what the country looked like, that is, whether it was wooded, steppe, or something in between. Explicitly incorporating biome type into the analysis is interesting because biome type does not always represent a proxy for long-term trends in climate. It is true that in a warmer, more humid climate, you'd expect to see greater forest cover and a greater abundance of energetically dense plant foods available above the surface. But the series of brief (500–1,000 years) cooling pulses that occurred in Europe between the end of glaciation and the onset of the Holocene left a rather open, steppe-like environment. This is an environment where plant foods, typically underground storage organs, would have demanded a considerably higher effort of harvest and preparation than what you'd find in wooded environments. It is here that late Upper Paleolithic foragers exhibit the shift toward a more diverse diet with greater plant content. Late Upper Paleolithic dietary diversity, and its degree of decoupling from ecological pressures, contrasts with what you see among Middle Paleolithic foragers, who seem to vary their diet according to what is easier to find, leaning more heavily on meat in steppe environments.

Does this mean we need to revise our statement in the previous chapter about Neanderthal behavior being just as "modern" as that of *H. sapiens*? This gets to the question of what made it possible for one clade of humans, in the context of growing climatic volatility and on the eve of a cold stage for which nothing in the African climate of the previous 150 ka could have prepared them, to begin to decouple their subsistence habits from the contingencies of their environment. What, that is, allowed this population of Upper Paleolithic humans to substitute planning and cooperation, facilitated by symbolic storage in speech and more durable media, for a resource-rich environment? Neanderthals did not want for planning and symbolic communication. Did they simply not have enough? Did a genetic mutation, as one influential pair of authors has proposed, afford *sapiens* humans an enhancement in working memory, invisible in cranial anatomy and thus, for the moment, in the archaeological record? Such an enhancement might have affected the *episodic buffer,* the inner screen on which we recombine memories to reflect on the past and formulate scenarios for the future. It might have affected the *phonological loop,* enhancing the fluency with which its beneficiaries attended and responded to speech even while engaged in other tasks.

There is something bracing about this hypothesis, which causes the history of humanity to pivot on a chance event. But it is unlikely to be the whole story. As we've seen in Australia, material culture betokening the kinds of symbolic exchange and episodic interiority that characterize humans today does not appear, fully formed, the minute humans arrive in a new setting. When it does arrive, it comes piecemeal—petroglyphs here, burials there, long-distance exchange at a third place—and not in an orderly implicational hierarchy, with *Z* only appearing in assemblages that also feature *Y* and *Y* in assemblages that also feature *X*. The emergence of material markers of enriched interiority seems to be conditioned as much by demographic as ecological context. This jibes with the Australian story: if any type of event creates a demographic bottleneck, it is a migration over open water. The demographic hypothesis also makes a certain heuristic sense if you're trying to work out a selection cascade. It takes a long time for the effects of enhanced working memory, if that is what we're seeing, to appear in the subsistence tool kit. But if you're surrounded by more people, being a better communicator or a better reader of others' intentions might well enhance your reproductive success. If these traits became widespread in a community, they might well boost the community's success in reliably providing enough calories, protein, and neurologically essential fatty acids to meet its growth and maintenance needs. Increased fertility might drive interiority, planning, and social complexity rather than the other way around.

Increased fertility, incidentally, would have the effect of shifting the demographic structure of the community toward younger cohorts. Among contemporary foragers, it is often the young, sometimes accompanying women, who forage for the small but reliable sources of energy and nutrients—nuts, fruit, small animals—that support their growth. Consumed on the foraging round, away from camp, and in any case leaving fewer archaeologically legible traces, these are the foods that mark the arrival of a human-as-in-us life history and subsistence strategy.

Before we move on, I must acknowledge that despite what I said previously about biases in the definition of behavioral modernity, all the examples I've discussed come from Europe and the Mediterranean. They draw on evidence and methods that for the most part have become available only in the last couple of decades. Even so, the legacy of biases in the places accessible to and of interest to archaeologists casts a long shadow over the places for we have enough data to make rigorous diachronic comparisons. If I were writing this book ten or twenty years from now, the story might be otherwise. Imagine for a second how this chapter might read if it were written from a Sahulian perspective. We'll catch of a glimpse of this possibility when we return to ethnographic sources.

Megafauna Extinctions

First, we need to make a quick detour to talk about the consequences of intensification. Among the great controversies in the literature on Paleolithic foraging is that surrounding *megafauna overkill* hypotheses. First proposed by paleoecologist Paul Martin in 1967, megafauna overkill hypotheses start by noting that archaeofaunal assemblages—of any origin, not just those that represent human occupations—suggest that in many parts of the world, the late Pleistocene was host to a variety of large animals that have since gone extinct. "Large" is kind of vague, so zooarchaeologists have proposed arbitrary cutoff points for "large" and "mega-": 44 and 1,000 kilograms, respectively, for herbivores and 22 and 100 kilograms for carnivores, whose predatory tendencies makes them "behaviorally larger" for their size than herbivores of comparable mass. The extinctions of these large animals seem to have unfolded in waves. Often these waves appear in the archaeological record shortly after humans arrive. In the Americas, for instance, we have skeletal remains for thirty-seven genera of now-extinct mammals in North America and fifty-two in South America. Of the thirty-seven extinct genera for North America—Martin's original overkill scenario focused on North America—thirty-two come under the "large" or "mega-" categories, mostly herbivores, including three kinds of proboscideans (mammoths, mastodons, and gomphotheres). The Clovis occupation, the first peopling of North America by humans with a hunting repertoire capable of bringing down something the size of a mammoth, began shortly before 11 ka. By shortly after 10 ka, thirty-two genera of large fauna have ceased to appear in the archaeological record, prompting some observers to characterize peri-Clovis large fauna turnover as a "blitzkrieg."

If this sounds suspiciously like the trophic dominance scenarios we had to contend with in Middle Paleolithic Eurasia in the previous chapter—a people maniacally fixated on large game, forever on the edge of protein toxicity—perhaps that should give us pause. But it's possible the Clovis hunters did specialize in large game. As we saw above, mid- to late-Holocene communities have been observed that specialized in fish and aquatic mammals, getting more than 60 percent of their calories from animals without suffering hyperaminoacidemia (by comparison with the Northern Dene, the Inuit, or the inhabitants of Tierra del Fuego, the Chumash appear moderate in their reliance on meat). In fact, there is evidence that Clovis communities hunted large fauna. These include species still with us, such as mountain sheep, caribou, muskox, elk, and bison, and others that are extinct—including a type of mammoth thought to have weighed upward of 7,000 kilograms. If humans did instigate fauna turnover in North America after 11 ka, it could not have been through some indirect means such as burning; there is no evidence that Clovis people practiced habitat modification on this scale at this time.

The difficulty, as we saw in the Upper Paleolithic Mediterranean, comes when you shift from taxonomic cardinalities to statistical counts of the relative abundance of different taxa. For while it clear that Clovis people hunted large fauna that are now extinct, it is not clear from the archaeological record that they hunted them intensively enough to drive thirty-two genera extinct in a thousand years. Relative to their abundance in the fossil record in the 12 to 10 ka window, it is striking how infrequently individuals of the extinct taxa appear at Clovis kill sites: just fifteen assemblages, featuring just five of the extinct genera, as opposed to more than a hundred kill-site archaeofauna featuring taxa that have survived.

Proponents of overkill hypotheses respond that *agent-based models*—simulations that represent the stochastic behavior of individual actors, such as animals, assigning each individual a set of properties and constraints on behavior and allowing their interactions to unfold as if in an experiment—consistently show rapid extinction of large fauna following the arrival of humans. These models rely on assumptions about how foragers rank prey that, as we've seen, warrant closer inspection. Is it necessarily the case that large, slow, nonaggressive animals will be highly ranked simply because they represent easy targets that generate a high return in calories and protein? I don't intend the question to sound like a joke. In fact, the ranking of large animals as subsistence resources depends on community structure, in two ways.

First, you have to have enough adults on hand to kill and butcher one or more of these creatures, and someone needs to be empowered to coordinate the effort. Even today, with high-powered rifles that reduce the effort-of-kill to well below what it would have been 10,000 years ago, the work of dressing and transporting the carcass is considerable. So at a minimum, you need to have residential camps large enough to send out hunting parties equipped to butcher such an animal and haul it back to camp. You probably also need a certain degree of *hierarchy,* institutionalized channels of deference and authority, in your band structure.

Second, assuming they manage to get the meat back to camp, they're then faced with the problem of how to distribute all this meat fairly and keep it from going to waste. Even today, with refrigeration, it is impossible to transform a feral camel, say, into a kind of very large bundle of the type of small, on-the-go resources we imagined in the Howiesons Poort culture and the late Upper Paleolithic Mediterranean. This is because a big part of the value of large game lies not in energy or protein but in the *indexical value* of redistributing it. This indexical value consists in the fact that the act of sharing affirms and reinforces the obligations of mutual support—the symbolically elaborated community structure—that make collective provisioning and defense possible. We will have more to say on this theme below. For now, the key message is that sometimes it's not worth the pain—the social friction, the accusations of selfishness—of going for the big kill. Prey-rank models that focus exclusively on energetic balances (calories out, calories in) miss this.

This is not the end of the story. Not all models of megafauna extinction require the imputation of behavior to hunters. Ecologist Lewis Bartlett and colleagues compiled global time series estimates of climate change, large fauna extinctions, and human colonization dates for the past 80 ka. To account for the time-averaged nature of first appearance and last appearance dates in the archaeological record, they generated a large number of colonization and extinction scenarios for thirteen regions, ranging in scale from islands to continents. Then they modeled the effects of climate and colonization on extinction. Uniformly, they found that models that included colonization as an independent predictor yielded a better fit with observed extinction data than models that included only climate parameters. In models that included both colonization and climate change as predictors, colonization accounted for roughly 60 percent of the variance in the timing and tempo of extinction phenomena in different places.

Does this mean the extinctions were caused by overkill? Not yet. This model says nothing about the mechanisms of extinction, simply that the timing of extinction events is best predicted by models that incorporate the arrival of humans. We are nowhere near understanding the wide range of effects humans have on the environments they colonize.

In Sahul, as we've seen, a population with the cultural and technological sophistication to cross open water and establish continental-scale trading networks arrived by 50 ka, well before the Last Glacial Maximum and during a Marine Isotope Stage (MIS 3) understood, in Africa and Eurasia, to have been a period of relative warmth, humidity, and stability. What do megafauna extinctions look like there? Archaeofauna from Australia include eighty-eight taxa, marsupials and lizards, that have disappeared from the fossil record at some point over the past 450 ka. No more than fourteen overlapped with human occupation. The numbers of identified specimens are exceedingly low, with many taxa identified from just a single specimen, so there's considerable uncertainty about the relationship between last appearance date and date of extinction. There are, however, other proxies for the presence of megafauna, including palynological (pollen and spore) data indicating the relative abundance of scrub vegetation and dung fungi. It is possible, on the basis of dung fungus spore counts, to infer a drop-off in large herbivore numbers between 50 and 40 ka. But: there is no sign of the extinct herbivores in faunal assemblages from human occupations in this time.

We cannot dismiss out of hand the possibility that human predation contributed to the trophic truncation of late Pleistocene Africa, Eurasia, Australia, and, later, North America. But we do need to recognize that overkill hypotheses are not as parsimonious as their advocates would have it appear. They entail a large number of hidden assumptions about human behavior. Targeting large herbivores simply because they're slow and carry a lot of meat does nothing to smooth out uncertainties in access to energy and protein, not for individuals, not for the community. Diversification, by contrast, does serve a buffering function. So does treating the whole trophic web, as opposed to discrete plant and animal taxa within it, as the subsistence base. This is what we saw the Martu doing at the top of the chapter. Let's look more closely at the social structure and material culture that subserve this kind of coordinated buffering.

Subsistence Strategy and Social Structure

What role does social cognition play in how you get your living? Earlier, we might have put the question this way: Does cooperative provisioning, that is, the coordinated sharing of the effort and yields of foraging, foster the longer-term forms of trust and other-directedness implicated in cooperative child rearing? Or is it that cooperative rearing emerges in response to pressure from increased fertility and fosters an intensification of cooperation in other domains? (Remember: "Both.") The buffering afforded by enhanced social cognition was of two types, one to do with how we engage the material world (stone, bone, fire—operative chains that demand coordination), the other with how we manage social relationships. The first we can track through artifact assemblages. The second is trickier. To formulate a compelling story of how human social cognition emerged—emotional entrainment in dyads and groups, inference of others' states of mind, imitation, kinship systems, and altruism—you need to be prepared to depart from the archaeological record. Taken together, the picture we've formed is one in which growing sophistication in the material and social realms has accompanied increasing diversity and reliability in the subsistence base, with pockets of specialization appearing in a broader mosaic of versatility.

I've alluded to three new things. One is what I've called *planning*: activity oriented toward manipulating the environment over time and space horizons that exceed the here and now. The second is *interiority*: a tendency not just to rehearse past experiences on an inner screen and recombine them to fashion alternative pasts and futures, but to fit them into abstract patterns that become filters for future experience. The third, implicit in the first two, is the close integration of technical, social, and symbolic dimensions of behavior. I've offered these as an alternative to the trait lists of the behavioral modernity literature. What implications do they have for subsistence?

To start, let's get more precise about what planning is. Earlier I held up prescribed burning as an example of planning. Clearly, the Martu understand the long-term effects of their actions and see their intervention as critical to the health of the country—above all, to its productivity for foraging and to its resilience to perturbances such as wildfires caused by lightning. The biome properties (flora, fauna, trophic network, "patchiness" or heterogeneity) that characterize Martu country are the products of Martu intervention. These properties increase the odds of finding prey on the hunting round. This sounds like planning, but we need to be careful. After years accompanying Martu on foraging rounds, Bliege Bird and colleagues have concluded that the Martu motivation for burning is not landscape modification: it is simply to clear the brush to make it easier to hunt sand monitors, a type of lizard that represents a staple in the foraging diet. What we see here is something we could call *emergent planning,* awareness of the beneficial longer-term effects of everyday actions alongside near-term motivations.

Next, let's return to large fauna. Hunting large animals incurs a logistical problem that is also a social problem: you have to share the meat. By and large, among foragers from different parts of the world, the greater the variance (from one day to the next, from one individual to the next) in returns on a particular type of resource and the less predictable the relationship between labor and yield, the more equitably you're expected to share. But isn't institutionalized sharing exactly the type of other-directedness and recurrent smoothing of yields that we associate with human sociality? Why would humans *not* specialize in sharable resources?

This question points to a tension at the heart of *immediate-return* forager economies, that is, economies where food is consumed shortly after the activity by which it was gained—within hours to a couple of days. Sharing is a prominent feature of immediate-return foraging communities today. In the parts of Australia where aridity and seasonal variability in precipitation made redistribution essential to getting a consistent living, sharing is institutionalized in two complementary ways. One is via censure for selfishness. Among the Martu, for instance, a strong aversion to being labeled *malya,* selfish, one who produces food exclusively for the benefit of her dependents and close kin, exerts a profound influence on people's day-to-day decisions about what kinds of foods to look for when they go out foraging. The second way in which sharing is institutionalized is via a strong expectation, also backed up by public censure, that you will share *on demand* from those who have a right, by virtue of their relationship to you, to ask things of you. If you were looking for a functional explanation for the prominent role of sharing among immediate-return foragers, you would not have to stretch your imagination to arrive at the hypothesis that institutionalized sharing facilitates social buffering, helping to ensure that everyone in the community gets enough calories, protein, and fat even when not everyone has a good day foraging. Institutionalized sharing would also support the decelerated life history and prolonged postreproductive life that support cooperative rearing by making it possible for some members of the community, especially those who no longer have the strength to go out every day, to stay in camp taking care of the kids who are too young to go out with their mothers. If you squint, you can see this history inscribed in the practice of demand sharing: you are responsible to yield part of your own yields, especially windfall surpluses, to those who "raised you up."

But for all that sharing is unique in the degree to which it confers social capital on an individual—that is, makes that person seem appropriately invested in relatedness and the collective responsibility to hold the country and its inhabitants—sometimes it's a pain in the ass. This is particularly the case when the thing to be shared comes in the form of a large-bodied animal whose carcass must be lugged back to camp and distributed. In the age of the Land Cruiser, the lugging is less of a problem, but equitable distribution might be more of a problem than previously. This is because camps today tend to be larger and more permanent, so there are more people you need to stay on good terms with.

Let's make this more precise yet. Should we not expect foragers to be experts at estimating the returns from a given type of resource and planning their foraging strategy accordingly? Yes. So what is the basis for this estimation of returns? In the prey rank theories already mentioned, behavioral ecologists have tended to use energy—calories—as a rough proxy for the utility of a foraging resource and the mean return over a long run of foraging bouts as the expected utility for that resource. To take an example germane to the current discussion, the mean energetic value of a hill kangaroo in Martu country, averaged over a long run of foraging bouts, is over 3,500 kcal. The mean return of a sand monitor is just over half that. The sand monitors, however, have much lower variance. You might go out many days without killing a kangaroo—eighty-five days in a hundred, to be precise. But so long as you're burning the surface, in the dry (winter) season if you go out for three hours, you can expect to come home with a sand monitor. Even then, the expected rate of return, in kilocalories per hour, is just two-thirds what it would be if you focused on kangaroo, if by "expected" you mean "mean."

But the mean is a poor way of operationalizing expected returns if what we're interested in is a cold-eyed appraisal of competing survival strategies, because *the value of a resource does not scale linearly with its energetic content.* Once you've satisfied your energetic needs for the day, the surplus is not much use as a source of food energy—it has declining marginal value. A better way of estimating returns on a mix of resources that differ widely in variance is by explicitly including *saturation utility*—here, daily energetic needs—in the model. This gives you an S-shaped curve—not the logistic curve we encountered in the prologue, but generically similar. When mean energetic return is too low to satisfy your needs, you might be better off emphasizing the high-variance/high-yield resource—kangaroos, say—and hoping for a windfall. But as mean energetic return approaches saturation, you're much better off sticking with predictable (low-variance) resources—here, sand monitors and other goannas, along with plant foods.

We've seen, through archaeological and ethnographic examples, two complementary strategies of subsistence intensification. On the one hand, you can focus on a portfolio of small, diverse, and reliable resources, some amenable to capture by children for their own consumption, some requiring coordination in both the camp and the bush (as in the use of nets to hunt birds and fish), most of them favoring either immediate consumption or a low-key form of sharing. This is what we saw in the eastern and northern Mediterranean and on the Iberian coast. Or you can make sharing, including a respect for relatedness and the mutual obligation to hold and support, the community's preeminent social value, so that unpredictable yields will be equitably redistributed. Cutting across both strategies, you can practice intensified forms of habitat modification. These range from intensive exploitation of one resource type (such as shellfish or possibly megafauna) to the point where you modify the trophic web without intending to all the way to burning surface vegetation with the express intent of producing a successional mosaic, with a gamut of strategies in between that demonstrate varying degrees of awareness of the longer-term effects of one's actions. The first and the third strategies evince a distinctly human degree of pattern recognition and long-term buffering. The second, sharing, evinces a quality of interiority—a capacity to reflect on experiences and organize them according to abstract symbolic registers such as kinship and reciprocity—that is unique to humans.

In relatively stable, resource-rich climate refugia such as the eastern and northern Mediterranean and the Iberian coast, we saw that diversification supported a wave of demographic pulses. In the Western Desert, a combination of diversification and enforced sharing has enabled communities such as the Martu to survive at low population densities in one of the most marginal environments on Earth.

I have not yet said anything about how diversification and sharing function together. To do this, we need to look at how foraging strategies diverge along gender lines. Recall from the prologue the work of the Goulds, who camped with foragers in a different part of the Western Desert in the wet (summer) seasons of 1966–1967 and 1969–1970. "In a sense," they write, "it is the dependable efforts of the women in gathering that free the men for more chancy hunting activities. . . . *Yet from the point of view of time expended, hunting ranks as a major subsistence activity.*"

Fifty years later, Bliege Bird and colleagues observed something similar among the Martu: women emphasize reliable resources, plant and animal, and men emphasize high-variance/high-yield animal resources that afford an opportunity to demonstrate generosity through sharing. These trends are coupled in that women's emphasis on low-variance resources that meet daily needs makes it possible for men to focus on high-risk/high-reward prey.

In the Martu case, for women and men alike, this is *hunting* we're talking about. When Martu women choose to hunt goanna as opposed to bustard or kangaroo, they're choosing reliability of yield, not low effort of capture. In the wet season, goanna cannot be smoked out of their burrows. They must be tracked on the surface, something that demands considerable skill, endurance, ecological expertise, and physical courage. Even then, goanna don't come close to bush tomatoes and honey as far as expected energetic yield goes, nor, for that matter, do bustard or kangaroo. Even grubs—caterpillars of *Endoxyla* species, which grow to about 7 centimeters (3 inches)—represent a more reliable, if lower-yielding, source of protein and fat than sand monitors. In Bliege Bird and colleagues' observations, more than 70 percent of the Martu diet, when they camped in the bush, came from things that must be hunted. Of the rest, more than half was store-bought. That is, *there is way more meat in the Western Desert forager diet today than was the case historically.* Women's foraging strategies have shifted toward the more risk-prone strategies of men. This reflects three developments. The first is the introduction of a novel tool kit that includes four-wheel-drive vehicles and high-powered rifles. The second is the introduction of a novel subsistence cushion in the form of store-bought flour and jam. The third is the trend toward a less mobile way of life where community members have regular contact with a wider range of individuals with claims of relatedness to them. The first two have lowered the stakes of a high-variance/high-yield foraging strategy. The third has raised the stakes of appearing selfish.

This provides a clue as to what hunting might be for, what function it might serve, if it is neither the most reliable source of food energy available, nor, historically, did it provide the bulk of the protein in the foraging diet. At least in some cases, the impetus to hunt is less meat's metabolic value than its value in a symbolic register predicated on relatedness and holding. To provide meat not just for close kin or those you regularly share a camp with but for an extended network of classificatory (totem-sharing) kin is to reaffirm the web of relatedness that makes it possible to thrive in the desert. To provide meat is to express your commitment to a constellation of interdigitated forms of custodial responsibility: for children and the community, for the country and the living things in it, and for a cosmogonic order in which kinship, animals, and country are three faces of a single phenomenon. The fact that meat is unreliable makes it costly to provide, all the more so because high-variance resources are subject to such extensive sharing that *hunters incur a net energetic penalty for hunting.* If your sole object were to ensure you were adequately fed, you'd be better off not going out at all and simply waiting for others to get home with small but reliable yields than going out to hunt kangaroo.

Hunting, that is, functions as a form of *costly signaling,* a way to demonstrate one's commitment to the community. Does this mean that women, because they adopt a lower-risk provisioning strategy, are less committed to sharing? No. It simply means they are less given to this one form of peacocking. What is clear is that the decoupling of two stages of provisioning, foraging and distribution, represents a long-term trend in human economy. As human behavior comes to exhibit the marks of modern sapience, meat's value comes to derive less from the physiological exigencies of growth and maintenance, more from its status as an emblem of cooperation.

This changes when defensible storage encourages the emergence of property as a social norm equally compelling to sharing. In this sense, livestock represents, among other things, a way of storing value, including but not limited to food energy. This we'll see in the next chapter.

4 Domestication

In the prologue, I said that meat has become an emblem of global capitalism. Yet so far we've seen nothing resembling capitalism or even an economy in the conventional sense. Toward the end of chapter 3, I started referring to the "forager economy." This usage was intended to underscore a shift in the tone of the discussion as we moved from relying mainly on paleontological and archaeological evidence to evidence from behavioral ecology, with its characteristic use of food energy as a metonym for economic value: calories expended, calories consumed. In fact, I argued, foragers are keeping two sets of books, that is, they operate with two implicit rubrics of value: the *acquisition* and the *redistribution* of energy. All *regimes of value,* all systems of social structure oriented toward the regimentation of economic behavior, incorporate multiple forms of capital, multiple *registers* of valuation and exchange. Some of the richest work in economic anthropology is that which seeks to elucidate the *register boundaries*—the places, literally and figuratively, where one form of capital gets transformed into another.

In this chapter, the question of how different activities generate value comes into the foreground as we canvass the emergence of a new economic relationship between humans and other terrestrial vertebrates: the keeping of livestock. The economies we look at in this chapter are not capitalist economies. But they are much more "like ours" in that they turn on the deferred redemption of value across spans of time and space significantly greater than what we have seen before—and sometimes on the *accumulation of surpluses* in the form of herds and flocks, captive food supplies that, with proper management, are self-replenishing and mobile. By the end of the period dealt with in this chapter, livestock formed the basis for a distinctive family of administrative and political orders, including some that archaeologists and historians have had no trouble recognizing as empires.

There is no longer any question that the people discussed in this chapter are human. This chapter continues the discussion in a broader channel in that it asks about the role meat played in making us what we are. The previous chapters have construed this "what we are" variously in physiological, cognitive, and social terms. This chapter introduces the economic and political dimensions.

As we started to see in the previous chapter, the value ascribed to meat, and to animals, is both economic (that is, something that can be translated, without too many hops, into a contribution to the satisfaction of basic metabolic needs) and symbolic. I am hesitant to draw a bright line between the two. It is tempting to imagine the symbolic as being built on top of the economic like a layer cake. But as in our treatment of niche construction and culture, a better image would be of a rope formed of many filaments braided together, no one of them more fundamental than any other. In chapter 3, we saw that interiority, the capacity to organize experiences in symbolic registers and to reflect on these registers and their episodic manifestations over time horizons longer than those of the episodes themselves, is central to human economy. In this chapter we'll see how the symbolic ordering of encounters with animals changes when animals become captive participants in the domestic scene.

What Is Domestication?

For all that we have a clear sense of the *outcomes* of domestication, it is not so clear at what point an animal is domesticated. Nor—a recurring theme since chapter 1—is it clear what kind of time relationship we should expect between the onset of a domestication process and the appearance in the archaeological and genomic record of markers of that process.

In fact it is misleading to speak of *the* domestication process. Domestication has unfolded in response to at least three different kinds of instigating phenomena. It's also misleading to characterize domestication as a historical process if by *historical* we mean "in the past." Here I intend a more generic usage: historical simply means "occurring over time." Domestication is not something that happened once or in one period of time. It is an ongoing phenomenon, clearest today in the domestication of fish via aquaculture. So domestication is not the same as *neolithization,* the shift to a more elaborate technological tool kit incorporating the ubiquitous use of hafted projectiles and finely worked bone, the construction of houses of stone and brick, and, at length, ceramic industries. Neolithization preceded and accompanied domestication in two key centers of plant and animal domestication at opposing ends of Eurasia, as we'll discuss. But it would be a mistake to treat domestication simply as a component of neolithization.

Domesticates are not the only outcomes of domestication. We tend to imagine the domestication process as one in which humans inserted themselves into the evolutionary process, assuming responsibility for providing selection cues to a population of animals while at the same time shielding them both from other cues (from trends in climate, vegetation, or demographic pressure, say) and from the possibility of mixing with the wild population—in this way, over time, coaxing a new species from the captive population. This type of scenario flows, again, from the episodic limits of our imagination: we see exemplars of the domesticate before us, we can compare these individuals to individuals of a corresponding wild antecessor, fossil or living, and we fill in the gap between wild and domesticate with a fantasy of human volition. This type of scenario gives humans way too much credit. More than that, it leaves out most of the picture, the dense network of changes in our own behavior, and in our own physiology, that unfold in the course of domestication, not to mention the network of changes that unfold in the shared biome that humans and their vertebrate *codomesticates* create. Domestication is a process of intensifying mutualism. From a human standpoint, domesticates come to represent what anthropologist Pat Shipman has called "living tools." But if we step back, domestication, in its early stages, looks less like the human appropriation of animals bodies as a form of capital—that comes later—than like the joint implication of two kinds of large, gregarious vertebrates in a shared process of niche construction.

In the previous chapter, we saw how difficult it can be to ascribe intent, to say, Here is a case where humans have acted out of a desire to alter their environment. Intent is not always sharp-boundaried, even when you can ask the people in question what they're doing and why. Take prescribed burning: even where people have a clear understanding of the cascade of changes that will come of burning surface vegetation and a clear understanding of the benefits those changes will bring, they often play down suggestions that the benefits of a successional mosaic, including a greater abundance and variety of edible plants and animals, are the reason for burning. In domestication, the ambiguity of intent is magnified. Domestication is not a process in which humans manufacture living tools the way we manufacture tools of stone, bone, and cane. It is, rather, a process in which humans and other gregarious vertebrates come to play tightly coordinated roles in a shared economic and reproductive niche.

Pathways to Domestication

The archaeobiologist Melinda Zeder has proposed a model that recognizes three distinct pathways to domestication: the commensal, the prey, and the directed pathways.

The commensal pathway starts with the forms of niche construction we've considered in previous chapters and with *synanthropy,* a tolerance of humans. Synanthropy varies among individuals in a population. Individuals who are less susceptible of responding to chance encounters with humans with aggression or aversion would have better success at exploiting the novel opportunities afforded by human presence, specifically, the refuse from human food preparation and consumption along with any smaller prey attracted to that refuse. Over time, synanthropes would form a breeding pool distinct from less synanthropic conspecifics as the population diverged into two distinct *ecotypes* defined by distinct mixes of food sources. One ecotype, the subpopulation that keeps its distance from humans, continues to elaborate the dietary niche it had established prior to the arrival of humans, though, depending on the intensity and extent of human activity, this niche may undergo substantial modification. The other ecotype, that of the more synanthropic subpopulation, establishes a new dietary niche in coordination with the human community whose waste provides part of its diet. In this way, even occupying a single biome type and in close geographic proximity, the two populations could at length form separate species, albeit with continuing gene flow in both directions across the species boundary. The outcome of this *sympatric speciation* would be a population of animals selected for their ability to ingratiate themselves to humans, even if the humans in question had done little, at least initially, to encourage ingratiating behavior and did not anticipate the long-term outcome of recurring gestures such as sharing food. The dog is the emblematic commensal domesticate. Dogs most likely originated in a single sympatric speciation from gray wolves in Central Eurasia at least 15,000 years ago, on the downslope of the MIS 2 glacial maximum but prior to the warming trend that marks the onset of the Holocene at 11.7 ka. If the domestication of wolves did not require, at least initially, any particular effort on the part of humans to segregate semidomesticates from the wild population, you would expect to see wolves spontaneously forming multiple ecotypes with distinct breeding pools in a single biome. In fact you do see this today, with migratory caribou specialists sharing the North American boreal forest with a population that adjusts its feeding to the season rather than following its prey.

The prey pathway starts with a different initial relationship between humans and their animal counterparts, one in which the animals in question are targets of human hunting. In chapters 2 and 3, we saw how archaeologists have borrowed from behavioral ecologists a set of rubrics for describing "optimal foraging" behavior to interpret faunal assemblages. These rubrics center on the interpretation of mortality profiles—the species, size, sex, and maturity of animals, as far as these can be determined from skeletal remains—with a preponderance of larger specimens of a given animal species taken as evidence for human specialization for large prey and growing prevalence of smaller species interpreted as a sign of desperation in the face of declining prey populations. In chapter 3, I expressed skepticism about some of these interpretations, which seemed guided by a prior conviction that early humans were large-prey specialists who diversified only under the pressure of falling yields—the Man the Hunter myth. But just because mortality-profile evidence can be misused does not mean it is without value. In Southwest Asia starting with the onset of the Holocene, mortality profiles show a tendency on the part of human hunters to cull young males while allowing females to live to a much older age, presumably producing more offspring in the interim. This suggests a hunting strategy, well developed in some parts of the region as early as 10 ka, oriented toward sustaining prey populations—or perhaps toward regenerating populations that had been driven into decline by intensified culling.

Kill-profile evidence from one early Neolithic sequence in the northern Jordan River valley (8–6 ka) suggests that for both cattle and pigs, overhunting preceded the appearance of domesticates by not more than a millennium. Faunal assemblages in the earlier part of the sequence are dominated by younger and smaller animals, including females in their reproductive prime. This is followed by a rapid shift to patterns that indicate domestication—delayed killing of cattle, with adult skeletal remains showing morphological signs of domestication, and the preferential culling of young male pigs.

Zeder's third pathway, the directed pathway, is something of a catchall defined by exactly the type of reflexive intent that is absent in the commensal and prey pathways. In this sense, it depends on the other two pathways to provide models of the possible outcomes of domestication: once you're familiar with domesticates, it becomes possible to project the outcome of domestication on new species, in the process imagining new roles that domesticates could fill, notably transport and traction, as with horses and camelids.

What Caused Domestication?

If domestication initially was not the product of conscious design, what pressures nudged humans and other gregarious vertebrates toward the construction of a mutualistic niche?

In the three-pathways model, both the commensal and prey pathways presuppose some kind of intensification of human subsistence activity that serves as an instigation—in the commensal case sharpening a population gradient in synanthropy into a fissure between two ecotypes, in the prey case forcing humans to assume custodianship over weakened populations lest they disappear. In the commensal discussion, I glossed this intensification as the "arrival" of humans. In some cases, *arrival* may be the word for it. As we saw in chapters 2 and 3, some of the most striking changes in both biome structure and human material culture and dietary niche occur when a community colonizes a new place. There is evidence of this in Neolithic sequences at both ends of Eurasia in the early Holocene. In other cases, the instigating intensification may represent an in situ change, whether in technology, population density, the ideology governing the community's approach to resource exploitation, or residential strategy, for instance, a shift toward spending much of the year in permanent dwelling places. But was some kind of intensification of human economic activity, perhaps incorporating sedentism, the only trigger for Neolithic domestications? Or is it a limitation of Zeder's model that it seems to take intensification, perhaps specifically demographic pressure, for granted as the proximate cause of domestication?

In the previous chapter, we reviewed arguments that increasing population density spurred a broad-spectrum revolution in late Paleolithic subsistence strategy across the eastern and northern Mediterranean—a new emphasis on a broader range of foods, many of them, at least on the surface, requiring greater effort (birds, lagomorphs) relative to caloric yield. We contrasted the Mediterranean to the coast of Portugal, where Epipaleolithic diversification of tool kit and diet preceded increasing population density and declining *residential mobility*—spending more time in one place. In both Southwest Asia and the Yangtze and Yellow River basins of north central China, you see a similar causal ambiguity in the early Neolithic.

To bring rigor to the question of what instigated domestication, we need to ask two further questions. First, what is the array of possible causes whose signals we'd like to separate? Second, what were these causes *of*? Domestication per se? Or neolithization, a more capacious network of changes that included not just enhanced lithic, bone, and antler industries but also, for the first time, facilities to *store* food and amass *surpluses,* the concentration of populations in residential centers or *villages,* and a cascade of changes in ideology and ritual culture that encouraged the creation of captive animal populations? There is nothing in the three-pathways model to suggest neolithization was a necessary prerequisite for animal domestication. It is worth keeping in mind that the same set of upstream pressures may have encouraged both processes, and at the same time, either may have mediated the other. That is, Neolithic technology, ideology, and settlement patterns facilitated the enclosure of zoomass—animal biomass—while captive zoomass provided an incentive toward denser settlement and a more expansive view of the human role in shaping the cosmos and other living things.

What were the possible instigators? We've already seen that economic intensification includes within it at least three distinct phenomena: pressure to increase yields driven by growing population, yield increases driven by technological enhancement, and increased rates of exploitation of particular patches of the biome driven by seasonal or year-round settlement and the availability of storage for plant resources. To these we may add climate change: the cooling pulse at the end of MIS 2 is hypothesized to have spurred technological innovation and a shift to village life, whereupon the warming trend of the early Holocene, less than a thousand years later, increased the abundance of plant and animal life, not to say the human population.

Domestication was rarely an all-at-once phenomenon; in most places, foraging continued alongside planting and herding for thousands of years. Nonetheless, the change in the modal economy of human subsistence across Eurasia, Africa, and large swathes of the Americas between 10 and 5 ka is astonishing. So whatever the effects of climate change, either peri-Holocene cooling pulses or the Holocene warming trend itself, it is more likely that these effects were mediated by other factors that served to amplify the climate signal.

In the same spirit of "both"—recall our guiding heuristic of historical causation—we need to attend to how feedback loops may have entered into the process, creating self-sustaining pressures for economic intensification, including domestication, even in the absence of steady extrinsic pressure. We have seen this already in the northern Jordan valley, where intensified reliance on cattle and pigs incrementally forced early Neolithic foragers to assume increasingly specific responsibility for ensuring the continued availability of their prey. The archaeological record does not afford us a season-by-season or year-by-year view of the domestication process. But we can imagine a scenario in which decreasing prey numbers and smaller body sizes prompt a shift in hunting strategy, away from targeting reproductive-age females, perhaps coupled with the use of captive decoys to attract prey to a place where they can be more efficiently killed and butchered. The shift in strategy partially quenches the instigating factor, the decline in prey, but in the process, it encourages further intensification, say, by allowing the community to support a denser population or to achieve equivalent yields with less effort. More likely in light of what we saw in chapter 3, what the shift in strategy brings is decreased *variance*. Yields may still be lower but they are more consistent.

Lines of Evidence

For Neolithic domestications, we have three lines of evidence. One is faunal assemblages. At time depths of 1 Ma, 100 ka, or even 50 ka, a number of factors—the small numbers of specimens, the difficulties of dating them, and the tendency of finer bony structures to degrade to the point where they go missing from the record—conspire to limit the interpretive resolution we can bring to skeletal remains. At 10 ka, these problems no longer present quite the obstacles they did earlier. Carbon-14 dating and ^{18}C:^{16}C ratiometry are more accurate, and skeletal remains often include enough preserved collagen to date them directly. It is as if we are now trying to figure out what happened on the beach a year ago rather than a hundred years ago.

On top of that, the people from a year ago tended to leave a lot more stuff behind than did those of a hundred years ago, and their kitchen middens tend to be a lot more obvious, sometimes enclosed within permanent structures made of stone, clay bricks, or bermed earth. Archaeologist Jean-Denis Vigne and colleagues, in excavations of Shillourokambos on Cyprus, identified faunal assemblages with between 500 and 5,000 identifiable specimens per stratum for a chronological sequence of seven strata of continuous early Neolithic occupation. Faunal assemblages of this size afford adequate statistical power for quantitative time series analyses of species, sex, and age ratios. Some specimens are well enough preserved to allow for *morphometric analysis*—comparing the sizes and shapes of skeletal and dental remains not just to identify sex and age but to distinguish between wild and domesticated individuals or wild and domesticated species in a single clade. Domestication sets in motion a characteristic constellation of changes not just in behavior but in skeletal morphology (including, the anthropologist Helen Leach has argued, in *humans*). Morphological aspects of this *domestication syndrome* lag the onset of domestication by tens or hundreds of generations, but when they appear, they leave a signal in the skeletal record. CT scanning makes it possible to recover this signal in some detail.

The second line of evidence also comes from faunal skeletal remains. Here what is of interest is not the intensity with which humans exploited them or the degree of management that can be read off mortality profiles but the mere fact that the animals are found outside their natural range. Stocking—the deliberate transport of animals from one place to another to provide something to hunt—is an example of what Vigne calls "control in the wild." Here again Cyprus provides a case study, since even at the peak of the MIS 2 glacial maximum, it was separated from the mainland by too much water to imagine boar and deer colonizing the island by swimming. Yet charred boar remains appear in an Epipaleolithic midden on Akrotiri, an islet off Cyprus, dated via collagen to 12.5 ka, 4,000 years before domestication syndrome appears in suid—pig—remains in the eastern Mediterranean. Persian fallow deer, never domesticated, appear at Shillourokambos in Cyprus at 9 ka.

The third line of evidence for the timing and pace of domestication is genetic. We've seen this already with the domestication of dogs. To estimate the time and place of dog domestication, investigators used *linkage disequilibria,* divergences in the rates of co-occurrence of identifiable sequences in the genome from what would be expected in a genetically uniform population. These divergences provide signatures of population bottlenecks, events when a small number of dogs were used to found a new population geographically isolated from the source population.

More commonly, population genetic studies of domestication in both plants and animals have relied on mutations in a small region of the mitochondrial genome that does not code for any transcribed genes and thus is subject to neutral selection; mutations in this region do not threaten the viability of the lineage. By estimating the rate of mutation and comparing sequences for this region of the mitochondrial genome in domesticated and wild populations of related species sampled from different parts of the world, geneticists elicit a set of *haplotypes,* classes of individuals defined by the fact that they share the same base pair sequence in the part of the genome subject to neutral mutation. These haplotypes form the basis for cladograms, trees describing possible histories of divergence among populations identified by the mitochondrial line.

Of course there are problems. For one, it turns out that the rate of mutation, even in parts of the genome that are not subject to strong selection pressures, varies depending on the time horizon over which the comparisons are made. For another, the trees generated by haplotype analysis are a lot messier than you might expect. In the case of dogs, there is virtually no overlap between mitochondrial haplotypes sampled from domesticated dogs and those taken from wild wolves. But regression analysis generates cladograms with a lot of clades featuring both wolf and dog haplotypes. The populations identified by these mitochondrial sequences seem to have diverged from a common ancestor more recently than other clades that encompass domestic populations alone.

These results raise new questions. First, how much genetic divergence should we expect to see over 5,000, 10,000, or 15,000 years? Enough so that wolves and dogs share practically no marker sequences today, even if they arose from a single population 15,000 years ago? Mutation rates derived from studies over much longer time horizons suggest we should not see many new haplotypes emerging over the spans of time implicated in domestication. The domestication signal should be one of *partitioning* among haplotypes already present in the wild population at the time domestication gets underway.

Thus we see that *domestication is not a one-time event.* Domestication does not mean a sudden and complete cessation of interbreeding across the wild–domesticate population boundary. Ongoing bidirectional gene flow has been the norm rather than the exception, and distinguishing introgression of wild genes into the domesticate genome on the one hand from multiple domestication events on the other requires a detailed understanding of the history of the migration, colonization, and settlement processes by which humans and their commensals arrived in different parts of the world.

Once you learn to take introgression, rather than distinct domestication episodes, as the null hypothesis for clades that feature both wild and domesticated populations, genetic evidence offers a new window on colonization and diffusion. There may have been as many as twenty distinct centers of domestication for economically significant food plants, if you include rices, cereals, pseudocereals such as buckwheat and quinoa, legumes, fruits, nuts, and underground storage organs. By contrast, it appears that Neolithic livestock domestication was concentrated in just three regions—Southwest Asia, China, and the Andes—and most domesticated animals were domesticated in just one of these. Cattle, goats, and sheep originated in Southwest Asia by 10 ka and spread to Europe and Africa. Zebu cattle of South Asia may be descended from a separate domestication event, but there are also signs of introgression from domesticates introduced from Southwest Asia. Pigs were domesticated in both China and in Southwest Asia, with dental morphology suggesting complete domestication by 8.5 ka. For chickens, chronology has been hampered by ongoing difficulties distinguishing the bones of wild jungle fowl from domesticates. But evidence from transport of chickens beyond the natural range of the red jungle fowl suggests origins in southern China or Southeast Asia at least 4,000 years ago. For horses, an exemplary "directed" domesticate, there are clear signs of domestication, including bridling and milking, at 5.5 ka in what is now Kazakhstan. In South America, a long record of exploitation of vicuñas and guanacos is marked by a change in mortality profiles after 5.8 ka that suggests the emergence of domesticated alpacas and llamas.

Even these "single domestications" have a certain meshiness to them. That is, the divergence between wild antecessor and domesticate is not like the branching of a tree. Rather, it is a process with many small branches that later come together and diverge anew. It is unlikely that jungle fowl, say, or aurochs (the wild ancestor to cattle), or any other animals were captured in the wild and bred in captivity just once. When we speak of single domestication events, we're defining "single" down to the resolution afforded by current methods. But we're also acknowledging that domestication emerges in distinct social contexts, and these are defined not just by shared environment and biota but by the circulation of material culture, beliefs, and customs. You will be more inclined to take an animal captive, rather than kill it in the course of capture, if you have the kinds of organic implements (snares, lassos, nets) that facilitate nonlethal capture. You will be more likely to attempt captive breeding if you have heard of others doing the same, and you will be more likely to persist if your social environment provides continuing reinforcement of the view that this kind of intervention in nature is a good thing for humans to do. Economic transformation is also a transformation of the ethical schemas by which a community makes sense of its place in nature.

Scenes of Domestication

Southwest Asia

By far the largest volume of evidence exists for Southwest Asia, and archaeological assemblages from this part of the world continue to provide the template for chronologies of Neolithic material culture. Epipaleolithic assemblages in what is today the Palestinian territories and Israel provide evidence of some residential sedentism as early as 14.5 ka, including pit dwellings with walls of clay and stone, along with clear signs of reliance on the seeds of wild cereals for food and, perhaps, incipient domestication of cereals. By 12 ka, there are clear signs of neolithization: arrowheads featuring notches near the base to facilitate hafting, the use of bone for combs and other household implements, and figurines. Symbolic artifacts have a deep, if uneven, presence in the archaeological record, and by the Epipaleolithic, in Southwest Asia and Europe, these included a number of *representational* artifacts, including rock art and animal figurines. What is new in the earliest Neolithic assemblages are figurines depicting humans in a more or less naturalistic fashion, particularly women. In the millennia that follow, these are succeeded by women in increasingly aggrandized and fantastic postures that have suggested, to some observers, deification: women accompanied by lions, or seated on panthers and giving birth to bulls. Bulls themselves seem to become the object of a cult, even in places where cattle were not a major food source. Alongside all this, architecture grows more confident. Larger rectangular structures appear that may have been dedicated to ritual purposes, including animal sacrifice. All of this precedes the earliest signs of the domestication of goats just before 10 ka.

The archaeologist Jacques Cauvin has argued that the evidence betokens a change in mind-set that in turn engendered animal domestication. Residential sedentism did not compel people to adopt agriculture, by either limiting the foraging range or increasing population density. Indeed, foraging, certainly under the conditions in Southwest Asia in the early Holocene (far more wooded than we think of it today), took less energy and fewer bodies than growing and raising food. Nor, in the initial transition to food production, was growing one's own food a more reliable way to produce the minimum yield necessary to maintain the labor force and its dependents. If anything, agriculture represented a new source of volatility. In Cauvin's view, the only way early Neolithic communities could have been induced to adopt agriculture long enough to give rise to domesticated species would be if the coordinated labor were coerced. Coercion, in turn, demands some form of durable social hierarchy, perhaps originating with an uneven distribution of foraging surpluses stored in households or with an uneven distribution of the charisma by which certain individuals became acknowledged as cultic specialists and formed a proto-priestly caste. The cults themselves, in combination with the very fact of settled life, would promote a view of the world in which individuals and lineages occupy fixed positions in a hierarchy of productive roles, with gods and priests—those with the power to bring about an increase in the abundance of plants and animals—at the top and others below.

A number of researchers have placed political ideology at the center of their hypotheses for the emergence of domestication in Southwest Asia. But newer perspectives, inspired by new attention to the time course of cereal domestication and signs of periodic abandonment and subsequent reoccupation of residential structures, have complicated Cauvin's picture, suggesting that foraging continued alongside the use of domesticates for as long as three millennia. In this scenario, foraging provided for everyday needs, with domesticates reserved for public events—perhaps cult propitiations, perhaps feasts whose purpose was to underscore political hierarchy.

China

Evidence of ceramic industries appears in southern China as early as 21 ka. By 14 ka these spread as far as Japan and Pacific Siberia. The makers were mobile foragers who visited kiln sites on their seasonal rounds. Further signs of neolithization do not appear until 12.5 ka, when sites in northern China (contemporary Hebei province and the Beijing vicinity) show bone and antler industries, specialized tools for seed processing, dedicated butchery spaces, and signs of domesticated dogs. As in western Eurasia, residential sedentism, suggested by pit dwellings, middens, food caches, and cemeteries, predates domestication by a considerable time. Whether these were villages as we understand them is unclear; lower Yellow River sites offer evidence of continued residential mobility. With respect to animal consumption, wild taxa are a consistent presence in faunal assemblages throughout Neolithic and into Bronze Age strata. The evidence for increasing reliance on domesticates at the expense of hunting is inconsistent. Domesticated pigs appear in northern China from 8 ka. In the Yangtze River basin, however, deer (wild) dominate mammalian fauna as late as 4 ka, while fish remain a key source of animal food throughout. In the Yellow River basin to the north, pigs edge out deer and fish from 6 ka, eventually comprising as much as 60 percent of identified specimens, save at Jiangzhai (Shaanxi province). There, between 7 and 4 ka, pigs *decline* while reliance on deer increases. Again, *the transition to food production is not a one-way process.*

As in Southwest Asia, domestication is accompanied by an efflorescence of symbolic material culture. Jiahu, a site in the interior of China, between the Yangtze and Yellow River basins (present-day Henan province), is exemplary. Jiahu is the site of the earliest rice farming identified thus far in China outside the Yangtze basin, with storage pits from the earliest level of the sequence (9.0–8.6 ka) yielding mainly domesticated (that is, nonshattering, threshable) seed spikelets. Signs of pig domestication appear around 8.6 ka. Ceramic vessels from Jiahu provide the earliest traces of fermented beverages in China. Burial goods include rattles made from tortoise shells inscribed with characters that prefigure, though have no established genealogical link to, *hanzi*. Most tantalizing of all, burial excavations at Jiahu have yielded a set of six end-blown flutes, made from the ulnae of red-crowned cranes, with five to eight holes, remarkably intact, at least one of them playable.

Again, when we look at these sites today, it is difficult not to view them through the filter of historically attested peasant societies. The rapid emergence of durable shelter and storage structures, combined with signs of domesticated plants and animals, biases our interpretation. But in China, as in Southwest Asia, gathering, hunting, and fishing all remained economically central even as some sites demonstrate a decisive turn toward reliance on domesticated millet, rice, and pigs.

Diffusion

If animal domestication occurred in just a handful of places, how did domesticates come to be so widespread? There are a couple of scenarios. First, it's possible that the spread of domestication represents *population replacement*. In this scenario, as populations of humans with domesticated plants and animals colonized new areas, they brought their "living tools" with them. The colonizers pushed any existing local populations to the margins of their former range, where they no longer had access to adequate resources to maintain themselves. Eventually the indigenous populations died out or were absorbed into the colonizing population, most likely in a role of casted subordination if not outright slavery.

Another possibility is a *skills transfer* scenario. Again, the scenario opens with a population of Neolithic food producers diffusing into an area occupied by Epipaleolithic or Mesolithic foragers. This time, however, the indigenous populations do not get displaced. Maybe the herder-cultivators have been pushed to migrate out of their own home base by population pressure, a change in local climate, the need to find more land for livestock, or an ideology that impels them to make land. Whatever the impetus for out-migration, there is no reason to expect that they will be better suited to getting a living from their new country than the people already living there. The climate, biota, and physiography may be different from what they, and the plants and animals they brought with them, are accustomed to. Daily photoperiod (hours of daylight), not to say seasonal and annual variation in photoperiod, may be different, with implications not just for the viability of domesticated grasses but for the health and morale of vertebrates, humans included. This was the case in the diffusion of agriculture from Southwest Asia into Europe and, to a lesser degree, in that of rice and pigs from the lower Yangtze basin into the interior of northern China. In both cases, a subsistence package that emerged in a warmer coastal region nearer the equator was forced to adapt to a colder, more continental climate with less sun and substantial variation in daily photoperiod over the course of the year.

As we've seen, just because a community made extensive use of domesticates does not mean it had lost its foraging skills. But again, migrants would have been faced with an unfamiliar environment and possibly unfamiliar plants and animals. In the face of all this, the technological advantage enjoyed by the Neolithic migrants over the Epipaleolithic and Mesolithic peoples they encountered in the course of migration was not necessarily decisive. So we can entertain alternatives to the population replacement scenario in which the vector of colonization was not the herder-cultivator community per se but its knowledge, which local populations fused with their own knowledge of local environment and biota to establish domesticates locally, perhaps using captives from local populations of animals similar to those previously domesticated by the colonizers to seed new domestic lineages. We can also imagine hybrid scenarios in which knowledge diffuses along with domesticated biota, which get taken up as a package by local populations without their being wiped out or subordinated. It could even be that "migration" in this case means not the wholesale migration of herder-cultivator communities but the establishment of long-distance trade relations in which domesticated plants and animals made their way into a new region, perhaps as prestige goods, in the absence of large populations of people.

Now that we've identified type scenarios, let's look at some evidence. The Mediterranean coast of Spain offers a good place to start for two reasons. First, the climate and photoperiod are not so different from the area to the east (Liguria, northwestern Italy) that represents the best candidate for the source of the earliest Neolithic material culture in Iberia. By contrast, biota differ in a key respect: Iberia at the time of neolithization had no wild goats or sheep, or emmer, einkorn, or wheat, so domesticated populations must be descended from populations imported via trade or colonization. Therefore, we can limit the number of variables—local redomestication was not an option, while the confound of contrasting climate is absent. Second, the

Mediterranean coast of Spain presents a striking array of petroglyphs—rock art—that we can call on to support one scenario or another.

The establishment of a Neolithic economy in present-day Valencia and Alicante unfolded over just 500 years. By 7.5 ka, herder-cultivator assemblages with decorated fired ceramics, polished lithics, and a consistent kit of domesticated plants and animals appear at sites scattered across the coast and into the interior. At some sites, domesticates account for two-thirds of specimens recovered from faunal assemblages. These assemblages do not occur at sites with earlier Mesolithic strata. But the Mesolithic foraging economy does seem to decline around the same time as the Neolithic is established. So this looks like population replacement.

Can rock art help us refine the story? The rock art in the area displays a mix of styles, some more schematic, some more naturalistic and narrative laden, including scenes of war. It would be easy to interpret these differences as signs of population replacement—two communities, two styles. But while the superposition of some tableaux on others provides evidence of chronological sequence, it does not say anything about the time between successive mark-making episodes. Some of the more naturalistic tableaux feature depictions of chronologically late tools. But secure dating has proved elusive, prompting divergent interpretations. For those who would argue that local populations adopted imported technology, it is tempting to read the rock art as evidence for the adoption of an imported cult, which might have been a condition of receiving instruction in new ways of making a living.

Part of what makes petroglyphs so exciting in this part of the world and elsewhere is the preponderance of animals, wild and domesticated. Rock art exemplifies the ways in which other-than-human animals have served as a screen on which humans projected their budding interiority. We can say more: across the frontier marking the transition from hunting to herding, human relationships with other vertebrates have been a key domain in which we've worked out our understanding of our role in the world—the degree to which humans alone may be said to exercise culture, the degree to which humans alone are responsible for the upkeep of the world or are destined to master it. This is a theme we'll return to.

Elsewhere in Europe, the evidence argues for a mix of these scenarios, including population replacement, interbreeding along gendered lines, and reacculturation of local communities to imported habits. By and large, populations of domesticates are descended from imported plants and animals, even in cases where appropriate local populations were present (though pigs exemplify the complexity of the diffusion process, with evidence of a population turnover after 6 ka—the reestablishment of domestication from local wild stocks). But no matter how strong the role of outside populations, human and animal, in promoting diffusion, the need to adapt to local conditions shaped the history of agriculture wherever it was established. In the Orkneys, north of Scotland, carbon isotope data suggest sheep were foddered on seaweed as early as 5 ka.

Domestication Syndrome

Up to this point, I've been speaking as if domestication yielded a more-or-less stable set of morphological, physiological, and behavioral outcomes in animals. I've alluded to difficulties spotting the outcomes of domestication in the archaeological record and stressed that it takes time for domesticates to appear even once captive breeding has taken hold. But we have not yet examined what makes for an archaeologically visible domesticate. Let's look at what distinguishes a domesticate from a wild animal and how a distinctive package of physical and behavioral features, a domestication *syndrome,* might emerge in the absence of human intent.

The morphological changes that mark domestication in animals can be glossed in terms of decreased skeletal robusticity and, in some cases, neoteny, the persistence into adulthood of features associated in the ancestral population with juveniles. Body size decreases, as does cranial capacity. Domesticates are lighter boned. Often adults exhibit less sexual dimorphism than wild counterparts. Endocrine changes include precocity—sexual maturity at a younger age—and an extension of breeding season. Most striking are the behavioral changes, which include not just reduced aggression among males and reduced aversion to humans but a broader pattern of docility that in some cases encompasses attenuated sensorimotor exploration—domesticated animals seem less alert to their surroundings than do their wild counterparts.

In an extraordinary forty-year series of experiments initiated in 1959 in Novosibirsk, the Russian physiologist Dmitry Belyaev demonstrated that selectively breeding foxes for nothing more than tameability (nonaversive responses to hand-feeding and petting in pups) rapidly yielded the entire constellation of changes commonly seen in domestication. By the fourth generation, pups were demonstrating tail wagging and by the sixth, the arousal response seen in dogs on the return of a favored human. Though tameness is commonly observed in the context of a dulling of sensorimotor vigilance, the foxes in Belyaev's study developed heightened sensitivity to key aspects of their social environment, above all gestural cues from human minders. Mating became less seasonally dependent, and a variety of coat colors not observed in the wild emerged in the selected population.

The population that served as the source for these experiments had been farm-bred for many generations, so these foxes were in the funnel of pre-domestication at the time the experiment began even if their behavior was within the range of that observed in the wild. Still, the results of the experiment were illuminating. It transpired that the neoteny characteristic of domestication emerged because selection for tameability was, effectively, selection for a prolonged window of *heightened* social exploratory behavior—the number of days from birth to the appearance of fear behavior in pups tripled to four months. Domestication seems to represent selection for a muted stress response. In endocrine terms, this means reduced glucocorticoid expression and enhanced serotonin expression. These in turn drive swathes of the broader domestication syndrome via epigenetic control.

At a certain point, of course, humans do begin to selectively breed their animal counterparts for things other than nonaversion, notably sexual precocity, relaxed seasonality of estrus and rut, and, at length, in livestock, higher *conversion ratios,* that is, the ability to put on weight faster. But the fact that domestication initially selects for reduced body size and diminished hardiness lends credence to the argument that most early domestication encounters grew out of short-term reinforcement of mutualism with no thought to long-term outcomes.

A Landscape, Not a Membrane

Three times in this chapter I've referred to a *transition,* from hunting to herding, from foraging to food production. At the same time, I mentioned that in northern China, there is clear evidence at one site of a shift *away* from reliance on domesticates, at least as far as animal source foods go, more than two millennia after their use was established. Rather than simply acknowledging that the transition unfolds in fits and starts, we need to question whether to refer to these phenomena as transitions with defined end points is to prejudice our evaluation of the variety of strategies of economic intensification evident in the archaeological record. The space between foraging and herding-cultivating is not, in archaeologist Bruce Smith's elegant metaphor, a "one-way membrane." It is, rather, a territory or landscape through which societies past have charted a wide range of itineraries. In the past generation, a small number of archaeologists have called for greater attention to this landscape and the paths that mark it.

Toward the end of chapter 3, I alluded in passing to the distinction between *immediate-* and *delayed-return* or *complex* foragers. The latter are exemplified by the coastal peoples of the Pacific Northwest, who got their living in large part by fishing, spent the winters in permanent villages, and accumulated sufficient disparities in hereditary social status to sustain a tradition of competitive feasting immortalized in the anthropological literature as the *potlatch.* The potlatch was so central to regional politics that in the second half of the nineteenth century, colonial authorities felt compelled to outlaw it. Clearly, neither intensification nor the accumulation of surpluses depends on a community's adopting domesticates as its main sources of food. But complex foragers have been treated as outliers in the taxonomy of human economic behavior.

Smith sees the peoples of woodland eastern North America around 2 ka (collectively known as the Hopewell societies) as an object lesson in how societies get classified as complex foragers even when it is clear they are deriving a substantial part of their energy budget from cultivated plants, simply because there is nowhere else in our classification schemas to put them. Hopewell sites show evidence of the use of seven cultivated seed species, four of which exhibit markings of domestication. Grass domestication in this part of the world goes back to at least 5 ka, but the shift to the maize-centered agriculture known from postcontact histories does not happen until 900 CE, when maize sweeps the eastern woodlands from Florida to Ontario. To characterize the intervening 4,000 years as simply a drawn-out transition is to do injustice to both the stable period of partial reliance on domesticates and the suddenness with which maize comes to dominate the economy around a thousand years ago.

Smith proposes a *domestication continuum* defined by the proportion of the caloric budget that comes from domesticated and nondomesticated food sources. This is a start, but it does not go far enough. For one thing, we would do well to consider the fact that seasonal alternation among subsistence bases was long the rule, not the exception. It is easy to imagine communities that relied on domesticated plants and animals in certain periods of the year. It is also possible to imagine, as I noted for Southwest Asia, that the use of domesticates was differentiated from the use of wild sources in *social-indexical* terms, with domesticates serving as prestige goods in feasting contexts.

We can go further. There are subsistence strategies that unequivocally entail significant human intervention in the life cycles of other living things yet where, by conventional standards, there is no domestication. A case in point is agroforestry as it is practiced in eastern Indonesia and Papua New Guinea, where human intervention over long periods of time has fostered the presence of trees whose products are used for food and medicine, not to mention the plant, insect, and animal communities that depend on these trees. None of these living things remotely qualify as domesticated, yet their distribution reflects a long history of mutualism with human communities. Once you become aware that this is possible, you start to see it in the archaeological record—for instance, in New Guinea, where signs of extensive forest and wetland modification (drainage, clearance) appear by 6.5 ka.

What is at stake is our capacity to recognize changes in subsistence strategy for the political acts they often have been. Take the Lacandon Maya of Chiapas, Mexico, and neighboring Peten, Guatemala, described by anthropologists John Edward Terrell and John Hart:

> Over the last 150 years, the Lacandon have been alternately portrayed by explorers and anthropologists as either hunting-and-gathering bands, small permanent agricultural communities, or a semisedentary farming society. . . . Lacandon subsistence and adaptive strategies differed between groups, and they changed within a group or family depending on social, economic, and environmental circumstances.

This sounds remarkably like what political scientist James Scott has described for Southeast Asia. Since the emergence of lowland river delta empires fed by wet-rice surpluses, the history of Southeast Asia has been characterized by the tendency of highland peoples to adjust their subsistence strategy to suit their political interests, becoming more mobile and shifting upcountry whenever the state threatened their autonomy. Wet-rice empires are an archaeologically recent phenomenon (less than 2,000 years). But we should not expect the strategic deployment of ways of getting a living that entail different degrees of mobility and different levels of reliance on domesticates to be anything new. In the case of mobile pastoralists, it is becoming apparent that transhumance, seasonal shifting of camp, far from being the burden of a specialist livestock economy, has often been the reason for maintaining large herds. That is, *livestock support a type of mobility that has been valued for reasons other than the needs of livestock*. Transhuming pastoralism emerges in the Jordan River valley of Southwest Asia as early as 9.5 ka. Excavations running up through the Islamic era suggest that mobility waxed and waned over time.

Domestication and Nutrition

What were the nutritional implications of increased reliance on domesticates?

Most arguments about the nutritional status of Neolithic people come from stable-isotope ratio studies on collagen recovered from human skeletal remains together with osteopathology—characteristic signs of nutritional deficits in the mineralized skeletal remains themselves. The degree of ^{13}C enrichment relative to ^{12}C in skeletal collagen and dental enamel can be used as a proxy for degree of reliance on C4 plants, while ^{15}N enrichment tells us something about where in the trophic network an individual stood with respect to protein—more ^{15}N corresponds to greater reliance on animal-source protein, that is, more hops from primary nitrogen fixation. Carbon-13 enrichment also serves as a marker of trophic distance from primary production and has been proposed as a proxy for use of marine-source foods. These relationships are heuristic. Legumes, for instance, are ^{15}N-depleted by comparison with cereals, so high reliance on legumes may overestimate the degree to which a diet is plant based. Conversely, the relationship between animal-protein reliance and ^{15}N enrichment appears to be sublinear, so high levels of ^{15}N may not discriminate between diets rich in animal and plant protein. Carbon-13 discrimination is similarly limited.

There are also problems of sample bias. As we've seen, food production and storage tend to foster social hierarchy. In Neolithic, Bronze, and Iron Age societies, it is predominantly elites who received burials in archaeologically legible graves. If the skeletal remains that provide the sources for collagen and enamel studies come from burial sites, these are likely the skeletons of the most privileged people in the community. Presumably, they were also the best fed.

In spite of these concerns, stable-isotope studies do tell us something about the changes in diet and nutrition that came with the adoption of herding and cultivation. What this something is varies from place to place. Across the southwestern edge of Eurasia from Greece to Iberia, the transition from Mesolithic to Neolithic is marked by a decline in reliance on aquatic foods at coastal as well as inland sites. Some places show diminished ^{15}N enrichment in the Neolithic, consistent with reduced reliance on animal-source foods, while others show variance from site to site. In Spain, for example, an analysis of skeletal collagen from twenty-five individuals from seven sites around 5 ka suggests that animal-source foods accounted for less than 25 percent of the diet at most sites but upward of 40 percent at two.

The causes of declining reliance on marine-source foods are unclear. In some cases, it might reflect a time-budget conflict—the greater labor demands of agriculture made it impossible to keep up aquatic harvesting. This explanation makes most sense in population-replacement scenarios, where newcomers bring agriculture with them and never acquire the familiarity with local biota that the foragers who preceded them had. Places where the aquatic-food signal remains strong in the transition to agriculture may be places where agriculture arrived via cultural colonization rather than population replacement and existing local knowledge was not completely lost. The turning away from aquatic resources provides support for the view that ideology had a strong hand in driving increased reliance on domesticates. Neolithic people seem to have been adequately nourished in energetic and amino acid terms. But there is some evidence, in some places, that Neolithic people suffered chronic anemia, not what you would expect if nutritional benefit drove the shift to food producing.

The evidence comes from mineralized traces of blood corpuscle overproduction in the cranium. Corpuscle overproduction is accompanied by an expansion of the spongy, marrow-containing cancellous tissue of the interior layers of the cranial orbit at the expense of the dense outer cortical layer. The cortical layer displays conical lesions called cribra. The anemia that engenders red blood cell overproduction may have a number of origins, some infectious, some hereditary, some linked to deficits in dietary iron and its absorption cofactors, including vitamins B_{12} and D and ascorbic acid or vitamin C. Endemic anemia was at least partly caused by want of heme iron and ascorbic acid in the diet, but it was probably partly infectious in origin too. Keeping herds of animals brought humans into contact with a novel range of *zoonoses*. Today, upward of 60 percent of infectious disease in humans is caused by pathogens also found in other gregarious vertebrates. The ones we tend to hear about are epizootic, that is, they achieve high rates of human-to-human transmission. But historically, *enzootics,* pathogens with stable patterns of mostly animal-to-human transmission, have accounted for the greater part of chronic infectious debility in humans, and domesticated herds represent the main reservoirs. So anemia in early agricultural populations might be related to domestication in ways that have nothing to do with a drop in meat consumption or dietary breadth.

Japan offers an opportunity to examine the role of dietary diversity in micronutrition and skeletal health in early agricultural societies. In Japan, Holocene assemblages are dominated by the Jomon culture. Jomon is sometimes characterized as a complex foraging economy, but Smith cites it as a "low-level food-producing" economy comparable to that of eastern North America. In any event, around 2.5 ka, a new, rice-producing economy appears in Honshu, known as the Yayoi culture. Jomon and Yayoi crania exhibit orbital cribra at roughly comparable rates—there is no significant difference in rates of anemia, as far as this measure goes, between the two. By contrast, Yayoi teeth exhibit a decline in linear enamel hypoplasia—places where enamel deposition was interrupted, by infection or nutritional stress, in childhood. That is, in Japan, food producers seem to have been at lower risk of developmental malnutrition than foragers in comparable environments and did not experience an increase in skeletally salient micronutrient deficiencies. One explanation is that in Japan, the adoption of agriculture did not coincide with an abandonment of marine foraging. To the contrary, there is even some evidence that Yayoi people practiced aquaculture, releasing wild-caught carp into rice paddies and harvesting them at the end of the season.

Empire

From a distance of 10,000 years, the advantages of food production are far from obvious. Cultivation and herding required more labor than gathering and hunting, and that labor had to be coordinated and timed in ways that demanded a new kind of corporatism and deference to authority. The products of agriculture, in turn, became bound, in imagination and then in law, to the particular episodes of labor that had yielded them. This, coupled with novel technologies of food storage, encouraged the hoarding of surpluses, undermining mutual assistance. Food, not to say livestock, pasturage, and other things implicated in food production, came to be understood as property. Food production engendered entrenched hierarchies of access to the basic means of living that worked to the disadvantage of the vast majority of the community.

On top of all this, in many, and perhaps most, cases, the diets of early food producers were less abundant in iron and other trace nutrients, and despite the Yayoi evidence, they may not have been more secure even in terms of meeting energetic needs for development. Dietary versatility is itself a form of insurance against environmental volatility and other sources of nutritional stress. By adopting a diet that was less diverse in its key constituents and in the knowledge needed to acquire them, food producers put themselves at risk of a shortfall. There is something more to say about the relative homogeneity of the food producer diet: perhaps it was less interesting—less surprising, in tastes and textures, less inspiring. There is something oppressive about eating the same thing day after day.

Food producing was not a necessary concomitant of settled living, nor was it everywhere subject to runaway feedback. We have evidence of long-term stable economies at many different levels of reliance on raised foods short of total commitment, along with periodic alternation between greater reliance now on foraging, now on producing.

And yet across most of Eurasia and Africa and large parts of the Americas and the western Pacific, we do observe something like a transition to agriculture. So it must have had something going for it.

We need to be careful not to project our own perspective on people living 5,000 years ago. Whether to cultivate seeds or breed animals in captivity was not a decision people made, weighing up the pros and cons, the way we might make a decision about a career or where to live. A better analogy would be urbanization. A majority of humans now spend the bulk of their lives in urban or periurban environments. This represents a dramatic departure from the past. Imagine observers a thousand years from now looking back on the moment humanity became urban. *How could this happen,* they might ask, *when, at the time, urban life posed higher risks of schizophrenia and pollution-related disease?* Of course, we as a collectivity have not *decided* to live in cities any more than Neolithic people *decided* to domesticate plants and animals. Rather, domestication and food production unfolded as a mesh of gestures guided by immediate concerns—declining prey, a gradual realization that it might be possible to make the rice come to the settlement rather than the other way around. Opposing signals—the realization that it takes more work to produce rice than to harvest it in the wild, chronic anemia in children, social inequality—manifested over longer time horizons and, as a consequence, exerted a more relaxed selection pressure on everyday behavior. Over time, ideologies arose to justify this everyday behavior—deference to big men, human mastery over the land and its animals, labor equals property. At length, these ideologies became self-reinforcing.

In certain places, notably the cold, arid steppe of central Eurasia, livestock offered one particular advantage: they served as a *trophic capacitor*, concentrating and storing energy, fixed nitrogen, and micronutrients from the grasslands in forms humans could use: meat, milk, fiber, and dung. Pasturage made the steppe productive.

How productive? The *Shiji*, a Han dynasty court history completed circa 94 BCE, describes the Xiongnu, a political formation to the north of China in present-day Mongolia, as a state much like China itself, replete with class stratification, hereditary elites, and a central government that exercised substantial control over the circulation of prestige goods. Some archaeologists today would go further and say that the Xiongnu was not just a state but an empire: a political formation in which territorially and culturally diverse peoples were brought into a single network of trade, with agricultural surpluses and prestige goods moving consistently from the frontiers to the centers of elite power. If the Xiongnu was an empire, it violates our expectations in at least one key way: its economic backbone was mobile pastoralism.

Xiongnu archaeology has yielded signs of wheat and millet cultivation, foraging, and fortified permanent settlements with iron workshops, but this was country best suited to keeping herds on the move. The herds in question included sheep and goats, along with horses, cattle, and smaller numbers of pigs, yaks, and camels. Our rubrics for talking about political complexity are so deeply tied to sedentism that at first it is difficult to imagine how an empire could emerge from this kind of economy. Indeed, as we have seen, mobile pastoralism has lent itself to resisting state control. But if we let go of evolutionist taxonomies of political complexity—chieftainship, confederation, state, empire—and start to see deference and autonomy as contingent features of an economic landscape that varied with season, climate, and the charisma of elites local and distant, livestock come into focus as an unparalleled medium of the concentration of wealth, for two reasons. One is trophic capacitation: specialization for mobile herding allows productive use of large swathes of land that are not suited to other kinds of economic activity. The other is that livestock *are well suited to use as currency*. This is something we see across Africa, Eurasia, and the Pacific. In places where livestock are used as currency, they tend to occupy the apical slot in a hierarchy of currencies graded by the kinds of things it is appropriate to use them for. Livestock are the currency of bridewealth and blood debts. Under certain conditions they support the formation of imperial elites.

In the Xiongnu case, the elites in question participated in a remarkably well-integrated prestige economy across an immense territory. Grave goods include precious metals and gems, textiles, ceramics, and lacquer wares from as far away as India and the Mediterranean. There is evidence of the consolidation of wealth and political power—fewer, larger monuments, more consistency in the distinctive indicia of nobility—in the centuries leading up to the appearance of the Xiongnu. Does integration of elites betoken submission from subsistence herders? On the evidence, the Xiongnu was not born of the kind of warlordism we associate with early empire. Deference to distant elites came not of conquest but of the fact that local elites were themselves embedded in a chain of deference leading to those who, from the Han perspective, were the "rulers" of the state they called Xiongnu. Could the Xiongnu elites have raised an imperial army in the manner of Chinggis Khan 1,300 years later? Perhaps not, but they were organized enough to repel Chinese adventurism.

In Iron Age Eurasia, animals raised for food and the people who rely on them occupy coordinate positions of subjection to institutions animated by the accumulation and concentration of wealth. The contemporary world is similar in this respect. It is to the contemporary world that we turn in part II.

Bridge: The Topology of History

In *Space Is the Machine*, the architect Bill Hillier makes the case for a topological approach to urban form. By this he means that we cannot understand how a city evolved or how people use it today simply by measuring distances and areas as they appear on a map. Instead we must think of cities as movement economies, phenomena whose evolution and function are governed by the recurring need people have to get from one point to another. When we look at a city as a network of street-level itineraries, Euclidean measures of distance and area fade into the background and something new becomes salient: the topological distance between two points, defined as the number of segments one must travel to get from one to the other. In walking networks, segments are bounded by lines of sight. For transit networks, you might substitute change of line (a two-seat ride feels longer than a one-seat ride of equivalent travel time). For auto networks, you might add merges and exits. The topological view does not jump out at you when you look at maps or aerial images. You must first imagine yourself tracing one route.

Something similar is true of history. In the prologue, I promised a comprehensive unpacking of the Meat Question. For the Plio-Pleistocene, this was straightforward. The evidence is sparse, the resolution in the time domain poor, the catalogue of human nutritional niches limited. Once we enter the Holocene, things change. In chapter 4, we began to encounter the challenges of geographic breadth as the circumstances of animal–human coevolution at the western and eastern ends of Eurasia diverged. In the modern era, this challenge is compounded. We must be more selective in our coverage and more thoughtful about how we choose what to focus on.

One way to manage the explosion of economic strategies we see in the modern world is compendiousness. I could offer a dictionary of animal–human relations, arranged by geography or mode of subsistence. This has its appeal. But like the city viewed from above, the compendious approach would blind us to many of the key determinants of the evolution and function of meat eating.

Instead, I've chosen to focus on a small number of cases, itineraries whose features illuminate features of the whole. The danger with a selective approach is the risk of bias in choice of cases. In the prologue, I expressed dissatisfaction with the glib way in which observers from a range of disciplines—geography, economics, behavioral ecology—have invoked conjecture about meat's role in human evolution to justify assumptions that income elasticity is driving growth in demand for meat today. I pointed to weaknesses in the ethnographic evidence for the Man the Hunter thesis and contradictions in the consumer behavior data about income and meat eating. In part II we explore these contradictions. Just as in part I we focused on the problems of evidence that attend claims that "meat made us human," so in what follows, we do the same for claims that "affluence must mean meat."

This is not to say that it is never the case that rising incomes release demand for meat that has been pent up by want of consumer market power. As we'll see in chapter 8, income elasticity may be part of the story—but it is not the whole story. A full reckoning of the Meat Question demands that we attend to all the things that are not salient in the aerial view—that is, those things that do not show up in the aggregate statistics.

In chapter 3, I made the case for a Sahulian perspective on behavioral modernity. My point was to loosen the grip that western Eurasia—Europe, the northern Mediterranean, and Southwest Asia—has exerted on the stories "we" tell about who "we" are. That first *we* continues to be dominated by people of European ancestry, with implications for what counts as modernity in the archaeological record. In chapters 6, 7, and 8, I do something similar: I offer an Asia-Pacific perspective on the modern meat economy. My aim is to nudge the food systems literature away from the North Atlantic and toward those parts of the world whose tastes, expertise, and climate will dominate global patterns of change in diet over the next two or three generations.

The story I tell in part II is not universal; you could find counterexamples from other parts of the world. But it is broadly significant in that it illustrates a recurring relationship between economic coercion and meat eating across divergent political environments—Indigenous Australia and North America, urbanizing China. The pattern that emerges runs counter to the story we most often hear about meat and affluence—and gives us cause to ask whether some other set of arrangements between humans and the animals we eat might be possible, perhaps necessary, in the near future.

II Must Affluence Mean Meat?

5 Enclosures

My first time in Port Hedland, Western Australia, I was driving. The drive from Perth had taken a few weeks, with stops all along the coast and a detour up the North West Cape to Exmouth, where a US naval communications station sits cheek by jowl with what was then the major scuba diving destination on the west coast. In Carnarvon, I stayed at a hostel that catered to seasonal workers on the fruit plantations, mainly young people from the United Kingdom and other points abroad. When you checked in, they issued you your own crockery, presumably to minimize conflict in the kitchen. One evening I sat at the table, pounding Coca-Cola until the whole world seemed to be vibrating. A thirteen-year-old girl from Scotland, traveling with her mother, got into an argument with a man three times her age and was obliged to recite the radio operators' alphabet—*alpha bravo charlie*—to prove a point. When I asked people how long they'd been there, they all said, *Too long*. The town gave off an ominous reek of ripe papaws, and I was glad to leave. When I returned from Exmouth, I stayed just long enough to fill the tank and pick up a hitchhiker. At the next gas station, three or four hours up Highway 1, the manager, hearing my American accent, professed his love of Frosted Grape Pop-Tarts and asked if I would send him a box (I did).

After weeks of tropical desperation, hostel owners piss drunk at midday and no radio in the car save the regional news (heroin busts, mango futures), Port Hedland came as a relief. I knew the port was shipping out salt and iron, but for a regional mining hub, the town felt remarkably quiet. The one attraction, apart from the port itself, was a tidal flat just east of Cooke Point known as Pretty Pool. At low tide during full moons, puddles left by the receding sea caught the moon in such a way as to create a staircase illusion. One evening I went down to Pretty Pool and walked out. When I returned to shore, the light had gone, and it took me half an hour to find my shoes. Later, I was told I might have stepped on a coelacanth buried in the sand.

A tourist office staffer a couple of towns back had let slip word of a controversy then brewing over Wittenoom, a former blue asbestos mining town in the interior. There were twenty-some residents remaining. The state was looking to close the town, citing the dangers posed by asbestos and other toxic airborne particulate matter. The residents had sought an injunction against the withdrawal of essential services. They argued that the closing of Wittenoom was a diversion intended to draw attention away from the greater airborne particulate hazard at active mines elsewhere in the state. They wanted to establish Wittenoom as a tourist attraction. Complicating matters, an Aboriginal group, the Banyjima, had lodged a Native Title claim encompassing Wittenoom Gorge. This was 1997. The previous year, the High Court of Australia had ruled in *Wik v. Queensland* that the issuance of pastoral leases such as those held by mine operators did not, of itself, extinguish Indigenous claims to territory under the nascent regime for adjudicating such claims known as Native Title. No one knew what *Wik* meant for the state's authority, say, to close a town. People at the tourist offices and, later, the State Geological Survey in Perth got nervous whenever I brought up Wittenoom. In this context, Port Hedland did not seem all that interesting.

When I returned in 2010, this time flying up from Perth, the vibe was different. Port Hedland had cleaned up well. The hostels and campsites had closed, and motel rooms went for A$500 a week. A new development, two-storied single-family houses, each worth more than A$1 million, abutted Pretty Pool—"BHP managerial class," said my host that week as we drove past one night, BHP Billiton being the world's largest minerals concern and a principal beneficiary of Port Hedland's new prosperity. The iron boom had started in 2004 with a spike in demand from China. By 2016, it would be over. Remarkably, iron ore exports continued to surge, peaking at nearly 43 million metric tons for the month of August 2016, more than four-fifths of which went to China, even as the price of ore threatened to bottom out at less than a third what it had been in 2010. Port Hedland had become the highest-volume bulk export terminal in the world.

If this seems like a strange way to open a discussion of meat in the modern world, consider that for a long time—from the 1860s, when Europeans first established permanent settlements in this part of the world, through the onset of iron extraction in the 1960s—livestock was at the center of the economy in the Pilbara, the region where Port Hedland is located. Livestock and minerals have been closely intertwined, not just in the Pilbara but across Australia and other parts of the colonized world. The pastoral leases alluded to earlier were, as the name suggests, originally issued to the operators of cattle and sheep runs, and stock and mineral booms have often unfolded in cyclic alternation. An area is stocked; a gold discovery follows. When the gold runs out, the prospectors turn to livestock.

We have no trouble thinking of minerals—gold, iron, aluminum, uranium, today the rare earths essential to semiconductors—as substances that shape the world in profound, difficult-to-foresee ways, with scarcities and gluts cascading through shipping and construction, manufacturing, consumer goods. The same could be said of petroleum and other fossil fuels. There is something about these *extractive commodities* that compels us to take them seriously. They are inaccessible, obstinate, hard. To get at them takes brute force, violence, toward the earth and toward human beings. We must really want them to expend such effort.

Now I want you to start thinking about meat in the same way, as something extracted from captive pools of zoomass assembled and maintained at great expense and with considerable violence and whose movements, be it as live animals or refrigerated cuts, shape our lives in deep, unexpected ways. In this chapter and the three that follow, we turn our attention to the modern era, roughly the past two hundred years. If part I asked what role meat had in driving human evolution and fostering humanity's expansion beyond its early range, part II asks what role meat has in our world now that human economic activity has come to dominate biosphere dynamics. The sources and interpretive rubrics I use to address this new question will be different from those I relied on in part I. But the themes of part I will continue to occupy us as we ask, at every turn, How deep are the evolutionary and historical forces guiding these developments? Were these outcomes inevitable? Should we want them to be otherwise in the future? Must an affluent world—where the operative sense of affluent is something we'll work out as we go along—be a meat-eating world?

We begin, in this chapter, with enclosure.

A Metabolic View of Colonization

In chapters 3 and 4, I used the term *intensification* without taking much care to define it. In principle, it should not be difficult to provide a precise operationalization for intensification, say, in terms of change in the rate of turnover of various factors implicated in the procurement of food—energy, water, carbon, nitrogen. If a band of foragers uses 10 calories to gain 100 in some unit of area and time, and a village of cultivator-herders uses 100 calories to gain 1,000, then the latter are practicing a more intensive way of life than the former. Notice that this says nothing about the relative efficiency of the two ways of life—the ratio of calories in to calories out is the same, but in the second case, the rate of turnover is ten times as great for a given unit of area and time. You can vary the unit of analysis—intensification per capita or intensification for a group occupying a given extent of land and water—to look at the relationship between population density and intensification. When I say "calories used" or "calories in," I mean not just energy expended in human labor but the full range of energetic resources that get drawn into the calorie life cycle, as it were—for instance, the energy contained in the grass that ungulates, be they wild or domesticated, eat. Intensification in this usage amounts to something like *concentration of biomass in space and time.* This is more or less what I had in mind in previous chapters.

Intensification is difficult to quantify archaeologically, in part because of the time-averaged nature of material debris—Was a system of irrigation earthworks used for two crops a year, or one crop every third year? Were the earthworks built in one generation, or over ten?—and in part, as we saw in chapter 4, because intensification is not a one-way phenomenon. A single panel of archaeologically legible artifacts might have been used to support more and less intensive ways of life at different times. Alas, historically, the concept of intensification has been closely tied to a model of economic history that did in fact take it for a unidirectional phenomenon culminating in *modernization,* construed here to mean the adoption of industrial agriculture and liberal capitalism.

So before we become too enamored of intensification, let's take a step back and ask a question that on the surface seems simpler: *How do we define the units of space and time over which economists and archaeologists argue about intensification?* Or, rather, not how do *we* define these units, but how did the people in question define them? How have groups of people imagined the extents of the Earth's surface—not to say forest canopy, rivers, and bodies of water surface and subsurface—where *their* economic life played out, along with the rhythms—seasonal, annual, decennial—over which they made use of different parts of their range? When did it become difficult to imagine configurations of space and time other than contiguous blobs of land occupied continuously by one group to the exclusion of others, unfolding across the surface of the Earth in a gapless tessellation? How, that is, has land become *enclosed?*

Generally, when historians use the term *enclosure,* they're referring to a constellation of legal and economic processes associated with the transfer of common pasturage to private title—often a literal enclosure or fencing in—starting in England in the seventeenth century and spreading in the centuries that followed across northern Europe and more recently to other parts of the world. Here I have a broader usage in mind, encompassing not just land but the metabolic and life cycles of plants and animals. In this usage, the growth of large herds of livestock represents a kind of enclosure: it is a fencing in of the biological and social processes embodied in the growth and reproduction of a population of gregarious vertebrates. The beneficiaries could be a household, a multihousehold seasonal pasturing group, a village, a state, or a privately capitalized stock operation. In this usage, enclosure is not necessarily something that pits landowners and capitalists against smallholders.

Expanding our use of enclosure this way does two things. First, it helps us see that large herds represent *open-air bioreactors*—biomass factories, if you will. A bioreactor is any kind of enclosed environment designed or evolved to support biological activity, tissue synthesis in particular. It encompasses a *scaffold,* a physical surface where metabolic activity unfolds, and a medium, a fluid enriched with the nutrients required for that activity. This image, the herd as bioreactor, will be useful when we discuss the industrialization of animal feeding.

The second reason for expanding our use of *enclosure* is that it focuses attention on relationships between the captive exploitation of land, animals, and human beings. The metabolic view of colonization stands at the heart of the claim I advanced in the prologue—that the contemporary meat economy is one in which humans and animals play coordinate roles and suffer coordinate forms of violence.

Grazing

Before we look at how livestock—open-air bioreactors—facilitated settlement colonialism in Australia and the Americas, it is important to note that the role of livestock as instruments of colonization did not originate with the capitalist forms of stocking that characterized Australia and the Great Plains of North America. In the previous chapter, we saw how specialist mobile pastoralism, practiced at subsistence grades of intensity with even modest surpluses, could support the expansion and integration of elite networks to the point where the total institutional configuration—mobile flocks and herds, town-based craft specialization, a chain of deference that pumps wealth and prestige from the periphery to the center—comes to resemble an empire. This was the case with the Xiongnu, which embodied a livestock-based expansionary state without much in the way of settlement colonization. Herders and elites at the frontiers were *enrolled* in the state's apparatus of surplus extraction, not displaced by an advancing wave of livestock. In Northeast Africa at a much earlier date, we see the complement: expansionary colonization without much, if anything, in the way of a state. Cattle from Southwest Asia appear in Northeast Africa by 8 ka, interbreeding with local aurochs or, possibly, with cattle previously domesticated *in situ*. Sheep and goats follow, along with donkeys. Mobile pastoralism did not emerge here on the margins of settled cultivation: domesticated herds appear in the Nile river valley at least a thousand years before domesticated cereals. Initially this was not a population replacement scenario: indigenous foragers simply integrated herding into their economy. Livestock, with their capacity to convert dryland scrub into usable biomass, allowed forager-herders, and then simply herders, to thrive in the desert. As early as 7 ka, cows' milk was an essential part of the herders' diet in what is now Libya. Over time, herding, and herders, pushed south and west.

But what happened in Australia and the Americas in the nineteenth century was new in at least three ways. First, speed and scale: it happened a lot faster over a wider area and at higher levels of intensification than did Neolithic, Bronze Age, and Iron Age episodes of livestock colonialism or even those of the early modern Atlantic colonial empires. Second, modern livestock colonialism was a commercial enterprise underwritten by outside capital. In Australia in particular, stockists saw themselves not as homesteaders but as the founders of a new landed elite. They were there to get rich. Third, in Australia and some parts of the Americas, in particular the United States and Argentina, grazing frontiers took form in the context of expansionary states that used grazing to extend the reach of their claims to territorial sovereignty. This is not to say that graziers and the state colluded in pushing back the frontier. Often they were at odds, and grazing thrived in those places where the state lacked the enforcement power to impose its own vision of settlement. But ultimately there came a time when graziers would appeal to the state to recognize their de facto claims to title over pasturage and forcibly pacify or remove the indigenous population.

Southeast Australia

The first penal colony at Botany Bay, near present-day Sydney, was established in 1788. Exploratory settlements at Port Phillip (now Melbourne) and in Van Diemen's Land (now Tasmania) followed in 1803. The former was quickly abandoned, but Van Diemen's Land, which had seen sporadic French occupations prior to British settlement, became a key settlement zone for transported convicts. In Van Diemen's Land, as in New South Wales, commercial livestock operations played an essential role in the colonization process, with wool exports to England providing a key source of income for free settlers. For convicts, transport to the Antipodes was not intended to offer a fresh start. The colonies served as open-air prisons, with convicts assigned to private station (ranch) operators and often denied a ticket of leave—effectively, a pardon—even after many years of service. In Van Diemen's Land after 1820, commercial livestock operations relying on assigned convict labor became the rule rather than the exception. By 1830, settlers, including free colonists and convicts, numbered 22,500, their cattle and sheep close to a million. Three British Army regiments were garrisoned in the colony, both to control the convicts and to repel or remove native communities that interfered with settlement. The population of Indigenous Tasmanians in the parts of the island occupied by settlers had fallen from perhaps 6,000 at the time of the colony's establishment to 250, if that, and was pacified in 1831 after a decade of intensifying low-level war.

Around the same time, squatting took off on the mainland, driven by the growing export market for wool. Pressure had been building on the colonial government of New South Wales for fifteen years to adopt a more liberal policy of land alienation. The government responded with a series of strategies intended to vent this pressure while maintaining control over the settlement process. Initially, the colonial government made grants of land on the basis of would-be graziers' social status and capital. Grants were succeeded by "tickets" of occupation conferring the right to graze livestock, which were succeeded in turn by renewable one-year licenses. In 1835, a privately backed expedition from Van Diemen's Land reestablished a colony at Port Phillip and attempted to subvert the colonial government's authority, "purchasing" 1.5 million square kilometers (580,000 square miles) from Indigenous occupants for trade goods worth £200. Squatters quickly established stock routes, simply driving their flocks beyond the limits of New South Wales into what is now Victoria and, by 1838, South Australia. Fencing was uncommon until the 1860s. Shepherds' huts emerged as a way of signaling de facto occupation, and squatters evolved an informal system of dispute resolution to minimize white-on-white violence, lest skirmishes create an incentive for the government in Sydney to clear the country. Squatted sheep and cattle runs were immense. When, in 1847, the Colonial Office in London instituted a new system of pastoral leases to regulate squatters' claims, leased claims ran 10,000 to 14,000 hectares (25,000 to 35,000 acres). In 1860 the colonial government of Victoria, now a separate colony, put in place a system of "selection" intended to break up squatters' claims when pastoral leases expired. In practice, a successful squatter, possessed of extensive capital, social networks, and knowledge of the land, could preempt essential parts of his run (say, those with water) and in this way thwart selection.

From the outset, it was clear to everyone on the ground, from colonial surveyors to squatters to the convicts who occupied the shepherds' huts that squatters deposited at strategic points across their runs, that the country they were entering was occupied. An 1836 survey of the Wimmera basin found that the Jardwadjali erected tepees with daubed exteriors, one large enough to accommodate forty people; the surveyors decided the natives must have had help from an escaped convict. Stock drivers sometimes encountered bands of Australians, sometimes larger groups, who varied in their degree of familiarity with Europeans and their animals. Sometimes drivers would find that the country ahead of them had been burned. What was Indigenous Australians' first encounter with livestock like? This is a question we consider in the next chapter. Historian Robert Kenny gives us a start:

> Imagine you have lived your life in a world where kangaroos, wallabies, emus, echidnas, possums, wombats, snakes, and lizards were the most visible things; where the biggest things that moved, other than humans—kangaroos and emus—were bipeds similar in size to humans. . . . What could you think if all your life you had tracked soft-footed wallabies and bare-footed humans, and you suddenly found the tracks of iron-rimmed wheels and hard-hoofed oxen? The genre to turn to is science-fiction: the Martians have landed.

Though settlers saw country suitable only for grazing ruminants, for local inhabitants this had been prime foraging ground affording a broad panel of plant and animal foods. Livestock changed that. The country became a scaffold for enormous mobile bioreactors that trampled much of the ground vegetation, consumed the rest, and denied local fauna access to surface water. If enclosure is fundamentally about monopolizing access to resources—land and water, labor, or the specialized metabolic affordances of ruminants—then in Southeast Australia, livestock were the vector of enclosure, triggering a cascade of changes in local biome and social structure that made it difficult for anyone but well-capitalized stock graziers to use the land effectively.

Western North America

If there is any place in the world where the bioreactor metaphor makes sense, it is the dry grasslands of western North America. In the decades following US independence, Sonora and Alta California came to support 1 million head of cattle, New Mexico 3 million sheep. Comanche territory was home to 2 million horses domestic and wild. Across the grasslands of the Americas, feral populations of ruminants, descendants of those introduced by European settlers in an earlier wave of colonization, roamed free. In some places—the Argentine pampas, Texas—feral cattle formed the basis for a new mode of capitalist stocking.

In settler-controlled parts of western North America before 1800, livestock were raised on a combination of pasturage and cereals, stimulating the market for cereal production in coastal and riparian zones. This was the tail end of a 500-year Northern Hemisphere cool-dry interval known as the Little Ice Age. The period of European colonization had coincided with a time when Indigenous nations across western North America had adopted a way of life that entailed greater mobility and greater reliance on foraged grasses—a contrast with what we saw in the previous chapter for the mid-Holocene Hopewell societies of the eastern part of the continent. When Europeans first arrived in North America, the Great Plains supported a bison population of 30 to 40 million and comparable populations of elk and pronghorn.

In the first half of the nineteenth century, a number of Plains nations adopted a specialist form of equestrian hunting, establishing a bison ("buffalo")-centered grassland niche that was neither herding as Europeans understood it nor simply "control in the wild" or "low-level food production," but the effective enclosure of bison metabolism without domestication. The instigation for this shift came in part from the encroachment of settlers whose large herds of livestock and burn-intolerant fields of domesticated cereals made it difficult for Indigenous nations to sustain a more extensive (spread-out) way of life.

In the wake of the Sioux Wars of the 1860s and 1870s and the removal of the Plains nations to reservations, the Northern Plains became the setting for a cattle boom that bears comparison to the sheep stocking of Southeast Australia forty years before. Railroads played an essential role in the stocking of the Northern Plains, providing an efficient way both to get cattle to the rangelands and to send them to Chicago at the end of the season for finish feeding and slaughter. In some instances, as in Australia, stocking ventures were backed by investors in the United Kingdom. The US government was more supportive of preemption than the British Colonial Office had been, but cattle demanded such extensive pasturage that grazing ranges were effectively held in common. As in Australia, early arrivals sharing a commercial outlook quickly evolved an informal regime of dispute resolution. This took the form of cattlemen's associations, whose members cooperated to limit overgrazing and prevent theft during biannual roundups (muster) and colluded to exclude latecomers, placing ads in newspapers announcing a range closed to new arrivals.

When, in the 1880s, the trickle of would-be graziers turned into a flood, all expecting to exercise the same right of smallhold preemption, guaranteed by the Homestead Act of 1862 and its successors, that the cattlemen had relied on, they found themselves effectively barred from entering established ranges. The federal government declined to enforce the law, and the cattlemen were content to allow their claims to remain in legal limbo: they had neither title nor leasehold, but they did have exclusive use of large, corporate ranges now conveniently demarcated with barbed wire. When, in 1901, the Roosevelt administration did enforce smallhold preemption, the cattlemen pushed west.

Did cattlemen's associations prevent overstocking? No. In fact, even members had an incentive to maintain herds at unsustainable levels, lest neighbors, sensing a withdrawal, encroach on their informal allotment of rangeland. As in southeastern Australia in the 1840s, animals were not just units of capital; they were instruments of land appropriation. Anthropologist Thomas Sheridan describes the outcome: "die-offs of Biblical proportions: 85% of herds on the Southern Plains during the severe winter of 1885–1886; similar losses during the great blizzard on the Northern Plains in January 1887; 50%–75% on Southwestern ranges during the devastating drought of 1892–1893."

The recent history of Sagebrush Rebellions—the histrionic rejection of federal regulation among cattle graziers in the western United States—goes back to this earlier episode of livestock capitalism. (The January 2016 armed occupation of the Malheur National Wildlife Refuge in Oregon exemplifies a recent reescalation of Sagebrush tactics.) Graziers came to feel that the right to graze their cattle on public lands was an article of natural law. The Taylor Grazing Act of 1934 nominally put an end to unregulated public grazing, establishing a system of permits and advisory boards for graziers seeking access to lands now under the management of the Forest Service and other federal agencies. In practice, for a long time, the advisory boards consisted exclusively of permit holders. Permits are specified in terms of animal unit months (AUMs), an entitlement to graze one cow and one calf on a particular range for a particular period of time—the "month" refers to how much forage the "animal unit" is expected to consume in that span of time. Opinion varies as to how great a deal graziers are getting. On its face, a public land AUM is a lot less expensive than comparable access to private land, but the private fees incorporate a greater share of the costs of environmental remediation that public lands graziers are required to pay out of pocket.

Rangelands, Sheridan argues, represent a classic common-pool resource, "low[-quality], patchy, and unpredictable," and we should expect to see some form of flexible tenure on land held in common or leased from the state. In Central and Northwest Australia, cattle stockists did succeed in gaining exclusive, long-term access to large estates of dry land, with implications we examine in the next chapter.

The Bureau of Land Management, established in 1946 and the principal object of Sagebrush Rebellion animosity, has been tasked with unwinding the cattlemen's effective enclosure of western ranges, not to say staving off overgrazing and water depletion, in part by reducing grazing allotments. The BLM manages 100 million hectares of land. Its statutory mandate is to balance the interests of graziers with those of loggers, miners, conservationists, and recreational land users. This has made it nobody's friend, but cattle graziers have been especially vocal, and a small minority violent, in their opposition to the policy of multiple use.

In part, this is a product of how different kinds of capital with different material characteristics engender different corporate social structures. If mining and logging were the province of loose confederations of independent operators, we would expect those operators to behave more like graziers do. By the same token, what distinguishes livestock as a genre of capital is that it makes it possible for loose confederations to effect enclosures on a scale we associate with "bigger," "harder" forms of capital. Livestock represents a more fluid, less obstinate genre of capital than minerals or timber: a small number of individuals driving large mobile bioreactors across the land can occupy it with practically no implements apart from the animals themselves (or, in the case of railroad stocking, by leasing ancillary capital on flexible terms: you need not buy the railroad right of way to ship cattle by rail). But livestock's fluidity should not blind us to its extractive nature.

Milking and Shearing

I could multiply examples, but we've seen enough now to rough in a pattern: the enclosure of dry grasslands and the enclosure of ungulate life cycles are mutually entailed. You need herds of a certain scale, open-air bioreactors, to occupy a stretch of country to the exclusion of rivals. Herds of this scale demand vast expanses of land and immense quantities of grass. Let's pause to consider this second, metabolic form of enclosure more closely. When we talk about "enclosing" animal life cycles, what does this mean apart from captive breeding? Can we quantify the captive appropriation of animal metabolism? Can we identify grades of intensification?

Up to this point, in our discussion of domesticates, we've focused on meat, though I've mentioned other roles that domesticates fill and other pathways by which humans and other vertebrates enact a shared niche: commensalism and companionship, cultic valorization, traction and transport. Sometimes, as with llamas and alpacas in the Andes, a domesticate comes to fill multiple roles: meat, milk, traction, fiber. When I discussed the role of animal-source foods in the forager economy, it made sense to focus on meat, though eggs have featured at various times and places and though foragers have used animal bodies for things other than food. Now that we've shifted our gaze toward domesticates, we need to look at the other ways that animals function in the economy of food producers.

For a long time, the working assumption in Neolithic archaeology was that milk, fiber, traction, and so on, things that could be extracted from the animal without killing it, represented *secondary products*. These things, the reasoning went, could not have driven domestication, since, with the limited exception of eggs, foragers do not use them. Even if we assume people had no trouble making the imaginative leap from hides to felt or from suckling to milking, developing a felting or dairy industry requires a long process of trial and error with lots of source material on hand to experiment with. On top of that, there was no material evidence for dairy industries prior to 5 or 6 ka.

In recent years, this has changed. More precise mortality profiling suggests that cattle, sheep, and goats were all being kept for milk production as early as 11 ka. Long-chain fatty acid residues typical of ruminant milk have been recovered from ceramic vessels in Southwest Asia and southeastern Europe from as far back as 8 ka. The animal protein attributed to Neolithic cultivator-herders in Spain in chapter 4 was probably largely dairy in nature. As I have noted, milk seems to have been essential to the livestock colonization of Northeast Africa.

So here is an example of enclosure of animal metabolism. We can debate just how important dairy products were to the diet in different times and places. We can ask when and where ruminants were first bred to be capable of producing milk at all times of the year. These are questions of how to measure intensification. But we do not need answers to these questions to recognize that with dairy production, we have a new kind of enclosure. The animal is no longer something that can be harvested just once in its life cycle. It is, instead, a renewable resource whose capacity to transform low-grade vegetation into high-quality food we can draw on continuously over the course of its productive life.

The same goes for the exploitation of animals as commercial, as opposed to subsistence, resources. This is what we've seen in Australia: among the squatters, sheep were valued not as sources of meat or even milk, but as reliable converters of scrub into fiber, which could in turn be sold to textile manufacturers in England. In this way, animals get taken up in the economy as we know it—that is, not the subsistence economy of foragers and small-scale herders, the economy of calories, but the commercial economy, the economy of debt and cash.

From Persons to Property

In the previous chapter, I made frequent allusion to *ideology*. What I had in mind was a set of values and a set of rubrics for interpreting experience in light of those values. But the ideologies in question, about the nature of relationships between humans and other living things and between humans and unseen forces, were more capacious than what we usually mean when we refer, say, to political ideologies. *Worldview* might be a better word or, better still, *cosmology*: a theory of how the world came to be and how it is structured, its origins and constitution. I gestured vaguely at diagnostic features of the cosmologies of hunters and herders. Now we have a third category of animal-based economic activity, personified in the figure of the grazier. Let's take a closer look at how cosmology figures in the productive lives of these three figures.

The literature on the cosmology of hunting peoples runs deep, most of it derived from ethnographic studies on the northern taiga of Eurasia and North America, the circumpolar region, and Amazonia. Certain themes recur. Among these are stories of hunters losing their way in the forest. As it grows dark and the hunter wonders how he will get home, he meets a man or sometimes a woman. The stranger invites the hunter to return to his village to spend the night. In some cases, the hunter ends up marrying the man's sister or daughter, or the woman who found him, and living for some time in the village before realizing that its inhabitants are in fact animals: reindeer, perhaps, or some other locally prestigious prey. In other cases, the hunter sees what's going on pretty quickly and flees without spending the night. In some versions, the animals, upon reaching their own village, "remove their skins" to reveal their true animal nature. These stories are laced with anxiety about losing track of what kind of being one is, perhaps getting stuck on the side of the animal. They illustrate a common feature of hunter cosmology: *personhood depends on where you are situated.* To humans, *we* are the people, the encultured beings, and all the rest are animals. To animals, *they* are the people, and we are something else—perhaps predator, perhaps prey.

Not all animals are accorded this status of persons from their own perspective. It tends to be those that loom large in the life of the community that are recognized as having an interiority and sociality homologous to that of humans. Even then, variation is the rule. Depending on where you are, whom you talk to and when, and what kind of animal you are talking about, you may hear, variously, that individual animals have souls or that their behavior is guided by "spirit masters" or "masters of the hunt": that it is the animals who must be propitiated, lest they take offense and cease to make themselves available or that it is the spirit master. In some parts of eastern Siberia, the spirits form a third category of persons, with distinct personalities and their own perspective on which types of beings are encultured, predator, and prey. It may be the spirit master, not the animal, who welcomes the hunter into his village and offers his daughter in marriage. Whatever the role of spirits, the relationship between animal and human persons is not symmetric. In some places, animals understand human language, sometimes even when it is not voiced. Among peoples of the Canadian North, animals stand in a tutelary relationship to humans.

Hunting itself is suffused with a tension between viewing hunted animals as munificent coevals and viewing them as manifestations of a possibly antagonistic unseen force that must be coaxed and tricked into providing for human needs. Killing an animal by hunting or trapping is both a gesture in an ongoing chain of reciprocal exchange similar to that between trading partners or feasting rivals and a more one-sided act of overcoming the animal or its obstinate spirit master. In some places, hunters frame the obligation to share meat in terms of the obligation to receive gifts graciously: the animal, in offering itself to the hunter, has acted in the capacity of a feast giver whose generosity must not be spurned.

So the relationship between hunters and the animals they hunt, even when it has an adversarial dimension, is one of mutual regard, founded on the recognition that these others are people too, albeit people of a different kind, people we sometimes have trouble seeing as people. How does this compare to how herders see the world? The anthropologist Tim Ingold has argued that in herding, trust gives way to domination. Livestock are not people the way hunted animals were, and humans need not feel indebted to them for meat. Mind you, herded animals—say, in the Sámi reindeer economies that formed the basis for Ingold's observations—are not "production units" in the way they became under the capitalist stocking already discussed. They are empathic, sentient creatures, in some cases individuals with distinct personalities, but they are property, not persons, and, in the herding relationship, humans are indisputably in charge.

Ingold's transition from trust to domination has become the standard way of summarizing the relationship between mode of subsistence and cosmology. But lately evidence has accumulated that the story is more complex. For one thing, Bronze Age excavations in Scandinavia have revealed rectangular longhouses occupied at one end by humans, at the other by animals, suggesting a domestic intimacy, a coevalness, that belies talk of a loss of trust (as anyone who has spent time working on a goat farm will tell you, goats feel no compunction about making their desires known at close quarters). For another, anthropologists in eastern Siberia have observed striking continuity in how hunters and herders talk about animals—in this case, reindeer again—and in how animals figure in the kinds of ritual traditions that offer insight into cosmology. Reindeer domestication in Northeast Asia dates to at least 2,000 years ago, so we cannot simply say that cosmology is lagging practice. In some herding communities, class stratification predicated on herd size testifies to the fact that people have no trouble seeing reindeer as property: the way to become a big man is to acquire lots of stock. At the same time, shamanic interventions in the spirit world in these communities look remarkably like those in neighboring hunting communities that are much more egalitarian.

These cosmologies, whether we call them animist or perspectivist, are distinct from the totemist cosmologies that predominate in Australia and some parts of North America. In the latter, the relationship between humans and animals is conceptualized not as one of perspective taking and exchange across boundaries of material likeness, but of kinship, with lineages incorporating distinct species of animals and distinct segments of humanity running back to the time of the world's making (in Australia, *the Dreaming*, discussed more fully in chapter 6) and apportioning responsibility for the ongoing upkeep of the world today. Perspectivism and totemism are not really in opposition. They are more like poles in the structuring of animal–human sociality, the horizontal and the vertical, with different societies standing in different places along the axis between the poles. They share an understanding that humans have been tasked with maintaining a world made by animals. This has often been read as environmentalism before the word. But maintaining here entails not just ritual work (sacrifice, shamanic flight, singing the Dreaming) but the everyday taking of animal life. It is an economic no less than a spiritual ethic, and under the right combination of economic and ecological pressures, it can tip over into overexploitation. This is something that people acculturated to view animals as wildlife, pets, or stock but never as rivals, trading partners, or ancestors find difficult to understand. The rupture Kenny describes in his account of how livestock entered the Dreaming in the generation following the stocking of Southeast Australia ("the Martians have landed") is a rupture not just in cosmology but in a prior entente between the productive and contemplative aspects of life.

Indeed, in the Lakota Ghost Dance movement of 1890, which culminated, on December 29 of that year, in the massacre of some three hundred Minneconjou Lakota at Wounded Knee, one of the things that motivated people to take up the dance and the practices of ritual purity that went with it was the hope that it might convince the bison to return. Bison had not been seen on Sioux reservations since 1883. Mourning the bison was, of course, a way of mourning the loss of mobility, autonomy, dignity, and legal standing that had come with military defeat and removal to reservations. But it was also an expression of hunger, the stomach-gnawing kind. On the reservations, Plains people were dependent for their material needs on Office of Indian Affairs agents, often political appointees with little managerial experience and no sympathy for the communities they were now charged with "civilizing." Conditions varied from one reservation to the next, but as a rule, agents saw it as their mission to turn Plains people away from hunting and toward commercial farming and stock raising, using coercion if need be. In September 1890, the incoming commander of the Division of the Missouri, the Army division that three months later would conduct the pacification that ended at Wounded Knee, asked the Department of War to provide emergency rations for the Northern Cheyenne at Tongue River Reservation, Montana, who were practically starving. No wonder, in the ten weeks that followed, all but the one seasoned agent on the Sioux reservations saw the Ghost Dance as preparation for insurrection. As Louise

Weasel Bear, a Lakota woman present at Wounded Knee, recounted many years later of the moment when soldiers opened fire with Hotchkiss guns, "We tried to run but they shot us like we were a buffalo."

Industrialization and Confinement

The shift from herding to grazing was just one step in the enclosure of animal metabolism that led to meat as we know it today. There are three others we need to consider. Usually these would all be described in terms of industrialization. This has merit, but there's something more specific going on in how the extraction of food energy from animal bodies changes after 1870. Let's call it *confinement*: getting animals to put on weight in the absence of the kind of locomotor activity for which vertebrates are evolved. Confinement has three dimensions: breeding, confined feeding, and slaughter.

Breeding

I have mentioned in passing that the cattle boom in North America was seeded with feral cattle left over from earlier stocking episodes. Texas longhorns, for instance, were well adapted to the dry grass biome of the western rangelands, and in the two decades starting in 1870, some 3 million were driven north, both directly to slaughter and to stock ranges on the Northern Plains. But as consumers developed a taste for beef, the traits that made longhorns easy to work with, their ranginess and independence, worked in their disfavor (or, depending on how you look at it, their favor). Their meat was too lean, even with fattening in the north, and they did not take to stall feeding. Their horns made it difficult to pack them in railroad cars. What cattle producers wanted was something more tractable, more amenable to life in confinement. The solution was the introduction of European breeds, sometimes crossed with longhorns.

This story repeated across animal clades. Pigs represent an especially interesting case because, unlike ruminants, they are not herbivores. The dietary niche of early Holocene suids was in fact not so different from that of humans, and domestication amounted to getting pigs to subsist on something other than what humans ate. This has included human food waste. But pigs also do well with the woody fruit of deciduous trees—acorns, beechnuts. Allowing pigs to roam the forest living off so-called mast and to collect then for slaughter in late autumn was the common method of raising them in Europe through the early modern era. The animals were rangy and recalcitrant, but this seemed like a fair trade: raising them did not require much investment, and they served as living bioreactors, converting material that was inedible to humans into high-quality food. By the seventeenth century, deforestation and enclosure brought pressure on this strategy of *pannage,* while the growth of cities and commercial beermaking and dairying offered new opportunities to experiment with keeping pigs as backyard animals and scavengers.

In China, where suids were also domesticated early in the Holocene, pigs looked different. Perhaps because wet rice cultivation encouraged more rapid intensification, pigs had been bred to respond well to a higher-quality diet and spend their lives on the farm rather than in the forest. At some point around 1700, Chinese bloodstock, from two lineages in fact, was introduced into the English pig gene pool. Within a couple of decades, references appear to new breeds that displayed clear signs of Chinese influence. It was these pigs, bred for year-round sty feeding, that formed the basis for modern varieties, together with crosses between Chinese pigs and those being raised in the eastern part of what became the United States. In parts of North America where transport was unreliable, pigs converted an unwieldy cereal crop into something planters could get to market. Today pigs are valued in part for their high rates of feed conversion (under three to one) but also for the fact that the entire pig life cycle, from birth to slaughter, can occur in tight quarters.

But the poster species for animals bred to grow and reproduce in confinement is the chicken. Actually, *bred* is a mischaracterization here, since most of the interventions in the chicken life cycle implicated in the modern broiler—a chicken raised for its meat, at feed conversion ratios of under two to one—lean on phenotypic plasticity rather than breeding. Confinement came late to the chicken. Experiments in eliminating ranging from chickens' behavior did not get underway in earnest until the 1920s, when it was found that vitamin D, delivered via cod liver oil mixed into feed, offset the rickets-like atrophy of the legs that befell chickens denied sunlight. By the mid-1930s, half of all chicks in the United States, a million a year, were hatched in commercial incubators, and hens could spend their entire lives indoors. B vitamin supplementation to promote more rapid growth followed, along with improved feedstocks, energy denser and lower in fiber. The 1950s saw the introduction of the now-archetypal maize-soy feedstock base, which Paul and Anne Ehrlich, in their Malthusian tract, *The Population Bomb* (1968), warned could foreshadow the future of human food. The same years saw the widespread introduction of antibiotics into chicken feed. Confinement did, of course, raise the prevalence of infectious disease among chickens. But antimicrobial use was and remains principally *nontherapeutic*; for reasons still poorly understood, subtherapeutic doses of antimicrobials stimulate animals to put on weight faster. (Antimicrobial dosing also fosters the emergence of drug-resistant disease agents, vitiating the drugs' therapeutic value for humans and animals alike.) Breeding has come into play too, in particular in an effort to increase the proportion of breast meat. Chicken breeding represents a form of *metabolic involution*—high yield at high cost. Modern broilers are fragile animals. They attain market weight in under forty days and exhibit traits of value in selling meat. But they require ever more finely calibrated growing environments to offset the risks of skeletal defects and immune disorders. The chickens raised today in batteries of 100,000 or more are bred not simply to tolerate confinement but to require it.

Feeding

Designing animals, by breeding or by manipulating phenotypic plasticity, to convert plant matter to meat faster and more efficiently is one dimension of enclosure. But as the case of chicken shows, it is not always the most important. The design of the spaces of animal production—here the term fits—is critical too. If you drew up a list of the emblematic structures of our time, the spaces that exemplify how we live, what would they be? The airport would probably make most people's lists, along with the refugee camp, the containerized shipping port, the open-plan office, the classroom, the supermarket, the gym. To these we should add the concentrated animal feeding operation (CAFO). In fact, the CAFO encompasses three distinct types of space: the chicken battery, the swine operation, and the feedlot.

In the United States, concentrated feeding operations account for 99 percent of livestock-source foods. By now, there have been any number of exposés by animal protection activists and journalists of the depredations of confined feeding: the contamination of groundwater with untreated animal feces, zoonotic disease agents, ammonia, nitrates, phosphorus, heavy metals including zinc, copper (used as supplements), and arsenic (used as an antimicrobial), antibiotics, growth hormones, pesticides, and stillborn animals—all with the attendant implications for the neurological, psychiatric, endocrine, and respiratory health of the uniformly poor, often racially marginalized communities forced to host these facilities; eutrophication of aquatic ecosystems leading to algal blooms and dead zones, again stemming from the dumping of nitrogen and phosphorus; aquifer depletion; exorbitant use of fossil fuels; and the stress experienced by the animals, which, despite breeders' efforts to extinguish locomotor exploratory behavior, are no more at ease with crowding than you would be if you passed your whole life crammed in a train at rush hour. In most parts of the United States, as of this writing, swine production entails the use of gestation and farrowing crates that provide neither bedding nor room for the sow to turn around or turn over. This may sound like the product of a characteristically American regulatory environment, but it's only in the past decade that gestation crates have been banned in Canada, New Zealand, and the European Union. Workers in swine operations are at heightened risk of exposure to methicillin-resistant *Staphylococcus aurea* (MRSA) and hydrogen sulfide. In many cases, CAFO (and slaughterhouse) workers are kept in a state of debt peonage, both to people traffickers and to the corporation that owns the animal operation, which charges them for protective clothing and other essential equipment and sometimes housing. All this is pretty well known.

What gets less attention is that the *concentration* in concentrated animal feeding is a concentration not just of animal bodies but of the ownership of those bodies. Between 1980 and 2000, the mean number of animals per operation in chicken and pig operations in Canada and the United States more than doubled. Vertical integration of gestation, feeding, slaughter, and marketing has become the norm save in cattle. Where third-party operations and family farms enter into production, it is as contract growers, purchasing feed and other inputs from the integrators but bearing full liability for the environmental and occupational risks of the grow-out phase. The integrator owns not just the animal bodies but the animal life cycle, including the schedule of feeding, supplementation, and confinement that contract growers are bound to and in some cases trademarks to the animal breeds for which those schedules were formulated.

Feedlots for beef cattle are a bit different. They tend to be smaller in terms of the number of animals present at any one time, though feedlots exist with capacities of 100,000. The industry remains less vertically integrated, and cattle find their way to a feedlot in a variety of ways. In some cases, the feedlot does own the cattle; in others ,they've been purchased at auction, or provided by graziers who maintain ownership through grow-out, or by investors using cattle as a hedge. Again, concentration of production capacity is the rule. In the United States, feedlots with a capacity of over a thousand animals represent less than 3 percent of the total number of feedlots but account for close to 90 percent of the cattle brought to market. The diet is mainly maize and wheat, along with the by-products of ethanol production. "Some finishing diets," notes a recent US-centered review of the feedlot industry, "may include up to 3% added yellow grease or tallow to increase the energy density of the diet." This "yellow grease" is the rendered fat of other livestock. In the United States, more than four out of five cattle receive sex hormone implants to improve feed conversion. In the case of males, this is partly to offset the loss of endogenous androgens following castration.

"In regard to water-quality issues," the same review continues, "it is more cost efficient to manage the manure of and effluent from one 100,000-head facility than from 20 facilities with 5,000 head each." Economies of scale are often touted as the great advantage of concentrated feeding, and this extends to labor costs: a well-run feedlot requires just eight to ten people for 10,000 cattle. (By contrast with poultry and swine operations, cattle work is skilled, with "pen riders" responsible for assessing the health of as many as 12,000 cattle a day.) But it is easy to make too much of economies of scale. For one thing, feeding operations largely succeed in externalizing the costs of environmental remediation to surrounding communities. For another, in the United States, starting in 1997 integrators benefited from a twenty-year period of depressed prices for cereals and soybeans made possible by a federal agricultural policy that decoupled subsidies to farmers from production.

In chapter 4, I started by describing domestication in terms of the bringing of animal life cycles under increasingly captive control. But historically, the relationship between humans and domesticates has been dialogic: codomestication rather than domestication, the iterative unfolding of increasingly denser forms of mutualism between populations of metabolically divergent animals, humans among them, converging on a common niche. No question, flocks and herds on the eastern Eurasian steppe 2,000 years ago or, for that matter, in the Sahara 7,000 years ago, were open-air bioreactors, converting fibrous grass and scrub into milk and meat for the benefit of human cohabitants. Livestock have long been both chattel property and the currency of pan-regional prestige economies that in some cases gave rise to empires. But for most of human history since the onset of prey domestication, pastoral economies have also been zones of exchange, reciprocal if asymmetric. From one point of view, it is the animals who have domesticated humans, coaxing them to work more than they had as foragers and hijacking their culture so that much of human knowledge and cosmology came to revolve around the needs and well-being of the animals they lived with.

With enclosure, this changed. Animal bodies and animal life cycles became an extractive resource, as ethically inert, as lacking in claims against us, as iron or oil. Their growth and reproduction were decoupled from environmental *zeitgebers*—somatic synchronization cues—such as changes in daily photoperiod or ambient temperature. They were, in effect, walled off, however imperfectly, from nature.

Killing

Like feeding operations, slaughterhouses and animal processing facilities—again, here the industrial term fits—have been the object of voluminous documentation, much of it covert. By no means does the United States hold a patent on the banalization of violence, but it is above all in the United States that activists and journalists have risked their own safety working in meatpacking plants. The bones of the story are thus: commercial, as opposed to backyard, slaughter of livestock originated in France about two hundred years ago. The template for the modern slaughterhouse was the Union Stock Yard in Chicago, which opened in 1865 and set the standard for many of the practices we associate with meat processing today, not least the use of marginalized, often immigrant communities as reservoirs of cheap labor. Slaughterhouses have been responsible for a number of innovations in workflow design, including the use of conveyor belts and assembly (rather, disassembly) lines, but automation remains superficial. At the end of the day, for all the effort that the livestock industry has expended to standardize them, large-bodied vertebrates remain obstinately diverse in appearance and deportment. Here is how political scientist Timothy Pachirat puts it in his remarkable account of his half-year working in a cattle slaughterhouse in Omaha, Nebraska:

> Some [cows] balk when prodded up the chute leading to the kill box [where, ideally but often not, they are stunned by a captive-bolt gun prior to shackling and suspension from an overhead conveyor], some collapse from exhaustion

> or disease, some have horns that are especially difficult to cut off, some are pregnant and about to give birth, some are unusually large, and some are unexpectedly small.

To accommodate this kind of heterogeneity at speed, work roles on the kill floor are minutely fractionated—where Pachirat worked, into 121 different roles—only a small number of which are directly implicated in the killing of animals via captive bolts and knives. The cattle pass through the kill floor workflow or "chain" at 300 an hour or one every twelve seconds, over shifts of ten to twelve hours. Sightlines are carefully controlled to minimize the number of individuals who witness animals dying and, not infrequently, thrashing about in terror or escaping from the kill box. This is the "politics of sight" that, for Pachirat, mirrors the broader public invisibility of the slaughter process.

The Law

In 1816, an Aboriginal man known in the legal record as Daniel Mow-watty was tried and convicted of raping and robbing fifteen-year-old Hannah Russell, daughter of a freed convict, and put to death, becoming the first Aboriginal Australian to be executed at law, as opposed to war, in New South Wales. The trial presented a number of legal difficulties. For one, the complainant, being a woman, was not a reliable witness, not least in matters of sexual conduct. This was resolved when the stockman who came upon the assault *in flagrante delicto* corroborated Russell's assertion that she had resisted, testifying that he had heard her cries of protest. For another, it was not clear that Mow-watty could be brought before the court, and this for two reasons: first, because his racial otherness made him ineligible to give evidence, and second, because it was not established that he was subject to Crown jurisdiction. Aboriginal persons, it was generally held, were accountable to their own body of law and their own regime of legal proceedings. These difficulties were surmounted when the same stockman testified that he had at one point worked alongside the defendant, whose habits and deportment had been the same as any other farm laborer's. This observation was corroborated by the constable of Parramatta, the district where the assault was alleged to have occurred, who had known Mow-watty for a dozen years: the defendant was acculturated to white ways and thus subject to white laws.

If you want to understand enclosure, whether of land or of animal life cycles, the law is a key place to look. In the transcripts of legal proceedings, we see people forced to give reasons for their behavior, in the process making explicit the sometimes contradictory theories of value—how property and other durable entitlements get created and transmitted, who is eligible to hold them—that underwrite everyday economic life. The context of *R. v. Mow-watty* was an ongoing low-level frontier war in which the colonial administration was determined to expand the space of effective Crown prerogative to alienate land. Just months before the trial, the governor of New South Wales had issued a proclamation barring Aboriginal people from white settlements and farms. As far as colonial administrators were concerned, the British Crown had asserted sovereignty and dominion (ownership) over the eastern half of the continent with the establishment of the first penal colony in 1788. But *jurisdiction,* territorial authority to enforce law, did not flow from sovereignty and dominion. It had to be established by effective occupation.

A 1763 Royal Proclamation governing political relations between settlers and Indigenous nations in English-speaking parts of Canada had given some credence to a *law of the interface,* that is, a recognition that Canada was inhabited by an array of nations governed by their own laws, who must be dealt with as such. The Royal Proclamation made Indigenous people of eastern Canada subjects of the Crown, but it also underscored their jurisdictional autonomy. In the United States, vestiges of a law of the interface survived into the 1820s, when the US Supreme Court formulated the *discovery doctrine,* which held that Crown sovereignty, and with it a new lineage of dominion and jurisdiction, had been established with the "discovery" of North America by English-speaking Europeans. In a pair of subsequent cases involving the State of Georgia's claims to jurisdiction over Cherokee territory, the Court construed Indigenous nations as "domestic, dependent nations," sovereign but not quite. The United States would continue with the pretense of making treaties with Indigenous nations up to the time of the Sioux Wars.

Today, most people who give the matter any thought believe that at the time of colonization the Crown's agents believed Australia to be *terra nullius,* no one's land. But this is a legal fiction of recent vintage. No one involved in the colonization of Australia was under any delusion the country was uninhabited. Joseph Banks, the botanist who had accompanied

Cook on the circumnavigation that in 1770 had charted the east coast of Australia, had described the local inhabitants in his report to the Admiralty. What makes it plausible that a doctrine of *terra nullius* was operative in some inchoate form at the colonization of Australia was that subsequently, particularly in the scramble for Africa of the late 1880s, it was established at European international law that a territory could be declared empty even if there were people who lived there who clearly considered it theirs, so long as they were not using the land in ways that made it theirs in European eyes. What were the right ways of using land? For a start, agriculture, and here is where we see theories of value in operation. The liberal political order is founded on a labor theory of value: you create property by "mixing," as Locke put it, your labor with nature and thereby drawing forth new things of value. Foraging, no matter how intensive, does not qualify as the right kind of mixing. But keeping domesticated animals does. The most efficient way to establish legal control over a large extent of land is to run livestock over it. In this regard, it is significant that the assault endured by Hannah Russell occurred on or near land owned by John Macarthur, credited with introducing Merino sheep into Australia. Livestock are property, but they are also the basis for a system of land tenure.

In chapters 3 and 4, I referred to the problem of *intent*: How do we know to what degree people who modify the land and biota, say by burning vegetation or breeding animals in captivity, acted with a reflexive understanding of what they were doing and where it would lead? My answer was that it does not really matter, that planning, like mosaic biomes and domesticated species themselves, is an emergent property of a chain of gestures, no single one of which would qualify as the *aha!* moment. Here we see where our anxieties about intent come from: liberalism demands of its subjects a certain kind of intentionality. Property requires, as legal theorist Carol Rose has suggested, a kind of performance that amounts to saying publicly, *This is mine*. Over the past two hundred years, grazing livestock has been a singularly effective way of announcing, *All this is mine*.

The enclosure of livestock metabolism was not a product of technology. It did not wait for the arrival of barbed wire or machine guns, though those came to play a role. Railways accelerated the process, but they did not instigate it. Enclosure was, first, about a change in attitude—in cosmology. Imagine you are standing on a rise, gazing out over an open plain studded with patches of grass and scrub. Cattle or sheep are moving over the plain.

Look once, you see individual animals. Look again, you see cells in an open-air bioreactor spread across the range like butter on toast. As the distances and quantities of biomass increase, it gets more difficult to see individuals. Livestock become a stage in a chain of energetic transformations, as do the human beings tending them.

6 Assimilation

The second time I made it to Port Hedland was in 2010, at the height of the iron boom. I did not return to Hedland to talk about the iron boom, though of course it featured in practically every conversation I had there. Unexpectedly, so did food.

I was there to talk to people at a regional Indigenous language revitalization center. As a rule, we expect food to figure prominently in conversations about cultural revitalization. But the conversations about food I found myself having in Port Hedland had little to do with traditional foods. Instead I heard stories about working in a meatpacking plant and participating in a regional sheep station strike. One senior figure in the community offered her thoughts on how a new system of welfare escrow would affect how people bought groceries.

In the prologue, I quoted from the reports of the Arnhem Land Expedition of 1948. It was another section of the same report, recall, that provided anthropologist Marshall Sahlins with the key evidence for his argument that affluence as we think of it today, a constant stimulus to production driven by consumer demand, represents an inversion of the values that undergirded an earlier "Zen road" to affluence. It is easy to misread "The Original Affluent Society" as a paean to the nobility of the oppressed, but Sahlins's point was not that foraging peoples exhibit a stoic resistance to the narcotic acquisitiveness of the modern age. Rather, what Sahlins sought to show was that foraging life was less laborious than commonly assumed and no less secure for that. I noted that field studies appearing at the time Sahlins was writing indicate something further: meat was marginal in the forager diet.

Up to this point, I've been making arguments about long stretches of time. As we've approached the present, the timescale of the narrative has contracted, from periods of 100 ka to millennia to centuries to decades. In this chapter, we look at the day-to-day struggle for nourishment that dominates so many people's lives, starting with people in circumstances much like those discussed in the prologue. In this way, we begin to circle back to the relationship between meat eating and economic status.

Slaughter and Civilization

In Port Hedland, all conversation eventually turns to iron. But animals appear everywhere at the margins. My host kept chickens. When I went for a run, she warned me to be mindful of camp dogs, feral creatures likely to attack in packs. One of the language center's board members told me how working in a meatpacking plant had set him on the path to social justice activism.

This was in Aotearoa New Zealand. At sixteen, he'd gone to visit a sister who'd married a Kiwi and moved there. He ended up staying nine years. Racism, though not absent in New Zealand, was not the obstacle to social mobility it was in Australia. Pākehā—European–New Zealander—girls wanted to get to know him, and he did not know how to respond. At the meatworks, he met people from all over: Iranian inspectors who would bless the sheep before slaughter so the mutton could be exported to Iran, Tongans, Māori, Russians. When he returned to Australia, he got a master's degree in Indigenous and intercultural studies. When we met, he was supervising child protective services for large parts of the Northwest.

Reading back over my notes from this interview years later, I am struck by two things. One is how different a single set of events may appear to people situated differently with respect to them. The conditions described above—a multiethnic working environment that attenuated racial mistrust—were the outcome of a process of casualization in the New Zealand meatpacking industry similar to what we saw in the United States in the previous chapter. The same individual made a comment about the history of livestock in the Pilbara that embodies a similar phenomenon. The Indigenous people of the Pilbara were fortunate, he said, because the sheep stockists had arrived before the missionaries and, having no use for the missionaries themselves, kept them out. The outcome was that Pilbara people had not suffered the same pressures to abandon language and other forms of cultural connective tissue that the people of the neighboring Kimberley region, to the north, had.

The second thing that strikes me about this tableau—the slaughterhouse as place of awakening—is how it inverts meat's role as an instrument of the civilizing process. Again and again we see colonized people, particularly those from communities without the correct—that is, sedentary—relationship to meat, getting exposed to meat in the hope that it will reform them and make them modern. All the links in the meat value chain have been used in this way: range management, slaughter, and consumption. We've seen a glimpse of this already: the reference to trial herds of cattle and goats on the Yolngu feeding stations visited by the nutritionist for the 1948 Arnhem Land Expedition. But nowhere is the relationship between meat production and the imposition of new habits clearer than in the cattle economy that developed in the drylands of Australia after 1850.

The Station Era

The *Station Era* is the term commonly used to describe the period in the postcontact history of Central and Northwest Australia when livestock were the defining fact in the lives of Indigenous people. In most cases, this meant cattle. In contrast to Southeast Australia, sheep, it was discovered, were not well suited to the desert—birthrates fell, predation by dingoes was a problem, and it was difficult to draw skilled shepherds and shearers to the remote and forbidding country. (The Pilbara was an exception, something we'll return to.) Cattle required less labor. As in the western United States, cattle in the Australian drylands were mostly left to fend for themselves and sometimes had no human contact save for the annual muster (roundup). Aboriginal labor made the dryland cattle industry possible.

Sheep and cattle were introduced into South Australia and Queensland starting in the 1840s, at the tail end of the squatter invasion described in chapter 5. Sheep entered the Pilbara from the 1850s. The 1860s, 1870s, and 1880s saw the expansion of the cattle industry into the Gulf of Carpentaria, the Northern Territory, and the Kimberley, respectively. The interior of Australia features little permanent surface water and gets little rain. In the Lake Eyre basin in the interior of South Australia, recurring droughts forced the abandonment of stations in the 1860s and 1870s. The introduction of bore wells in the 1880s made it possible for stations to draw on artesian aquifers for their animals' water needs, stabilizing the advance of grazing into the dry center of the continent.

The pattern of contact between hunters and herders that played out in Central and Northwest Australia from the 1850s on was the last in a series of such contacts that spanned the Holocene: from the earliest appearances of mobile herders in Southwest Asia and North Africa, discussed in chapter 4, through the Bantu expansions into southern Africa 2,000 years ago and the colonization of the North American rangelands described in chapter 5. Rarely, if ever, have hunting peoples been so quickly incorporated into the livestock economy.

There were several reasons for this. First, until bore wells gave stockists access to subsurface aquifers, local knowledge of the land and climate was essential to finding water and vegetation to support livestock.

Second, convict labor was not available in the Northern Territory or, after the 1860s, anywhere else in Australia. The Indigenous population represented a natural successor to that of convicts. Both occupied marginal positions in the social landscape of the livestock frontier. If anything, Indigenous Australians enjoyed less protection from exploitation than had convicts. Their relative indifference to the extreme climate mitigated the risk they would collapse or walk off in the face of desert heat or the monsoon, as did the fact that this was *their country*—theirs not just in the sense that they had been living off its plants and animals for generations but in the sense that they felt a custodial responsibility for it that transcended its economic value: the Dreaming, the cosmic unfolding, could not continue without them. By the 1860s, Aboriginal people living near sheep stations in the remote interior of South Australia were doing both seasonal work, during shearing and lambing, and the day-to-day work of animal management in exchange for rations of flour and tobacco.

Third, the introduction of livestock represented a rupture in both the economic and social life of the local community. Livestock usurped sources of surface water and destroyed the vegetative mosaic that local communities relied on for food. In these circumstances, dry rations became an essential part of the nutritional niche of the Aboriginal communities most directly in the path of the grazing frontier. The only way to get these rations was to live and work on either a mission station or a stock station, with all the restrictions that came with these settings. The United Aborigines'

Mission in particular went out of its way to destroy Aboriginal social structure, encouraging young people to marry in ways that contradicted the system of classificatory kinship that was universal among the peoples of the Center and the Western Desert, in which unions can be sanctioned only between individuals from complementary classificatory patriclines or *subsections*. Though some anthropologists have argued that subsection or *skin* anomalies had been not uncommon in the Aboriginal world even before contact, those who married "wrong" risked being ostracized by the community and thus becoming even more dependent on the magnanimity of white institutions. For similar reasons, stock station managers also encouraged disregard for the subsection system, for it ensured that the parties to anomalous marriages would not be able to return to the bush should they grow tired of station life. Even those communities not initially attracted by the novelty of rations found themselves depending on them as the concentration of people in the vicinity of mission stations led to exhaustion of the surrounding land. As three-times-weekly ration distributions became a standing feature of the Aboriginal economy, hunting skills attenuated, as did the networks of reciprocal exchange that bound people together locally and over long distances. Disease, including syphilis and measles, was the first mark of European presence to make itself felt in the interior. But it was stock work that played the central role in eroding Indigenous sociality.

Life on the stock stations did offer one particular advantage to young Aboriginal men that is difficult to translate into economic terms: it gave them an end run around the gerontocracy of Aboriginal Law (ritual knowledge). In a society in which the rites that afforded young men—and women, though less is known about women's law in this period—access to social adulthood were controlled by elders, young people were obliged to participate in a cult of deference that, for all that it was closely bound to the ethic of holding we looked at in chapter 3, could chafe. The cattle stations represented an environment in which control of Dreaming knowledge, though still an integral part of the Aboriginal social world, no longer gave older people quite the same authority over their juniors that it had under the foraging regime of a couple generations back.

I've been writing as if the Aboriginal Australians who spent much of their time on missions and stock stations and in towns represented a homogeneous community, but of course things were more complex. Stations and towns drew people from a wide area who differed in fine details of law and

The Dreaming

The Dreaming, a term popularized by the anthropologist W. E. H. Stanner, refers to a cosmogonic epoch in which Ancestors, the progenitors of the living things and forces found in the world today, walked the continent performing deeds heroic and mundane. Often these Ancestors take animal forms, but without the large-animal bias of perspectivist hunter cosmology (chapter 5)—a Fire Ant Dreaming is no less significant than an Emu or a Crocodile. Some Dreamings are human; in some places, meteorological forces such as lightning have Dreamings. As the Ancestors walked, they shaped the land, and a record of the Ancestors' wanderings is impressed upon the Earth. Dreaming sites, places whose distinctive physiographic features—an escarpment, a water hole, a clump of gum trees—mark the peregrinations and land-making activities of the Ancestors, were, and remain, the focus of Australians' ongoing participation in the Dreaming. Affiliates of a particular Dreaming would gather periodically to ritually reenact the Ancestors' travels, thereby recreating the land itself and propagating any natural phenomena associated with those Ancestors.

Among participants in a Dreaming, responsibility for "holding up" the country at sites representing stages in the Ancestor's wandering was held by different groups. In some cases, the initiated men of a local group, or of a single patrilineage represented in that local group, had custodial responsibility for the sites of their Dreaming that fell in the vicinity of their common place of residence. In others cases, custodial responsibility for Dreaming sites was not tied to residence. You might refer to the territory surrounding sites for which you shared responsibility in the Dreaming as *my Country*. Commonly, but not universally, this responsibility was transmitted by patrilineal descent, with the Ancestor whose activities were the subject of the Dreaming understood to be the apex of a descent tree ramifying across groups delineated by, for example, residence or language. But there were multiple paths of recruitment to Dreamings. Not all of them revolved around kinship.

subsistence habits, not to mention, in Central Australia, language. Stock station managers preferred to recruit Aboriginal labor from places that did not adjoin the station so that workers would be less inclined to walk off in the middle of the season, not knowing the country and, potentially, not being welcome in it by the local Aboriginal community. Catherine and Ronald Berndt, anthropologists who, in the late 1940s, conducted one of the earliest studies of Aboriginal life on stations and in towns, identified three grades of Aboriginal integration with white town society: those who lived in camps at the edges of towns, those who lived in town but depended partly on the station economy, and those who were integrated socially and economically into the organs of white town life. The second group consisted mainly of Aboriginal women who had married white men (or occasionally Asian men, for Afghan and Chinese merchants were a regular feature of town life) and their children. The third were often women who had been adopted by white families as children and denied contact with the Aboriginal community; they were effectively unable to operate in the Aboriginal world though never fully accepted in the white world. To these, of course, we must add those Aboriginal people who spent most of their time on the stock stations, those who continued to pursue a foraging subsistence beyond the station–railway–town corridor, and a smaller number who entered into contact with white society by being arrested and subsequently took work as native trackers for the police. Except for town dwellers, the composition of these different communities was fluid, and relations among them were not uniformly acrimonious. Even police trackers, save when they had been cast out for violation of law, could maintain good relations with their old community. They served as brokers between the Aboriginal community and white law. Often they were called on to produce someone to pin the blame on when communities living in the bush were accused of destroying animals from the stock stations, lest station managers take matters into their own hands.

Indeed, violence lay just beneath the surface in all encounters between the Aboriginal and white communities, on the stations and off. Massacres on the Australian grazing frontier were not the compressed, state-sponsored events we saw in North America in chapter 5. They went on for months, a handful of deaths at a time. Some Aboriginal transgression against white person or property, real or perceived, would touch off a wave of attacks and opportunistic killings by settlers and police. The last of these unfolded in the vicinities of Forrest River, in the East Kimberley, in 1926, and Coniston station, in the Northern Territory, in 1928. The close of the age of massacres marked the crystallization of the station era as the state made its presence felt more firmly in the regulation of Aboriginal labor in the livestock economy.

What did this economy look like? By all accounts, it was miserable. The anthropologist W. E. H. Stanner wrote of the cattle industry in the 1930s, "It was the tail-end of a disastrous period in which nothing had gone right."

In the Northern Territory, a 1965 estimate put the total area under pastoral leasehold for stockraising at over 721,000 square kilometers (278,000 square miles), or more than half the area of the Territory itself. Official tallies of the number of cattle on stations in the Territory in the period 1957 to 1969 ranged from 1.03 to 1.25 million, but this represents an undercount of as much as a third: station managers had incentives to deflate the number of cattle under their charge both to minimize taxes and manage the expectations of corporate owners with little understanding of the day-to-day challenges of cattle grazing. Indeed, absentee ownership was common in the cattle industry, accounting for perhaps half of all stations, with one firm, the British-controlled Australian Investment Agency (AIA), popularly know as "Vesteys," maintaining large pastoral holdings across the north. Station size ranged over two orders of magnitude. The largest in the Territory, at over 25,000 square kilometers (2.5 million hectares or 6.2 million acres), was the largest in the world. A fifteen-year meat export agreement with the United Kingdom had entered into effect in 1952, guaranteeing Australian graziers a market with a comfortable price floor. By the time this pact was reaching its end, the United States had become the main export market for Australian beef. That, combined with state investment in rail and road infrastructure and slaughtering facilities and the prospect of new markets in the emerging economies of Asia, left cattlemen, as it were, sanguine.

The consensus among outside observers was that the industry was in crisis. Open-range pasturing—in some parts of the north, 90 percent of ranges were unfenced—had combined with unrestricted herd growth and low turn-off (the proportion of cattle sent to slaughter during the annual roundup) to yield irremediable soil erosion. In the Northwest, cattle populations had *declined* 10 percent from their peak fifty years earlier, and turn-off was 11 percent. Despite heavy investment from the Commonwealth (federal) government, the situation in the Northern Territory was similarly dismal. In Queensland, more reliable rainfall made for higher rates of sustainable turn-off, though the Millennium Drought would later make a mockery of stocking densities there. But across the north, one fact underlay the economics of meat production: it was dependent on coerced Aboriginal labor.

By the 1930s, Indigenous Australians had become essential to cattle production and the ancillary activities—domestic work, road and airstrip construction, tracking fugitives for the police—it engendered. The number of people involved, relative to the size of the ranges and the number of animals, was small. In the Northern Territory in the mid-1960s, fewer than 6,000 Aboriginal people lived on stock stations, perhaps 30 percent of the territory's Aboriginal population. Of those, 20 to 25 percent were officially employed by the stations: the rest were "dependents" of those employed, though "dependent," as we'll see, was a slippery term. All these figures should be taken with a large grain of salt. The "Welfare Branch" of the Northern Territory Administration, the bureaucratic apparatus charged with overseeing native "wards" in the territory, had but a vague grasp of its client demographic, and its inquiries to station managers were met with stonewalling and obfuscation.

The answer to the question, *Who is an Aboriginal person?* varied depending on where you were, whom you asked, and the context in which you were asking. Even limiting the context to that of working conditions on stock stations, standards varied across Australia. The Commonwealth government had assumed responsibility for the Northern Territory in 1910, and the Territory Administration, including the Welfare Branch, in principle implemented policy formulated by the central government. Stock stations in Western Australia and Queensland were subject to regulation at the state level: though Indigenous Australians had become Commonwealth citizens in 1948 (and had been understood to be Crown subjects since long before), it was not until 1967 that the central government gained authority over Indigenous Australians in the states. From the cattlemen's perspective, if you looked black, you were, though an individual of mixed ancestry might sometimes be recognized as white for the purpose of deciding which labor standard applied to him—it depended in part on how much the station manager knew about the individual's background. In the Northern Territory, Aboriginal people were considered wards of the state. In principle, from 1953 on, the status of ward was race neutral, and anyone could be declared a ward on the basis of poor standards of personal deportment. In practice, to be black was to be in legal custodianship. In the Northern Territory, the official minimum age for Aboriginal stock workers was twelve, but many station managers were adamant that black boys needed to be "broken in" starting around ten, else they would never develop a feel for the work.

Nominally, Indigenous cattle workers were wage laborers. In the Northern Territory, the Aboriginals Ordinance fixed a schedule of cash wages, to be garnished for the upkeep of a worker's dependents. These wages amounted to approximately 20 percent of those paid to white workers under the Northern Territory Cattle Station Industry Award, the official schedule of wages negotiated by the white trade union, the North Australian Workers' Union, since the 1920s. Often black workers did not receive any cash wages. As a rule they were paid in kind, in food, tobacco, housing, work clothes, and scrip good for purchases at the station store at inflated prices, along with time off during the wet season to visit relatives on other stations and conduct initiations and other ritual exercises. Aboriginal workers did not become eligible for the award wage until 1968, after the Workers' Union applied to the Commonwealth Conciliation and Arbitration Commission to bring them into the award. The Arbitration Commission handed down its decision in 1966, giving the cattlemen close to three years to prepare. When the award wage went into effect, many station managers simply ejected their Aboriginal population, bringing the station era to a close.

Conditions varied from station to station, but across the dry rangelands of central and northern Australia, Aboriginal stock station inhabitants were subject to living and working conditions that bordered on chattel slavery. In the Northern Territory, as late as the 1950s, blacks who left "their" station were sometimes hunted down by regional police patrols and forcibly returned; those who sought work at other stations found themselves blacklisted by station managers. Often the local police officer was also the local Protector of Aborigines, offering Aboriginal stock workers and their dependents no way to appeal to the territorial or state native welfare authorities in the event of mistreatment by station management or the police. In the 1930s, Stanner wrote, working conditions in the North were hard on everyone, but Indigenous people had it worst. "The working natives were virtually peons," and conditions had changed little by the early 1960s. For all that Aboriginal Australians were the objects of race hatred, this was not simply brutality for its own sake. By the 1920s, it was clear that the stock industry could not survive without slave labor. In a 1928 report on the cattle industry in the Northern Territory, the Chief Protector of Aborigines for Queensland, acting in a consulting capacity, observed that the industry was "absolutely dependent upon the blacks for the labour, domestic and field, necessary to successfully carry on."

As on any other colonial frontier, one form the enclosure of Indigenous bodies took was sexual. Visiting Wave Hill, one prominent AIA-owned station in the Northern Territory in 1945, the Berndts commented, "Most of the [European] men were interested in Aborigines for one or both of two main reasons—economic and sexual." Across cattle country, it was common for Aboriginal women to be held in sexual thrall. A man who objected to his wife's being brought to the station manager's house would be "hunted," systematically denied rations and other in-kind tokens such as the new set of working clothes issued, at best, every two or three months, and subjected to more than the usual share of casual brutality and humiliation. Alternately, a man might be compensated for his partner's absence with a bag of flour or a packet of tobacco. Indeed, sex between non-Aboriginal men and Aboriginal women on the stations was not just ubiquitous but strongly transactional in flavor. Among other things, it was the main way Aboriginal people acquired underwear.

It is difficult to convey the sheer thuggish nastiness Aboriginal people were subjected to on the cattle stations. Men were denied medical care for grievous occupational injuries. They could be kicked, or beaten, or chained up, or shot on any pretext or none at all. Girls as young as seven were raped and groomed for sexual service. "The authority of European men," wrote the Berndts of what they observed in their 1945 survey of AIA stations in the Northern Territory, "was largely based on the threat of force. Their ascendancy rested primarily on the maintenance of fear among Aborigines. Any manifestation or even hint of rebellion was met with instant physical punishment." White managers and owners were inured to their own brutality. Indeed, the Berndts' invitation to conduct fieldwork on the AIA's stations came about because station managers had observed falling birthrates in the Aboriginal population, and the firm was concerned about maintaining its supply of black labor, perhaps by recruiting among people still living a foraging life in the desert.

Nowhere was the misery of life on the cattle stations clearer than in what and how they ate. On the stations, Aboriginal living quarters, including cooking facilities, were rudimentary and poorly maintained. On some stations, Aboriginal kitchens included a brick fireplace enclosed in a shed. On others, the community made do with fire pits of the type they might have used camping in the bush. Firewood could mean a 5 kilometer (3 mile) walk; fresh water, if it was available, 800 meters (a half mile). Station managers railed against the injustice of having to provide food for their Aboriginal workers' dependents and spoke casually of culling the Aboriginal population when it grew too large, perhaps by providing a bag of flour laced with strychnine. In fact, dependents represented a standing pool of conscript labor from which only invalids and young children, but not women in the third trimester of pregnancy, were exempt, and they were essential to the intense bouts of seasonal activity that marked life on the station. Dependents were provided with dry rations, energy dense but nutrient poor: syrup, sugar, jam, wheat and maize flour, condensed milk, and sometimes raisins, along with the bones and offal of cattle that had been slaughtered to feed the manager's household and the station's employees. Station managers and bookkeepers consistently inflated the proportion of dependents to workers, demanding reimbursement from the state (in Western Australia and Queensland) or territorial (in the Northern Territory) government for rations issued to dependents and exaggerating the cost of these rations. In the Northern Territory, a variety of subsidies were earmarked for Aboriginal wards—child allowances, old-age pensions—and cattle stations relied on the skim from these subsidies to shore up an otherwise unprofitable enterprise, a practice known as "nigger farming."

What about the employees—the cattle wranglers, boundary riders, mechanics, and drivers? At Wave Hill in 1945, the Berndts observed a ration of "one slice of dry bread, one piece of usually cooked meat (sometimes in the form of a bone), and a dipper of tea"—three meals a day, seven days a week, with leftovers and kitchen scraps made available to take down to the Aboriginal quarters for family. As with everything else, conditions varied. As late as 1965, managers on many stations were not aware of the legally mandated ration schedule, while on others, Aboriginal and non-Aboriginal employees received the same meals, albeit sometimes at separate canteens. Managers estimated meat consumption at 900 grams (2 pounds) per employee per day, but it is difficult to know what part of this was bone and other inedible matter. Foraged foods played little role in the diet save during the monsoon furlough.

These observations were made in the course of wider-ranging surveys of Aboriginal life on the cattle stations, but they accord with a survey of Aboriginal dietary habits in the Northern Territory commissioned by the Commonwealth Department of Health in 1951. The author, Winifred Wilson, visited three kinds of places where Aboriginal people congregated under white supervision: missions, settlements run by the Territory Administration's Native Affairs Branch (the predecessor to Welfare Branch), and cattle stations. The panel of sites ranged from Arnhem Land in the north to

Alice Springs in the south of the territory. Wilson's mandate was to examine diet and eating habits, and she rated the diets she observed on a scale of A to E. The scale was meant to indicate how adequate the diets in question were by intake of key micronutrients, principally vitamins A and C, calcium, and iron. Grade A diets were those that were consistently no more than 10 percent below recommended allowances for these nutrients. Grade E indicated a diet more than 140 percent below recommended intakes. (The scale had been devised for an earlier study of household diet in white Australia, but Wilson had extended it with grade E for use in Aboriginal communities.) Across the panel—missions, reserves, and cattle stations—60 percent of the diets she observed earned an E, a further 24 percent a D. On cattle stations, sixteen of seventeen diets got a D or an E, but the territory-run feeding stations fared little better: ten of eleven fell in the D to E range. A single diet received a B: that prepared for young children at the Native Affairs Branch settlement at Yuendumu, in central Australia, and that because the mission school these children attended supplemented the official ration. Of the five cattle stations she visited, one, the corporate-owned station at Victoria River Downs, provided a C-grade diet to Aboriginal workers on one of its five remote outstations. The outstations tended to be autonomous, and the one Wilson visited—constraints of time and transport prevented her from reaching the others—maintained its own garden, tended by Aboriginal women. Not surprisingly, beef featured prominently on the menu:

> Typical Meals
>
> *Breakfast.* Beef—fresh or corned. Bread. Tea, sugar, milk
>
> *Dinner.* Beef. Vegetables. Bread. Pudding. Tea, sugar, milk
>
> *Tea.* Beef. Vegetables. Bread. Tea, sugar, milk

Smoking breaks featured a rotation of cake, brownies, and rice pudding, along with the ubiquitous tea and milk, though how cake was prepared remains a mystery given the "complete lack of eggs." In fact, there are a lot of mysteries here. Wilson admits that her estimates of consumption come from quantities supplied to the outstation by the head station; she was not in a position to check how much people actually ate. "The figure listed for the consumption of meat is more or less an arbitrary one," based on what she was told about how often a bull was killed. In light of these limitations, we should perhaps treat the macronutrition estimates—7,217 kcal daily per person and 262 grams (a bit over 9 ounces) of protein—with skepticism.

Again, this was the best diet observed in any Aboriginal population on any of the five cattle stations surveyed. Even at the same small outstation, the handful of "camp natives" (dependents) fared considerably poorer—1,540 kcal daily per person and 1.5 ounces of protein by the same rough method of estimation. By and large, when it came to meals, Aboriginal people were treated with grudging disdain. Thus, at a mobile stock camp at Wave Hill, the "typical meal" consisted of a slice of bread and tea with sugar, with beef at midday. "The natives collected the meal from the kitchen, took it to any convenient place, and ate it squatting on the ground or around a fire. No plates or other utensils were used and tea was drunk from billy cans [buckets used for boiling water on a campfire]." Wave Hill maintained a large vegetable garden and egg-laying chickens, but Aboriginal people received vegetables rarely and eggs never.

Short of placing people under observation in a laboratory and providing all their food—we'll come to that—it is remarkably difficult to determine with any precision what people eat. Wilson's report suggests one reason: it is awkward and inconvenient to weigh people's meals, especially with someone from the head station breathing down your neck. Later in this chapter and again in chapter 8, we'll consider the advantages and disadvantages of different ways of estimating food consumption and waste, but let's pause to consider the special headaches that attend efforts to reconstruct what people ate in times past. In some cases, as we observed in part I, we are aided in this enterprise by kitchen middens, dental calculus, collagen, and coprolites. But now we're dealing with times and places where archaeological sites are less likely to feature salient concentrations of human remains, excreta, and food detritus in close proximity. Under the best circumstances—say, when the people you're interested in were literate, privileged, and inclined to document their lives in detail—diet remains elusive. On the cattle stations, we're dealing with marginalized people and record keepers given to deliberately misrepresenting how much of what those people ate. In these circumstances, sources that offer insight into diet, even by omission, hold an uncanny appeal. Food is the most ordinary thing about animal life, and yet, seeing it laid out in the lives of people distant from us in time, space, and circumstances is chilling. This is when it hits you: these people were animals like us.

In the National Archives of Australia, we find all the interoffice correspondence leading up to the formulation, in 1959, of a new set of ration schedules for Aboriginal wards broken out by sex, age, and employment status, with contributions from the Pastoral Lessees' Association (the cattlemen) and commonwealth dietitians. The final schedules, for all that they reflect the input of the station owners (who were not inclined to follow them in any case), are best read as fantasy: they suggest what those operating under the sign of native welfare believed Aboriginal people *should* be fed to keep them in adequate health but also in a position of dependency.

The first row in the schedule is dedicated to meat, with working women and men to receive 3,200 grams (7 pounds) a week. Next comes flour, then "Potatoes or Rice." "Fruit or Vegetables" comes below sugar, with a recommended weekly ration of 900 grams (2 pounds) "tinned or fresh." Oleomargarine was to be supplied for palatability and vitamin A. The territory dietitian recommended that children and pregnant and lactating women receive a supplement of reconstituted orange juice, 350 milliliters (10 ounces) a week, presumably for the vitamin C (table 6.1).

This schedule represented a compromise. The original schedule, circulated two years earlier, had featured less meat and flour and emphasized a greater variety of fruits and vegetables. Over the protests of the Commonwealth Department of Health, the 1957 draft was deemed too complicated and too reliant on refrigeration. It should be noted that the 1957 schedule itself represented the outcome of five years of delicate negotiation with the cattlemen.

Recall from the prologue the Goulds' roughly contemporaneous (1966–1967) observations of Ngatjatjara foragers: 90 percent of the time, 90 percent of the diet came from plant sources. This might have been low in animal by historical standards, since cattle and mining had pushed foragers to the margins of their range. But this was also the wet season, the time of greatest abundance, and the Goulds' observations accord with what behavioral ecologists had observed in other parts of the world with comparable biota. It seems safe to say that Aboriginal Australians ate more meat on the stations than they had as foragers. We can go further: by Wilson's admittedly rough calculations, Aboriginal Australians living on missions, reserves, and stations in the Northern Territory consumed a third more meat than did white Australians, not to say more flour and sugar and two-thirds less fruit and vegetables.

Recall from chapter 3 that in hunting societies, more often than not, hunting's status is way out of proportion to its contribution to the

Table 6.1

Scales of Food to Be Supplied to Wards (1959).

Food to Be Supplied	Weekly Quantity for Wards over 10 Years of Age Other Than Nonworking Females and Aged and Infirm Wards			Weekly Quantity for Wards under 10 Years of Age			Weekly Quantity for Nonworking Females and Aged and Infirm Wards		
	A	B	C	A	B	C	A	B	C
Meat	7	7 exclusive of weight of bone	7 exclusive of weight of bone	4	5 exclusive of weight of bone	3 exclusive of weight of bone	4 2/3	5 exclusive of weight of bone	5 exclusive of weight of bone
Flour	5	5	5	4	4	3	3 1/8	4	4
Potatoes or rice	2	2	2	1	2	2	1 1/3	2	2
Sugar	1	1	1	¾	1	¾	11 oz	1	1
Peas dried	1	1	1 or dried fruit	½	½	½ or dried fruit	11 oz	11 oz	½ or dried fruit
Fruit or vegetables	2 fresh	2 tinned or fresh	2 tinned or fresh[a]	2 fresh	1 tinned or fresh	1 tinned or fresh[a]	1 1/3 fresh	1 1/3 tinned or fresh	2 tinned or fresh[a]
Dried whole or skim milk Vitamin A fortified or cheese	Nil	6 oz for adults 18 oz for children	6 oz for adults 21oz for children	Nil	18 oz	21 oz	Nil	Nil	6 oz
Margarine—vitamin A fortified	Nil	½	½	Nil	¼	½	Nil	6 oz	6 oz
Golden syrup, jam or treacle	1	1	1	½	½	½	11 oz	11 oz	1
Tea	3 oz	3 oz	3 oz				3 oz	3 oz	3 oz
Tinned orange juice[b]	20 oz	12 oz children only	12 oz for children and pregnant and lactating women only	10 oz	12 oz	12 oz	13 oz	Nil	Nil

Source: Redrawn from National Archives of Australia A1658 4/1/6, 150.

Note: Column A shows quantities in the draft regulation, column B the pastoralists' suggestions, and column C the suggestions by the senior dietitian.

[a]At least half of which should be yellow (excluding peaches).

[b]Substitutions may be made on the following scale: lemon, grapefruit, or fresh raw cabbage: 1 oz; pineapple, mangoes, or fresh tomatoes: 2 oz; tinned pineapple juice or tomato juice: 24 oz.

community's energy and protein budgets. What makes hunting special is that it is risky. It demands a prolonged investment in ballistic conditioning and deep reserves of physical courage, but it also entails economic risk. Hunting is unreliable. The greatest risk with hunting is that you will go hungry, and this is reflected in norms of redistribution that make it repugnant to hunt for oneself when there are others to be fed. In ideology, if not always in fact, hunting embodies selflessness. In the Australian desert, as in hunting societies the world over, meat is the emblem of holding.

On the cattle stations, missions, and reserves, meat became an emblem of something else: poverty, oppression, dependency. Whatever you want to say about the affluence or otherwise of foragers, it is difficult to avoid the conclusion that Aboriginal Australians were less well nourished under white control than they had been before. Even as they complained about how much meat their Aboriginal workforce consumed, cattlemen were happy to use meat to cover up inadequacies in the ration they provided. Raised meat was an instrument of undernourishment.

Weet-Bix Empire

One morning I sat in the conference room at the language center in Port Hedland drinking tea with A, a senior figure in the language center community for many years. She told me a bit about her family. Her father was from the Pilbara, her mother from Broome, to the north in the Kimberley. Before World War II, her father had been a stockman in the Pilbara. Later, he applied for citizenship and went to work for the government. During the war, when A was a baby, her father had done his army service in Queensland, since he had asthma. But she had uncles who had fought. Some died in the war—they had volunteered. Later she wanted to ask them, *What for?* The war produced no change in white attitudes. Aboriginal people couldn't even go into a pub in Perth.

When A was growing up, her family spent holidays out in the bush, with a car, her mother refusing to load the car until she saw her father had filled the tank with gas. As a child, A hated going out in the bush. It was through her involvement with the language center that she'd come to learn something about the plant and animal life of the country.

At the time we spoke, A was treasurer of the language center and managed a seven-figure budget. It had been her responsibility to navigate the opportunities and risks posed by the sudden influx of iron money into the Aboriginal community. Still, the conversation turned toward finances of a more mundane kind. The central government had recently announced its intention to extend the system of welfare escrow previously implemented in the Northern Territory to the whole country. Under the system, known as the BasicsCard, benefits were made available as credit on a debit card good for purchases at a limited number of outlets, principally major supermarkets. Part of the object of the BasicsCard was to prevent the redistribution of cash benefits through the community via demand sharing and, in particular, the redirection of money intended for groceries to alcohol, inhalants, and pornography. *The government,* A said, *are fooling themselves if they think this will prevent misuse of benefits.* Cardholders would simply exchange food for cash.

The BasicsCard represents just the latest in a long train of white interventions in Aboriginal eating habits, all of them linked to moral panic over either Aboriginal habits or recognition of the white role in producing those habits. Not all Indigenous Australians worked on the stock stations. But most experienced a metabolic colonization that unfolded in parallel with, and partly as a consequence of, the growth of the dry-range meat industry.

The Pilbara, as I've noted, had a stock economy of its own, mainly sheep, mainly for wool. It was on the stations of the Pilbara coast that Aboriginal stock workers launched the first black labor action against the stock industry in Australia, twenty years before the award dispute in the Northern Territory. But this part of the country, as A's story suggests, was also home to a more varied landscape of Aboriginal integration into the white economy. Some months before she undertook her survey of dietary habits in the Northern Territory, Wilson supervised a similar survey in Western Australia. Both copies of the Western Australia survey that I've seen, that on deposit at the National Library of Australia and that incorporated into the correspondence on the ration schedule for the Wards' Employment Ordinance, are missing all but the first part, that dealing with towns. So here we don't have the evidence to compare the experience of people living in towns to that of people living on missions, stock stations, and state-administered "ration camps." What the Western Australia dietary survey does offer is a sense of the range of experiences of nutrition transition at the household level, something that gets lost in aggregate statistics. We'll consider just the data for Port Hedland.

In this survey, Port Hedland fared well. Of the seventeen households visited, thirteen, or 76 percent, had diets in the D to E range, the median proportion among the towns surveyed. Despite the presence of the port, the estimated cost of food was the highest of any of the towns, perhaps in part because the groundwater was too saline to grow vegetables. Consumption of animal-source foods, including meat and fish counted together, was the highest among the towns. Aboriginal people played a number of roles in the town economy, which at this point was still dominated by the export of wool rather than salt and iron.

> Natives in the town [Wilson notes] were employed as labourers and tradesmen for the railways, as builders and storekeepers and casually as lumpers [dockworkers] when the boats came in. Natives were employed as seasonal labour on sheep stations in the district since there was a general shortage of labour [she makes no mention of the strike that had ended two years prior]. At the time of the survey casual labourers had finished working on most of the stations and were going south to mining fields around Marble Bar, to work there for the rest of the year.

Again, it's important to keep in mind how small these towns were relative to the land area and livestock populations implicated in their income. At the time of the stock workers' strike, five years before the 1951 survey, Port Hedland had some 200 white residents. Still, it illustrates many of the problems of provisioning in places not well suited to growing food. Eggs, for instance, were not produced commercially in Port Hedland, but five of the seventeen Aboriginal households included in the survey kept their own hens. Fresh milk was unavailable: the dairy had been closed for noncompliance with state health regulations. Kangaroo was sometimes provided by relatives visiting from the surrounding country, and "most native housewives," the report notes, "went fishing every day." Apart from these, the main source of meat was a station 15 miles outside town, which slaughtered sheep and some cattle on site and trucked the carcasses to a butcher in town twice a week. Fresh fruits and vegetables had to be flown up from Perth, while flour, canned goods, and hardier fruits and vegetables came by boat. Nothing kept well, especially during the wet season, and not all households had an icebox.

As in the South Australia towns that the Berndts visited in the late 1940s, the Aboriginal population was divided between "camp" and "town" groups, the latter mainly of mixed ancestry though not, among those visited by this survey, in mixed-race households. Here again, fieldworkers were not in a position to weigh portions. But unlike on the stations, they were able to talk directly with those responsible for household provisioning, universally women—"housewives"—who were asked to give an account of what had been eaten in their home and by whom over the week prior to the visit. The picture that emerges from these data is approximate, but it affords a view of the everyday experience of eating and coping in a poor community that, to my knowledge, left no diaristic accounts of its own (table 6.2).

Table 6.2
Sample Menus for Twelve Households Surveyed, Port Hedland

Breakfast	Dinner	Supper
Weeties, milk, sugar Fried steak Tea, bread, butter	Roast beef mashed potatoes bread Tea, milk, sugar	Stew-meat, onions potatoes Tea, bread & butter jam.
Tinned spaghetti corned beef (fried) Toast, butter, jam Tea, milk, sugar	Tinned beef stewed with onions and potatoes Bread & butter tinned peaches Tea, milk, sugar.	Fried salmon bread, butter Tinned peaches and Ideal milk. Tea, milk, sugar.
Rolled oats porridge sugar, milk Stew of tinned beef[,] onions & tomatoes Bread & butter Tea, milk, sugar.	Stewed meat with onions & potatoes Bread Tea, milk, sugar	Cold meat, sauce Raw tomatoes Bread Tea, milk, sugar.
Fried mutton flap, Bread & butter, golden syrup Tea, milk, sugar	Curried mutton[,] onions & potatoes Bread, butter Tea, milk, sugar.	Fried fish, bread and butter, golden syrup. Tea, milk, sugar.
Sago, milk, sugar Boiled eggs. Toast, butter Tea, milk, sugar	Grilled chops Mashed potatoes Tea, milk, sugar.	Irish stew Bread, butter, cheese. Tea, milk, sugar.
No breakfast.	Damper [camp bread], jam, Tea, sugar.	Tinned sausages. Damper. Tea, sugar.
Toast, butter Tea, milk, sugar	Fried fish Bread & butter Coffee, milk, sugar	Stewed fish with potatoes & onions Bread & butter Tea, milk, sugar.

Table 6.2 (continued)

Breakfast	Dinner	Supper
Fried fish, bread & butter, jam Tea, milk, sugar. Milk for children	Fried chops, Mashed carrots & parsnips, gravy. Bread, butter, jam	Fried fish, Bread & butter, jam. Tinned fruit Tea, milk, sugar.
Kangaroo pie, Bread. Tea, sugar, milk.	Kangaroo stew with onions. Bread Tea, milk, sugar	Kangaroo pie. Bread. Tea, milk, sugar.
Damper, jam Tea, milk, sugar.	Tinned beef. damper Tinned pears. Tea, sugar, milk.	Beef stew. Bread. Tea, milk, sugar.
Fried eggs, Bread [and] butter. Tea, milk[,] sugar	Fried chops, onions, tomatoes. Bread [and] butter Tea, milk, sugar.	Fried fish Bread and butter. Tea, milk, sugar.
Weeties, milk, sugar Bread, butter, jam Coffee, milk, sugar.	Stewed chops potatoes, cabbage[,] onions, parsnips[,] carrots, Bread & butter, tea, milk, sugar.	Stew as for noon meal Bread, jam. Tea, milk, sugar.

Source: Redrawn from Wilson (1951b, 31).

Again I am struck by the intimacy of these data—the way they evoke the vulnerability of a person interrupted just as she, or he, was about to put food to mouth. Perhaps we have all experienced this, at home, or at work, or traveling: the uneasiness of being watched as we eat, the anxiety that our food, however ordinary, is ridiculous or inadequate, or that our manner of consuming it is wrong, too fast or too slow, careless, overly fastidious. It is the feeling of being caught out, of being exposed as someone who does not know how to take care of herself or, worse, lacks the means to do so. How much worse this feeling must be for those whose entitlement to food is insecure, tied to the vagaries of casual wage labor, and whose familiarity with the methods of preparation appropriate, in the eyes of onlookers, to different foods is limited. In the archives, Aboriginal people are forever handling food incorrectly: cooking things outdoors that should be cooked indoors, omitting the critical ingredients from sandwiches, substituting damper—soda-risen bread cooked in the ashes of a fire or in a camp stove—for cake, storing flour where it is liable to get weevily, and failing to account for the special nutritional needs of children and pregnant and lactating women. There is no crueler insult than to be told you don't know how to feed yourself.

Whatever asymmetries of power entered into the survey process, it is clear that the respondents did know how to feed themselves and their families under circumstances that were trying at best. Certain patterns emerge. For one thing, the diet here, as in all the other towns and camps, is much better that what we saw on the stations and missions of the Northern Territory, where Aboriginal people had little control over provisioning. It is more varied in taste and texture. In some homes, onions make regular appearances, occasionally joined by cabbage, carrots, and even tomatoes. In most cases, it appears, household dependents, including children, have access to the high-value foods that on the stations were reserved for the officially employed. Port Hedland also stands out from the other towns in the survey. Milk consumption—as in all towns but one, exclusively powdered and sweetened condensed milk—is 50 percent higher than anywhere else. Meat intake is also high, though this is because fish, which was included with raised meat, stands outside the regime of cash entitlements that constrains other food choices—a household could eat as much as its members (more specifically, the female co-head of household) could catch. For all that, it is clear that bread, sugar, and meat are being made to fill in for an absence of fresh fruits and vegetables.

Across the board, with the exception of Broome, energy, protein, and iron intake were markedly *higher* in the Aboriginal town and town camp populations than in a sample of white Western Australian households canvassed seven years earlier—on average more than 25 percent higher, and well above the figures included in nutritional guidelines. Again: *meat was a mark not of affluence but of poverty.*

Of all the unexpected foods that appear in this report, one in particular gives me pause. "Weeties" or "weetbix" (shredded wheat to American readers) appears in "typical breakfasts" in three towns. Sometimes it is mentioned as being prepared specifically for the children. Even now, Weet-Bix is the top-selling cold breakfast cereal in Australia (today it's available in organic and, improbably, gluten-free varieties). No doubt its presence in the diet of survey respondents offered cause for hope to the members of Parliament, physicians, and dietitians in the Departments of Health and

Territories who read this report. What better sign could there be that assimilation was working—and working at a metabolic level?

The View from New Guinea

Thus far, we've looked at evidence from populations that, whether on the cattle stations or in the towns, were thoroughly integrated into the settlement state economy. It would help to have a comparative case, a dietary survey conducted with similar assumptions about nutrition and labor but with a respondent community that was not so well integrated into the wage economy and that maintained strategies of subsistence not much changed from the time before contact. In New Guinea, parts of which were under Australian colonial control from the establishment of the League of Nations up through 1975, we have such a comparative case. Colonial contact came late to New Guinea. In the highlands, a number of communities had no encounter with outsiders, save for seeing airplanes pass overhead, until a series of Australian police "patrols" in the 1930s forced things. Like the 1951 Northern Territory and Western Australia dietary surveys, the 1947 New Guinea Nutrition Survey was conducted in the context of efforts to formulate a ration schedule for indigenous wage laborers. In New Guinea, however, wage labor was not yet as widespread as it was in Aboriginal Australia. Colonial administrators sought to base rationing guidelines "principally on native foods." To this end, they needed a baseline for food production, eating habits, and nutritional status in villages with a subsistence economy. Such a baseline would also make it easier to identify and respond to periodic food shortages sparked by weather anomalies or intergroup conflict and to begin to think about how New Guineans might be induced to incorporate cash crops into their gardens without jeopardizing their food security.

The New Guinea survey was more elaborate than those we have considered up to this point, with two physicians, two biochemists, a nutritionist, a sociologist, an "agriculturalist," and, at times, a dentist and a photographer in the field, accompanied, in each district, by a patrol officer familiar with the area and its inhabitants. For analysis and logistical support, it drew on the resources of a number of research institutes and administrative organs in Sydney and Canberra. The survey visited five villages chosen to exemplify a range of geographies, from coastal to alluvial to 3,600 feet above sea level, and a range of subsistence repertoires. The base of the diet varied from site to site but generally incorporated a mix of starchy underground storage organs, including taro, manioc, sweet potato, and yam, along with sago (the pith of certain palms and cycads). These were enriched with fruits, legumes, pumpkins, leafy matter, pork, grubs, and, in the coastal zone, fish, crustaceans, oysters, and in one case the occasional crocodile. In each village, fieldworkers observed twenty to thirty households, sometimes visiting households on two separate occasions, taking in food procurement, preparation, and mealtimes and conducting physical exams and blood draws.

Some villages remained relatively isolated from the white economy, but one coastal village, Busama, stood 30 kilometers (19 miles) by canoe from the town of Lae, and villagers there made modest use of store-bought foods from town, including bread, rice, flour, sugar, and tinned meat. Busama also showed the effects of Christian missionizing, with women "forbidden" to enter the food gardens on Sunday even if not enough food had been harvested the day before. Busama, the report notes, had been a "battleground" during the war, its gardens destroyed. It was assumed that this contributed to the exceptionally low energy and protein intake observed there. But in the two other coastal villages, where conditions appeared better, daily mean energy intake was 1,600 kcal per person and protein less than half "computed requirements," yet the inhabitants displayed no signs of nutritional stress.

The report from this survey runs to 300 pages, and we cannot do it justice here. But taken as a whole, it offers insight as much into its authors' expectations as into the nutritional behavior of village horticulturalists. Repeatedly, the authors express concern about the high contribution of starchy underground storage organs to the diet and the low energy and protein intake. But in terms of villagers' clinical picture, they cannot find much to complain about. Energy intake seems adequate and villagers do not appear hungry. Serum protein is slightly higher than in the sample from a 1944 Australian nutritional survey. Edema is not observed. In other words, "signs of gross inadequacy of protein were not detected," and the authors forbore offering an interpretation of the protein intake data save to note that basic knowledge about the protein content of the types of plant-source foods prominent in the villagers' diet was lacking. Likewise, the micronutrient profile looks good. Beriberi, riboflavinosis, and signs of ascorbic acid and vitamin A deficiencies are absent. On radiological diagnosis, 9 percent of children under one year of age ($N = 101$) display signs of rickets, as against

47 percent in a white Australian study five years prior. Even the exiguous fat intake (less than 5 percent of total energy) has no clear implications for either growth in childhood or maintenance in adulthood. The only widespread micronutrient deficiency they identify is iodine. Away from the coast, enlarged thyroid and goiter are endemic. This is thought to stem from an absence of iodine in the water and food supply.

The authors appear conflicted about the role that meat and other animal-source foods ought to play in improving the indigenous diet:

> Wherever practicable, great nutritional value may be derived from increasing the consumption of animal products. In many places, however, it may be easier to provide good class proteins from vegetable rather than animal sources, but, increased consumption of animal products is desirable in almost every part of New Guinea. Not only cattle but also tethered milch goats, poultry and sometimes buffaloes, sheep and pigs may be valuable sources of animal protein.

It would be too strong to read this passage as a paean to meat's intrinsic value. But here and, as we'll see, more broadly in the nutrition science literature, raised meat is associated with development and modernity. This is ironic in light of what we saw about the relationship between meat consumption and health in the Australian surveys. It is something to keep in mind as we start to consider the role of nutrition science in shaping policy interventions, then and now, in the metabolic lives of the poor.

Hunger

In May 1976 a photocopy of a typed one-page summary of events in Warrabri, an Aboriginal settlement 720 miles south of Darwin by road, arrived at the desk of the assistant director of health, Northern Territory Administration, Darwin. The report came from one Sister M, who had been living at Warrabri for six years. It had been forwarded by a nurse with supervisory responsibility for Aboriginal health in the region that included the settlement. After noting deaths and remote medical visits and describing a successful three-day festival that had attracted 700 Aboriginal visitors, Sister M turns to nutrition:

> Over the past few months I have been concerned with the higher incidence of illness, especially amongst the children[,] with both diarrhoea and chest infection. There is also a marked increase in the number of children going under the 80% S.W.F.A. [safe weight for age] margin.

This she attributes to a recent decline in employment and a tendency among those with well-paying jobs to spend their wages on cars at the expense of food. She continues:

> The D.A.A. [Department of Aboriginal Affairs] kitchen is still functioning, [but] . . . recently we have been advised that the price for meals will be increased from 10¢ to $1.00 for children; 30¢ to $1.50 for adults. These prices still sound reasonable compared with town prices, but the family situation here is totally unable to support them. A family with six children would be paying out $30.00 per week for one meal a day each. When the prices increase I imagine people will not patronise the kitchen any more.

At that point, the kitchen would be shut down. She concludes:

> We are at a loss to know which way to turn. The days of hand-outs are supposedly past. What is the answer when faced with an obviously starving, miserable child whose weight is slipping down the graph to the 60–70% S.W.F.A. We cannot just wait until it is so undernourished that it has to be sent into C.H.U. [presumably a hospital or clinic].

Sister M wrote in the context of the new policy at that time of encouraging self-determination in the Aboriginal community. This policy had emerged in the wake of a flowering of social justice and land rights activism in the Indigenous community over the previous thirteen years. The first sign of a change of register in the Aboriginal response to white behavior came in 1963 when the Yolngu community at Yirrkala, in northeast Arnhem Land, demanded the withdrawal of a bauxite concession on Yolngu land. This they did with a typewritten petition affixed to a Yolngu bark painting, which the initiated men of Yirrkala sent to the Commonwealth Parliament in Canberra, where it was pointedly ignored. Thus began the first Indigenous land rights case in Australia, which led, at length, to the institution of a formal hearings process for land claims in the Northern Territory. The highly publicized wars then unfolding in the Brazilian Amazon and in Biafra, which had inspired the formation of Survival International in London and the Copenhagen-based International Work Group for Indigenous Affairs, contributed to an environment in which Indigenous Australians' demands for restitution attracted a level of public sympathy unimaginable ten years earlier.

Sister M's question is one that native affairs administrators had been confronting, in theme and variation, for more than twenty-five years, since it was first pointed out that the desert was getting less productive for foraging.

In 1950 the commonwealth government faced a choice between watching unassimilated foragers starve and inducing dependency. It opted not to intervene. But with the eviction of stock workers and their dependents from the stations, the problem became urgent in populations that had been integrated into the white economy in some cases for three generations.

By 1974, it was impossible to ignore the fact that Aboriginal children, and mothers and the aged and those without work, were starving. It transpired that educating young mothers on the responsible preparation of school lunches—"meals should consist basically of buns or bread with a meat, cheese, sardine or egg filling, garnished with fresh sliced vegetables or tinned beans, beet root, vegemite etc. A dessert is served consisting of a custard or a pudding or ice-cream followed by an apple or an orange. A fruit drink ends the meal."—would not be enough. It would be necessary to provide emergency food supplements. These must be in a form that could be stored without refrigeration, in lightly constructed shelters, in the monsoon, while providing an adequate dose of energy and protein. For most people involved in the conversation, this last point, the protein content of the supplement, was of special importance. To this end, the favored supplement relied heavily on cheese sticks. This, Dr. E. H. Hipsley argued, was a mistake. Citing the experience of the 1973–1974 Ethiopian drought, where livestock losses of up to 80 percent and a run of poor harvests contributed to widespread malnutrition and 50,000 to 100,000 deaths, Hipsley stressed that under starvation, the body's overriding need was for energy. Protein deficiency was a consequence of starvation, not a cause. Providing supplements in the form of an unfamiliar concentrated-protein preparation risked rejection and dehydration and represented a waste of an expensive and perishable type of food. He proposed an alternate supplement featuring Weet-Bix in place of cheese sticks and high-protein cereal, with just 10 percent of energy derived from protein.

Subsequent correspondence suggests they went with the cheese sticks. It was more than another year before supplement stocks were ready for distribution to community health centers along with guidance on incorporating maternal education into their use.

Twenty-five years earlier, Hipsley had authored the section on health and nutritional status for the *Report of the New Guinea Nutrition Survey Expedition*. Is this significant in light of his intervention in the food supplement discussion? At a minimum it suggests that exposure to a wider range of subsistence strategies might temper one's view of the salubrious properties of animal protein.

In Australia today, as in the Americas, the life chances of people in positions comparable to what we've looked at in this chapter—social marginalization via simultaneous dispossession and integration into extractive enterprises—are dismal. By practically any measure, particularly respiratory illness, mental health, substance abuse, domestic and intimate partner violence, and contact with the criminal justice system, indigenous populations endure levels of debility that would be politically intolerable were they to occur in a racially privileged population, no matter how poor.

Animal protein, its production and its consumption, has been focally implicated in the series of developments that brought us to this point. Meat made it both necessary and possible to enroll people who had been stripped of their subsistence entitlements in coercive regimes of labor ranging from pick-up work to wage slavery to outright slavery. To admit this is not to deny that meat was also highly valued, both among subjected peoples and among those who saw themselves variously as their benefactors, tutors, or masters. This is not about valuing one kind of meat, hunted meat, say, as opposed to raised. When all you've got is flour, sugar, caffeine, and meat, and generally not enough of anything, then meat, no matter what its source, becomes essential, just as flour, sugar, and caffeine become essential. But it would be a mistake, in these circumstances, to view increased meat consumption as a sign of growing affluence.

The enclosure of domesticated animals raised for food and the metabolic assimilation of the people made to raise them (and build the roads, and mine the gold) went hand in hand. In the colonization of the Americas and Australia, animals and humans became locked in complementary positions of marginalization and dependency. In the final chapters of the book, we'll consider whether something similar holds in the urbanizing world today.

Intermezzo: Race and the Science of Starvation

In the discussion of nutritional surveys, I skipped over a question that would have troubled us in part I: *Where are the authors getting their understanding of what makes for a high-quality diet?*

Recall from the prologue Sherman's *The Nutritional Improvement of Life* (1950). Writing for an American audience, Sherman urged his readers to consider the benefits of a diet lower in animal products, meat especially, and higher in fresh vegetables and fruit. These benefits were partly nutritional and partly political: a diet lower on the trophic ladder would make for a healthier population domestically, and it would free up resources to produce high-quality food for a larger part of the Earth's population. Sherman stresses the gap between a diet adequate to maintain homeostasis and that necessary to promote vigor. Wilson, in the station and town surveys discussed above, quotes Sherman to make the point that the oft-remarked inefficiency of Aboriginal workers stems not from racial inferiority but from poor nutrition.

Prior to the identification of the micronutrients we call vitamins in the 1930s, nutrition science was mainly a science of animal energetics. Animal energetics, in turn, was a science of animal starvation. It was also a science of race.

The questions physiologists asked about animal energetics were straightforward: How much energy was required to keep an animal from starving under various conditions (for example, physical regimen, ambient temperature)? How much protein—specifically, in the early days, how much meat—was required to maintain the animal in *nitrogen equilibrium,* that is, to ensure that the quantity of nitrogen lost as urea in the urine was equal to that ingested? Efforts to measure metabolic rate by gauging the volume of carbon dioxide expelled in respiration went back at least to Lavoisier's experiments with guinea pigs in the 1780s, but for a long time, respirometry remained cumbersome and subject to the concern that what an animal did under a respirometer hood did not represent a good approximation to what it did out in the world. So in most labs, the key methods of research into the 1910s were collecting animal waste and fasting animals, often to the death.

A variety of animals were sacrificed by starvation: rats, rabbits, guinea pigs, chickens, cats, and dogs. Physiologists were partial to dogs, and canine hunger artists were cited with approval in the energetics literature into the 1950s. A dog in Kumagawa's lab in Tokyo was reported in 1898 to have survived ninety-eight days without food before succumbing, having lost 65 percent of its body mass. Fourteen years later, physiologists at the University of Illinois reported they had fasted their dog Oscar 117 days before ending the experiment: Oscar refused to manifest the increase in excreted nitrogen typical of late-stage morbidity and in fact remained in such good spirits, as his handlers reported, that he had to be restrained as the fast went on from leaping out of and into his cage before and after his daily weighing lest he injure himself. Humans, of course, could not be involuntarily fasted to the death, but self-experimentation was rampant in the energetics world. After 1890, fasting gained popularity as a health cure and the key to vigor, productivity, Christian virtue, masculinity, and racial superiority. Interest in fasting cures continued into the 1920s even as fasting gave way, in energetics research, to respirometric studies of resting metabolic rate and controlled trials of calorie restriction.

The practical aims of animal energetics were twofold. One was to improve feed conversion in livestock and, more broadly, to formulate generalizations about the relationship between body size and basal metabolic rate. The other was to understand the energy and protein needs of humans under different occupations. To most of the people involved in the debate around these questions, the underlying policy concern was clear: *How much meat did you need to maintain an industrial labor force?*—not to say a modern army and navy.

Around 1900, conventional wisdom held that active men required between 100 and 120 grams of protein a day at a minimum, predominantly from animal sources, and an energy intake in the vicinity of 3,000 kcal. Periodically, reports would emerge of people getting by on considerably less—a community of fructarians in California, say—but these reports were mostly ignored.

The dominant voice in this conversation was that of German physiologist Carl Voit. Voit's laboratory at Munich had pioneered a number of the techniques then becoming standard in the physiology labs of the United States and Japan, notably the use of nitrogen equilibrium as a proxy for protein needs. Voit clove to a figure of 118 grams (4 ounces) of protein per day for a man of 70 kilograms (154 pounds) doing light work. This struck Yale physiologist Russell Chittenden as nonsense. In 1902 Chittenden undertook a series of clinical studies to demonstrate that 50 to 55 grams (2 ounces) of protein a day, and a considerably reduced energy intake, would keep young men in vigor and nitrogen balance indefinitely.

Chittenden put groups of Yale athletes and newly inducted US Army soldiers (*N* of eight and thirteen, respectively) on carefully controlled diets and exercise regimens and observed them over a period of months—their food intake, their excreta, and their performance on various measures of fitness. He also kept notes on his own food intake and physical activity. The diets in question were experimental only in the sense that portions and protein content were controlled. In other respects, the food was ordinary and not especially healthy. Opinion was divided as to the significance of his findings. One contemporary praised Chittenden's rigor but thought it was too soon to attribute participants' physical achievements to diet, since there was no control for the independent effects of the regimented way of life implicated in the experiments. Fifty years later, Sherman would hail Chittenden's work as a breakthrough in understanding just how elastic the human response to protein is. Others regarded Chittenden's results as a curiosity. But there were those who saw Chittenden's work as anathema.

Chief among these was Major D. McCay, professor of physiology in Calcutta. McCay, on the basis of long observation in India and a series of experiments with the diets of prisoners in Bengal, argued that Chittenden's conclusions were not just wrong but dangerously so, for they undermined the clear connection between a diet rich in animal protein and the masculine vigor of the more advanced races. McCay was not given to self-doubt. His discussion of diet in Japan, for instance, starts, "Before the emancipation of the Japanese from the strict tenets of Buddhism . . ." But for all the late-colonial puffery, there is something remarkably contemporary about his argument. "There is little doubt," he writes,

> that the evidence of mankind points indisputably to a desire for protein up to European standards. As soon as a race can provide itself with such amounts, it

> promptly does so; as soon as financial considerations are surmounted, so soon the so-called "vegetarian Japanese" or Hindu raises his protein intake to reach the ordinary standard of mankind in general.

That is, McCay argues, it is meat's income elasticity that determines its rate of consumption. As soon as a race achieves the income necessary to support a meat-rich diet—presumably by adopting the industrial labor discipline of Europeans—its meat consumption shoots up and, with it, the masculine vigor that distinguishes meat-eating races everywhere. As soon as incomes rise, what geographer Vaclav Smil, writing a hundred years later, calls the "cultural constructs of pre-industrial societies" fall away.

With time, the tone of arguments like McCay's changes. Talk of race becomes more muted, but concern about the implications of a vegetarian diet for national development persists. For Cornell biochemist William Adolph, writing toward the end of World War II, the "protein problem of China" was that for the 85 to 90 percent of the population living in the countryside, the diet was basically vegetarian. More precisely, 95 percent of the protein in the rural diet came from plant sources. Plant-source proteins, Adolph frets, are inferior both in that they are less easily digested and in that the protein they provide is lower in "biological value"; today we would say its Digestible Indispensable Amino Acid Score is lower. He expresses surprise at the success of the Chinese peasants he has observed in devising combinations of plant proteins that exceed those of any of the constituents—"another case of blind experimentation, examples of which are wide-spread throughout Asia." But his experiences in China do not leave him sanguine about the possibilities of diet modification in the United States in service of the war effort: "Do we know, for example, how far the change from the omnivorous diet to the vegetarian can be carried with impunity? Many of our blessings in health and vigor are, nutritionally speaking, related to animal protein."

Today we are faced with the opposite question: How far can the change to a carnivorous diet be carried with impunity? Despite vast differences of culture and economic environment, the role of animal protein in the nutritional niche of people in emerging urban markets bears comparison to what we saw in Australia. Here, too, growing meat consumption masks, and perhaps makes possible, growing precariousness. In the final chapters, we consider the relationship between meat and precariousness in the contemporary world.

7 Coupling

A Great Uncoupling?

Years from now, 2016 may be remembered as the year globalization ended. This was the year when, seventeen years after demonstrations at the World Trade Organization Ministerial Conference in Seattle drew attention to the predatory dimensions of free trade, it was no longer radical, or even progressive, to question trade liberalization. Every major candidate in the US presidential campaign disavowed the US-initiated effort to conclude a regional trade liberalization regime for the Pacific Rim, the Trans-Pacific Partnership (TPP). In August, Hanjin, the world's seventh-largest transoceanic shipper by capacity, went bankrupt in dramatic fashion—vessels, containers, and cargo stranded en route; creditors seeking liens in every port where a Hanjin-owned or -leased vessel happened to be at the time of the bankruptcy filing—triggering a spike in freight rates just as shipping was getting underway for Christmas. Eight weeks later, the Canada–European Union Comprehensive Economic and Trade Agreement (CETA) came within a hair's breadth of falling apart after seven years of negotiation when the Wallonia regional parliament used its veto to block Belgian ministerial approval, partly over concern for the treaty's effects on farmers (three days later, Wallonia granted CETA its provisional blessing). In the United Kingdom, a referendum to exit the European Union passed, with voters from regions that had benefited most from intra-EU trade and EU equalization (that is, development) funds most strongly supporting the exit. In the United States, rural voters used their disproportionate electoral power to rebuke not just trade liberalization but multilateral coordination in practically any form. By comparison with the trends toward integration and liberalization that characterized the period between 1980 and 2008, you might be tempted to call the time we live in now the Great Uncoupling.

And yet I've titled this chapter "Coupling." There are three reasons for this. First, it is too soon to say that globalization as we have known it is over. In part, this is because long-distance value chains are subject to a nonlinear lag in how they respond to market signals, a situation where present behavior depends not just on present conditions but on past conditions too. Second, the reversal in trade liberalization has been cross-cut by continuity in a different dimension of globalization—that in *income stratification*. Until recently, inequality of incomes between higher- and lower-income countries tended to be greater than that between income strata within countries, so that you could be poor in a high-income country but well off compared to most people in lower-income countries. Now that is changing. Income inequality between countries is declining even as global income strata matched by local purchasing power emerge across the divide between what we have been accustomed to think of as the rich and poor (or developing or emerging) worlds. In many places, notably the United States, income inequality is on the rise. But *global* income inequality has declined modestly, largely as a result of rising incomes in China. At the same time, the return on capital has outpaced that on labor. The gap between capital- and labor-derived income will continue to grow for a host of reasons, not least the fact that capital, in the form of capital-market instruments, has never been so mobile. This has significance for the global food system in general and meat in particular, something we'll return to.

Finally, meat as we know it today is both consequence and cause of the long-distance coupling of value networks that makes events such as the Hanjin bankruptcy newsworthy. We saw this in the prologue. A restaurant such as V Street—the "vegan street food" bar from the opening paragraphs—depends on refrigerated air freight, not to say the inexpensive air travel that allowed V Street's founders and clientele to develop a taste for street food from all over. Expertise, like ingredients and tastes, has become dramatically more mobile over the past thirty or forty years. Nowhere is the mobility of expertise and tastes clearer than when it comes to food.

In the prologue, I noted that meat has become an emblem of affluence. In chapters 4 through 6, we saw how meat became an emblem of capitalism. But affluence and capitalism are not the same thing. In this chapter and the next, we see how meat mediates the relationship between capitalism and affluence.

Geographically, our emphasis is on East Asia and the Pacific. As the economist Branko Milanovic notes, East Asia, specifically China, has been largely responsible for the modulation of purchasing power disparities among population segments matched by income quantile in higher- and lower-income countries. As I noted in the prologue, China has also played a significant role in growing global demand for meat and other animal-source foods, with meat consumption in China growing ninefold between 1960 and 2010. As you might imagine, livestock producers in Australia are eager to provide meat, milk, and other livestock products to satisfy growing demand in China and other parts of East and Southeast Asia. So while this chapter treats commodity-chain coupling as a global phenomenon, we focus on a China–Australia axis.

At the start of chapter 6, I pointed to a trend in the timescale of the narrative, from the million-year horizon of chapter 1 to the hundred-year horizon of chapter 5. Even then, we were still operating at scales that exceed the episodic scope of human imagination. To really grasp meat as an economic and political phenomenon, we needed to zoom way in, down to the scale of the day-to-day lives of people experiencing a nutrition transition. We've now done that, but we have yet to hook up the stories at different scales of time and space. It is as if the two narratives, that of the enclosure of animal biomass and that of life on the margins of the livestock economy, were unfolding in parallel. Now it is time to connect the story at these two scales.

A Heat Map Thought Experiment

Imagine a movie that compresses events unfolding over a long stretch of time and a broad expanse of space into something we can watch in a single sitting. The events in question are the changes in the human control of other gregarious vertebrates encapsulated in the term *enclosure*. We'll set the starting time to the onset of the events described in chapter 4. To construct our movie, we're going to attach some kind of easy-to-spot sensory marker to key events. For most readers, the best way to imagine this marker will be as some kind of visual signal, say a point of light that varies in luminosity, hue, and saturation to indicate changes in the intensity and quality of some event unfolding at scales too small to observe with the eye. For some, some other kind of marker might make more sense: a tone that varies in loudness, pitch, and timbre or even an olfactory or tactile cue. The point is, we're giving ourselves a way to observe gradient fields in the intensity of activity on screen at scales of time and space that would otherwise be below the threshold of noticeability. That is, we're designing an animated heat map.

What kinds of events should appear on our map? For a start, let's say that every time an animal comes into the world, it gets tagged with a point of light (or a tone or a scent—any kind of signal that can be resolved in time and space will work). The light gets brighter as the animal gets bigger, and it disappears when the animal dies. The lights vary in hue and saturation to indicate animals' changing economic, social, and cosmological relationship to human beings in the same part of the world—maybe red pixels represent animals that humans eat, with the degree of saturation indicating degree of human reliance on animals of that type. Maybe we have different hues for different modes of implication in the local human economy, say, red for hunting and blue for fully domesticated, with intermediate hues for the low-level food production and mixed regimes discussed in chapter 4. Maybe a green component signifies veneration, companionship, nonlethal exploitation, and other forms of mutualism. We don't need to get the imaging paradigm perfect in order to have the experience of watching what happens as enclosure unfolds at high speed.

We've designed our heat map with reference to human behavior. This is *not* to say that animals exist to serve human needs. Rather, it's a modeling decision motivated by the desire to construct a visualization of how human exploitation of other animals has changed over the past 10,000 to 15,000 years.

What other events should trigger signals? How about this: every time a human being consumes meat or some other animal product, the event gets tagged with a point of light, varying in intensity to indicate the quantity consumed and in hue and saturation to flag the type of product and the degree to which it has been processed or had value "added" to it, a concept we'll return to.

So now we have a way to observe changes in the mode and intensity of the coupling between animal metabolism and human consumption. Now it's time to run the experiment. Set the starting time to 15 ka and the timescale to 250 years per second, so that at the end of sixty seconds we arrive in the present. What do we see?

For the first twenty seconds or so, not much: a dim scattering of animal pixels and the occasional flicker as human consumption assumes a stable phase relationship with animal metabolism. This *phase locking* is localized and transient, and it does not seem to build into any kind of coherent pattern over longer periods of time or broader extents of space. If there is a trend over time in the pattern of bright pixels it is modestly in the direction of greater intensity and more even distribution as glaciation recedes and animals of all types, including humans, emerge from refugia to populate the warmer, more humid parts of Africa, Eurasia, and Sahul. At 12 ka or 12 seconds, migration into the Americas picks up. In some parts of the world, human consumption grows consistently stronger as nets and snares come into use. Correspondingly, the pixels for birds, rabbits, and fish grow more saturated as they become more intimately implicated in the human economy.

Around 10 ka or 20 seconds, a new pattern starts to appear, faint at first: pools of animal biomass take form at the western and eastern edges of Asia, superimposed on pools of human consumption. In some cases, particularly in the western pole, these standing pools take the form of *gliders,* stable formations that move in a periodic, localized pattern, the shape maintaining itself as it moves. Generally the patterns of movement are tight little circles or harmonic swings along a relatively short axis. With a full period occupying a single year or four milliseconds, they appear to the eye as nothing more than a blurred vibration. Superimposed over that vibration is a slower and more directional form of movement as filaments of the animal-human complex extend out into Africa, Europe, and the interior of Eurasia, stretching and then separating to form new localized pools with their own patterns of annual and infrannual (over periods of multiple years) harmonic motion. This process unfolds for some time, in parallel with lower-intensity forms of provisioning in southern Africa, the Americas, and Sahul. In some places, these lower-intensity foraging regimes teeter for a time on the edge of food production, with human landscape modification giving rise to consistently higher levels of both animal biomass and human consumption without the phase locking seen in some parts of Africa and Eurasia.

Between 36 and 40 seconds—6 and 5 ka—intensification seems to hit an inflection point in Eurasia as metallurgy and urbanicity take form. At 52 seconds we can detect the Xiongnu formation in eastern Eurasia. And then in the final second comes the period we've been waiting for, the last 250 years—and it is gone in the blink of an eye. We need to run the experiment again, this time stretching that last 250 years to occupy the entire minute. To simplify division, let's call the period 240 years. Before starting, we'll add a new signal to the model: a gold hue that gets triggered for human pixels whenever humans make financial investments in livestock production not for their own consumption. Now set the start time to 1780 and the timescale to four years per second, so that the last half-second runs through 2019.

For the first eight to ten seconds, or thirty to forty years, the salient patterns of coupling between animal and human metabolism appear not so different from what we saw from seconds 50 to 59 in the first movie. The lit-up pixels are brighter—that is, biomass is turning over at a higher rate—and more widespread. But the pattern of concurrent activation between animal growth and human consumption is still highly localized. And at a quarter second per year, it is still practically impossible to judge the *phase angle* between production and consumption, that is, the delay between the one and the other (if you consistently go to bed and get up at the same times, say ten in the evening and six in the morning, then your going-to-bed and getting-up times are phase-coupled with a phase angle of eight hours). Between 7 and 10 seconds, at scattered points across the Americas and in the southeast corner of Australia, we see the first signs of a new regime of coupling. In some parts of the Americas, animals that had been fully domesticated shift hue toward the wild, but the pixels in question remain highly saturated—they are still bound up in the human economy. This we recognize as the first sign of grazing with feral stock left to fend for themselves save when they are rounded up. In the southwest corner of North America, a cluster of pixels flares up and remains bright as the Comanche adopt sheep grazing. Farther north and east, across the Western Plains and into the prairies, we see the bison population enter a volatile and irregular pattern of coupling with the Pawnee, Arikara, Hidatsa, and Sioux nations. Then, at 10 seconds, something changes in Southeast Australia. Pixels flood into Tasmania, the interior of New South Wales, and what will soon be Victoria. This is not a diffusion of herding like that we saw out of Southwest Asia in the first movie: sheep are driven into the backcountry in pulses of a few months, so fast it appears to the eye that they simply materialize in the interior. Within eight seconds—thirty years—the squatting rush has played out, succeeded by a similar if smaller rush in Aotearoa New Zealand. Curiously, alongside the local patterns of production and consumption in Australia, we also pick out, faintly, traces of *long-distance coupling* between stockists in Australia and gold-hued investors in England and Scotland. Here there is a discernible phase angle built into the coupling, as it takes a period of years for investors to realize a return on their long-distance investment. A closer-to-simultaneous form of phase locking emerges through the wool trade, as sheep hair from Australia gets processed and consumed in the British Isles in the span of a year or so from shearing.

In Canada and the United States, another kind of long-distance connectivity starts to emerge as railroads, coupled with centralized slaughterhouses and hub-and-spoke distribution infrastructure, make it possible for livestock producers to sell to meat consumers at a considerable distance. This still accounts for a small proportion of human activity but one that grows in an accelerating or *convex* fashion (imagine a plot of consumption to time—convexity refers to the way the line bows toward the *x*-axis as the process accelerates, as in the first half of the S-shaped logistic curve we looked at in the prologue), especially from 22 seconds on, following the end of the US Civil War. We don't actually see the railroads in the movie, but we can infer them from the pattern of coupling at a distance. From 24 seconds or so, capital from England and Scotland begins to play a role in the stocking of the Western Plains with cattle, producing a new pattern of coupling with a visible phase angle. The transport of cattle across the Atlantic may also produce artifacts in the signal. At the same time on the other side of the planet, cattle and sheep begin to make their way into the Pilbara and the desert interior of Australia, forming new couplings with both consumers in the southeast and Perth and with investors in England and Scotland.

Now jump forward to 50 seconds—1980. Long-distance coupling between the production and consumption of meat is the rule on both sides of the Atlantic, with cities represented by bright clusters of consumers surrounded by areas populated less densely by humans but far more densely by the animals they eat. In the United States, chicken has assumed a dominant role in the meat economy, and chicken hot spots—broiler and layer batteries—pepper the Southeast. Any periodic phase angle between annual production and consumption pulses that was evident in the signal at 30 or 40 seconds has been smeared out by the use of selective breeding, confined feeding, and refrigeration to make slaughter seasonless, while refrigerated shipping and "boxed beef"—the modern apparatus of meatpacking—has made long-distance coupling nearly as strong at 1000 miles as it is at 100.

China, meanwhile, is shaking off the effects of the Cultural Revolution, though the one-child policy, promulgated in September 1980, augurs a new age of brutality directly at women and illicit children. The policy is intended to curb consumption at the population level, including consumption of meat and other resource-intensive foods, while the country industrializes. Even so, by 2010—eight seconds later in our movie—growth in Chinese demand for commodities of all types, from iron to meat to fresh fluid milk, is historically unprecedented. Watching the last two seconds of the animation, we see that in a shockingly brief span of time, China has come to represent one pole in a long-distance network with phase complements in Australia, North America, and Western Europe and, increasingly, as it develops its own asymmetric partnerships to hedge risks of disruption to the inbound flow of raw materials, in sub-Saharan Africa and South America. Long-distance coupling in the China-directed meat chain is complemented by a new kind of localized coupling as confined feeding for pigs and chickens becomes the norm and broiler batteries spring up on the outskirts of emerging cities to meet urban consumers' growing demand for chicken. China's growth is rivaled only by that of its neighbor South Korea, which has emerged from colonization, civil war, and a succession of military dictatorships to become a singularly vehement proponent of capitalism. Its transformation is made all the more poignant by the dimness on our heat map of the North, where a famine in the mid-1990s killed, depending on which estimates you use, between 1.0 and 3.5 million people, 4 to 16 percent of the population.

This second experiment has brought us closer to understanding the coupling at the heart of long-distance commodity networks, but we're still having trouble resolving periodic phase angles between production and consumption. What if we zoom in further still, say, to the 60-year period spanning 1960 to 2019, at a timescale of one year per second, or even to a single year chosen from the period 2010 to 2017, at just over six days per second? The 60-year version represents the best scale for observing the growth of long-distance coupling in the "emerging" world—Brazil, India, South Africa, perhaps Malaysia and parts of Indonesia, and of course China—though most of the activity is in the last thirty seconds. The one-year movie, by contrast, shows us little about how patterns of coupling grow and contract over time. It may provide insight into seasonal phase angles between animal and human metabolic activity—though of course seasonal pulses in the availability of meat have all but disappeared. As we zoom in, our visualization is also subject to greater noisiness—it becomes more difficult to distinguish short-term volatility from trends that would prove stable over the longer term.

So perhaps we have exhausted our thought experiment. It is time to look at the infrastructures that make possible the coupling at a distance our heat maps show.

Value Chains and Topologies

At this point we've visualized the dynamics of the meat economy, but the nature of the physical components of that economy remains vague. I've used the phrases *value chain* and *value network* in passing, and I've alluded to the *topology* of the food system. A *value chain* is simply a series of steps in the reconfiguration of a parcel of matter from its origins in some elementary productive process—photosynthesis, say, or, at a slightly less remote point, the growth of an animal—to human consumption. I say reconfiguration rather than simply movement because not all steps in a value chain entail movement. Some steps entail processing—slaughter, butchery, chilling, packaging. Others unfold in parallel to these material transformations, though for analytic purposes, we may insert them at a convenient point in the chain: think of marketing, for instance. All of these steps, at least in principle, "add value" to the parcel of matter in question in that they increase what a consumer would be willing to pay for it. A cow on a feedlot in Queensland is of no use to a Chinese consumer, whereas a cut of beef wrapped in modified atmosphere packaging—a blend of gases formulated to extend a fresh food product's shelf life behind an impermeable membrane—sitting in a butcher's case at the supermarket is of considerable use. By *topology*, I mean simply the set of relationships defined not by degrees of physical proximity but by the number of steps between two events in a value chain. Often topological distances matter more than physical distances for understanding behavior. In the remainder of this chapter, we examine the topology of the meat value network.

I'm going to emphasize structure—topology—at the expense of quantitative detail: the nodes of the network and the arcs that join them, with less attention to the lengths and diameters of those arcs. But one pair of figures does deserve mention before we go any further: as of this writing, roughly 10 percent of goods traded are agricultural in nature (including textiles, lubricants, and biofuels alongside food-related goods) and 25 percent of food produced in the world is traded across international borders. So agriculture represents a significant part of all trade, but *on average* most food is still consumed relatively close to its point of production. That "on average" is important. The role that international trade plays in agricultural markets varies significantly from country to country and commodity to commodity. Japan, for instance, imports more than half its food. And that 25 percent represents a historically unprecedented level of long-distance coupling in the food system.

Infrastructures of Coupling

For our purposes, infrastructure encompasses anything that facilitates the phase coupling of different parts of the livestock economy. When we talk about infrastructure, we tend to imagine things like shipping and the built environment of transport and communications in general. But transport and communications—*logistics*—represents just one dimension of infrastructure. For most people, it is the most salient dimension—it's the one you see at a port, for instance, or out on the road. Here I take a more expansive view of infrastructure, one that includes the legal arrangements and financial instruments that play a central role in bringing the metabolic cycles of animals and humans into coordination over great distances.

Legal Infrastructure: Free Trade Agreements

Agriculture has long been the bête noire of trade liberalization, the sector where outcomes have diverged most dramatically from trade architects' predictions and, arguably, with the most disastrous consequences for human well-being, especially in poorer countries. This is partly a product of the intrinsic season-over-season volatility of crop yields, partly of the efforts of developed states since the early twentieth century to reduce volatility through a combination of price supports, maintenance of public food reserves, and tariffs. Complicating matters, starting in the 1950s, the United States, Canada, the Soviet Union, and what is now the European Union used agricultural surpluses as an instrument of foreign policy through a combination of in-kind grants of food aid and loans to client states for the purchase of food from the lender. The resulting web of patronage and dependency, with the attendant suppression of local food-growing capacity in the developing world, formed the backdrop to the series of multilateral negotiations known as the Uruguay Round. These negotiations concluded in 1994 with the transformation of the General Agreement on Tariffs and Trade—an outgrowth of the 1948 Bretton Woods agreement, which created much of the international public finance infrastructure we know today—into the World Trade Organization (WTO). Liberalization of trade in agriculture was a key theme of the Uruguay Round. The final negotiations leading up to the WTO agreement included an Agreement on Agriculture laying out the commitments of affluent food-exporting countries to reduce domestic agricultural subsidies so as to afford less-affluent countries parity of access to consumer markets in the rich world.

That was the theory. In practice, the Agreement on Agriculture had the effect of instigating a drop in prices for food producers to the benefit of the integrators and processors who purchase food from farmers and add value to it before selling it to consumer markets. To many observers, the decline in *farm gate* prices—the prices independent producers command—in the decade following the implementation of the WTO Agreement on Agriculture was neither unexpected nor unintentional. The agreement created new long-distance markets for exporters while exposing producers to the volatility of those new markets, making the relationship between producers and exporters more unequal. The United States and the European Union mitigated farm gate price drops by maintaining farmer subsidies while barring developing countries from doing the same. The agreement amplified the effects of the structural adjustment policies promoted by another pair of Bretton Woods institutions, the World Bank and the International Monetary Fund, which had, since the early 1980s, aggressively encouraged developing states to reduce public spending on all manner of infrastructure and services, including food commodity reserve systems. The outcome, over the period 1995 to 2008, was that many less-developed states became more dependent on food imports than they had been before the WTO agreements came into effect. They were also subject to more aggressive food dumping, with market prices for basic agricultural commodities often trading below the cost of production in the affluent world. Dumping had the corollary effect that it became economically impossible for producers in the less-affluent world to maintain the fixed capital for domestic production in dumped commodities, since they could not compete on price with imported alternatives. The round of trade negotiations that succeeded the Uruguay Round, the Doha Round, fell apart in 2013 largely over the question of whether public food commodity reserve systems ran counter to the 1994 agreement.

So much for trade liberalization in the large. What about meat on the Asia–Pacific axis? As I mentioned in the prologue, Chinese imports of beef from Australia grew 600 percent to over A$900 million just in the three years ending with 2015. Over the ten-year period 2006 to 2015, the growth was more like 9,000 percent, most of that concentrated in the last three years. The Australia–China meat trade has shown remarkable convexity, and it is by no means clear that growth is about to level off. Indeed, overall Chinese beef imports grew by a factor of ten between 2010 and 2015. In 2016 China resumed imports of beef from the United States following a twelve-year ban imposed after US herds were found to be at risk of bovine spongiform encephalopathy, a.k.a. mad cow disease. The same year, Brazil and Uruguay overtook Australia as the leading exporters of beef to China.

Still, Australia remains positioned to absorb much of the new demand for imported livestock products in China, in no small part owing to a bilateral free trade agreement, ChAFTA, that came into effect at the end of 2015. The same year, the two countries signed a protocol on health standards for live cattle. Demand for pork has also risen in China, with concomitant growth in domestic confined-feeding infrastructure. Pork remains the modal form in which Chinese consumers get animal protein—but it is nowhere near as dominant as it used to be, with beef, chicken, fish, eggs, and dairy products all making inroads. Indeed, domestic poultry is a US$100 billion industry in China, with egg production outpacing that of the United States and broilers just behind.

China is not the only East Asia country where Australia has been eager to reduce tariffs on livestock imports. In 2014 South Korea and Australia concluded a free-trade agreement, KAFTA, that, like ChAFTA, gives prominent place to the reduction of import tariffs on beef and dairy products, with the complete elimination of beef tariffs over fifteen years. Three months later, in July 2014, Japan and Australia concluded the Japan–Australia Economic Partnership Agreement (JAEPA), which emphasized, again, greater access for Australian exporters to the Japanese beef market alongside tariff abatements in coal and minerals. For Japanese negotiators, concessions on agricultural imports carried significant domestic political risk, and the Abe government's willingness to expose domestic producers, in fresh produce as well as livestock, reflects its concern about Australia's growing entente with China. That is, Japan has come to use trade agreements to bolster strategic relationships, even at the expense of negative trade outcomes.

In the wake of the disintegration of the Doha Round, affluent countries have turned to bilateral negotiation to further their economic and strategic interests, in the case of Japan preferring to think of trade agreements in terms of partnership rather than the bald liberalization long favored by the United States, the European Union, and the Bretton Woods institutions. The one multilateral trade liberalization agreement that does seem to have a future is the Regional Comprehensive Economic Partnership, proposed by China as a way to draw its Southeast Asian and Pacific trading partners into a single regime that, like the WTO, CETA, and the moribund Trans-Pacific Partnership, would encompass trade liberalization and dispute resolution. Australia and New Zealand have indicated they will join—in 2013, Australia even hosted the second round of negotiations—as have India, South Korea, and China's key regional strategic rival, Japan.

Financial Infrastructures: Derivatives and Land Investments

Sometime in 2006, prices for a wide range of basic food and feedstock commodities, things such as wheat, maize, rice, and soybeans, started to climb. In the eighteen months through June 2008, the prices of key agricultural commodities doubled on international exchanges. Volatility shot up too. With the global liquidity crisis of August 2008, agricultural commodity prices fell, but two and a half years later, another spike unfolded. Initially, market analysts explained the 2007–2008 spike with reference to "market fundamentals," that is, a mismatch between demand and supply, perhaps exacerbated by the redirection of agricultural land toward biofuel production. It has since become clear that something else was at work: speculation in derivatives.

The use of forwards and futures—agreements to purchase a fixed quantity of some commodity at a future date at a price determined today—to hedge agricultural volatility is nothing new. Futures, as environmental historian William Cronon has demonstrated, were central to the emergence of Chicago as a hub for trade in cereals and livestock products in the middle third of the nineteenth century. Deferred-fulfillment contracts, whether exchange-traded or over-the-counter, serve as a sink for risk in agricultural production by allowing producers to lock in prices before they make the capital outlays necessary to deliver some good on the agreed-on date. They also provide a way to hedge one's exposure to price movements in the commodity market—there is nothing to stop you from purchasing instruments, whether deferred-fulfillment contracts or further derivatives of them, whose benefit curve varies inversely with that of your business, buffering you against losses in the market. Exchanges for these instruments provide an additional benefit: they aggregate opinions from a broad pool of market actors, most of them in principle with a deep understanding of the underlying commodities and the factors that affect their prices, about what kinds of risk the sector is facing and how much different goods and services are worth. That is, they provide a difficult-to-manipulate instrument for setting prices, a benefit known as *price discovery*. Today, derivatives markets provide liquidity and hedging in the food system not just via agricultural production contracts but via contracts for freight rates, as with the Shanghai Containerized Freight Index.

Of course, derivatives markets are susceptible to speculation and other forms of abuse—the cornering of Cronon's mid-nineteenth-century Chicago. For this reason, they've tended to be tightly regulated (in the United States since the 1920s). But since the 1980s, two things have produced a surge of interest in commodity derivatives. The first, particularly in the United States, was deregulation. The second was the proliferation of bespoke over-the-counter instruments that are intrinsically more difficult to regulate than exchange-traded products. The outcome has been a divergence between the individuals and institutions involved in producing, for example, rice, soybeans, cattle, and eggs, and the individuals and institutions that trade derivatives in these things. The market capitalization of one class of over-the-counter instrument, commodity index funds (CIFs; kind of like a mutual fund for futures), grew by a factor of more than twenty-five between 2000 and 2011, with some CIFs deriving 30 percent of their value from agricultural commodities. By this time, 2011, three-fifths of the capitalization in the agricultural derivatives markets came from so-called noncommercial traders, that is, those not directly involved in producing the underlying goods and services. At the same time, certain "commercial" traders, notably large agricultural integrators such as Cargill and ADM, established investment services divisions to market agricultural derivatives. It is still not clear what proportion of the 2007–2008 price spike was a product of derivatives speculation, but the years since have shown a clear correlation between noncommercial trading volume and price volatility in the underlying commodities.

Since 2013 there has been a loss of enthusiasm for commodity index instruments, especially among European investment banks, which faced greater pressure from civil society groups than counterparts elsewhere. But a new kind of financial infrastructure has appeared with long-term implications for agricultural trade: agricultural land acquisitions as pure investment. Land acquisition today differs in key respects from the expropriative acquisition we saw in chapter 5. It is conducted more or less exclusively by purchase and lease agreements, and there are no de jure transfers of sovereignty or jurisdiction from the country where the land is located to the foreign actors, be they public or private, making the acquisition. Nonetheless, land acquisition is characterized by strong asymmetries between buyer or lessee and the people who actually make their living from the land in question. Even more than over-the-counter derivatives, land acquisition is marked by opacity and contractual heterogeneity, making it difficult to form a picture of which states and institutional investors are picking up land where, and to what ends. Worldwide, the volume of cross-border land acquisition in the period of 2006 to 2010 was at least 200 million hectares (494 million acres). Two-thirds of this land was put to agricultural uses. The bulk of it, some 40 percent, seems to have been dedicated to growing crops for biofuels, with food crops responsible for 25 percent and pasturage or other modes of livestock production for 3 percent (bear in mind that a large proportion of food crop yield goes to feedstocks for confined animal production). The sociologist Saskia Sassen provides an overview of the variety of actors and venues involved:

> South Korea has signed deals for 690,000 hectares and the United Arab Emirates (UAE) for 400,000 hectares, both in Sudan. Saudi investors are spending $100 million to raise wheat, barley, and rice on land leased to them by Ethiopia's government; they received tax exemptions and export the crop back to Saudi Arabia. China secured the right to grow palm oil for biofuels on 2.8 million hectares of Congo, which would be the world's largest palm oil plantation, and is negotiating

> to grow biofuels on 2 million hectares in Zambia. . . . Pakistan is offering half a million hectares of land to Gulf investors with the promise of a security force of 100,000 to protect the land.

In some cases, as the Pakistan example hints, title transfers have led to the eviction of long-term de facto title holders, generally smallhold farmers. In this way, jurisdictions characterized by an absence of formal land title or a lack of enforcement of existing title may serve foreign investors well. The current wave of foreign land acquisition has generated the usual paraphernalia of elite capital income management, including over-the-counter hedging instruments. Agricultural land, like agricultural commodities, may no longer be less volatile than the market as a whole. But it does offer guaranteed long-term demand. Everyone needs to eat. And as one institutional land investor, the Australian investment bank Macquarie Group, has stressed in its promotional literature, as demand for animal-source foods grows in China and other emerging markets, more land will be required to yield a given quantity of protein and energy.

Land is one vector of foreign agricultural investment. Built structure, including meatpacking and dairy plants, is another, to say nothing of producer cooperatives and flocks and herds. Here too the China–Australia axis is exemplary, with investments by Chinese food and textile producers in Australian livestock concerns provoking public alarm and a level of regulatory scrutiny not applied, say, to American investments in the same industries. One of these investments, Moon Lake's purchase of the Van Diemen's Land Co., a dairy cooperative in Tasmania, is of special interest for what it shows about the role of consumer tastes in driving long-distance metabolic coupling. We'll return to this story in the next chapter.

Logistics: The Cold Chain and Live Transport

For all the influence they exert over the trade in agricultural goods and services, legal and financial infrastructures cannot physically move animals from the places where they've been raised to the places where they will be consumed. For that, you need road and rail networks, ports and shipping routes, not to mention communications networks to manage the dispatch, routing, and queuing of trucks, trains, and ships—in other words, logistics. We'll focus on two components of transport infrastructure that play complementary roles in the livestock value network: the cold chain and live transport.

The *cold chain* refers to the ensemble of artifacts, technologies, and operational guidelines—behavioral protocols—implicated in keeping something cold over the course of its transit from manufacture to use. The something in question could be any perishable organic matter—vaccine doses, cut flowers, fresh fruits and vegetables, eggs, milk, meat. Even with the advent of vacuum packing and modified-atmosphere packaging, temperature remains the dominant factor in determining how long perishable food remains palatable and safe to eat: how quickly levels of organic micronutrients such as vitamins A and C decline, how quickly bright colors fade, how long animal tissues maintain elasticity, and how quickly levels of *Pseudomonas* species and *Listeria monocytogenes* rise to the point where they threaten the health of human consumers.

For livestock products, the cold chain includes refrigeration at slaughterhouses and milking plants, en route to distribution centers and wholesalers, in storage at distribution depots, en route to supermarkets and other retail points of sale, on display at those points of sale, en route to points of preparation and consumption (food stalls, consumers' homes), and in storage at the point of consumption. It may also encompass transport in the reverse direction: from retail points of sale to distribution centers and from distribution centers to points of manufacture. We take for granted that at least one step in the distribution chain, from retail point of sale to the consumer's point of preparation, will entail a break in the cold chain, but even those links in the chain that are nominally intact may provide less-than-optimal climate control. There are, in fact, at least two cold chains, that for frozen goods and that for goods that are simply chilled so that they may be returned to ambient temperature without the risks of tissue damage occasioned by freezing. Even within these two broad categories, exactly how cold you want to keep something depends on what it is—ice cream needs to be kept frozen at –25°C (–13°F) degrees, fresh meat and dairy should be chilled to around 0°C (32°F), while eggs and tropical fruit do best at a so-called exotic chill of 10°C to 15°C (50°F to 60°F). As the distribution network ramifies from depot to retail to point-of-use, you lose economies of scale and it becomes less feasible to maintain separate cold chains for different kinds of products.

As I read through the cold-chain literature, I found myself coming back to the question of cost: mechanical refrigeration demands energy (not to mention the longer-term environmental costs of disposing of volatile organic refrigerants), but it is difficult to get straightforward estimates, say, for how much energy it takes to keep a cargo of dressed cattle carcasses or fluid fresh milk packaged for retail distribution chilled to 0°C (32°F) for the duration of a flight from Australia to China. In part this is because shippers treat operational details of supply-chain management as proprietary trade information. But measuring the cost of the cold chain also comes down to how you frame the opportunity costs. Is the alternative to keeping perishable animal products chilled in transit not producing those products in the first place, or is the alternative allowing those products to spoil for want of a sufficient market at the point of distribution? If you hold production of perishable foods constant, then it makes sense to reckon the energetic cost of refrigeration as the refrigeration footprint less the energetic cost of producing food that in the absence of refrigeration would go bad or not get consumed. The global energetic footprint for mechanical refrigeration, in the most recent figures I've seen, is approximately 1,300 TWh (terawatt hours, equivalent to 4.7 million terajoules). This comes to 8 percent of the global electricity budget and up to 10 percent of the total energetic footprint for food production. The food cold chain's relative carbon footprint is 2.5 percent of global CO_2-equivalent emissions. On the other side of the equation, global losses of food for want of refrigeration up to the retail point of sale come to 20 percent by mass across all categories of agriculture, a bit more in the less affluent world (estimating losses at the point of consumption is more difficult). Given the exceptionally high cost, in energetic, greenhouse gas emissions, water consumption, and pollution terms, of producing animal-source foods, refrigeration might seem like a good deal. Indeed, across all types of foods, the energy flushed away with food losses up to the retail point-of-sale comes to more than a third of the total energetic cost of food production. Even then, the International Institute of Refrigeration sees tremendous headroom in the cold chain, with less than a quarter of food output "requiring" refrigeration actually getting it.

But these figures make sense only if you assume that there is no feedback between infrastructure and production, that is, that cold-chain capacity has no effect on producers' decisions about how much meat and milk and how many eggs to push to the market. This is not realistic. If cold-chain capacity is implicated in overproduction of perishable foods for long-distance transport, animal-source foods in particular, then the return on investment in cold-chain capacity, relative to the energetic and emissions costs of the volume of food preserved by refrigeration, looks less appealing. Beyond the question of cold-chain feedback in production decisions, it's important to note that even for animal-source foods, primary production—the cost of growing things "on the farm"—represents a relatively small proportion of the total energetic cost of producing food. Transport, built structure, and "industry" (including fertilizer and feedstock production) represent the bulk, by a factor of more than thirty, of the total energetic cost of getting food to market. Most of the cost of maintaining cold-chain capacity comes under the transport and building headings.

If the cold chain is for dead things, its complement is the live transport of animals. Again, it is difficult to know exactly what is going on, since operational details are treated as trade secrets and most of the action unfolds en route. But a couple of things are clear. First, live transport is widespread. Chickens represent the most commonly transported animal across markets, with transoceanic live export of ruminants growing at around 4 percent per annum. Australia is live export's most enthusiastic proponent, exporting upward of 600,000 live cattle annually over the past twenty years and much larger volumes of sheep. The main market for sheep and goats has been the Middle East and adjoining parts of East Africa, while the cattle market has focused on Southeast Asia, Indonesia in particular. China, along with Korea and Japan, represents the growth market for cattle, including dairy breeders as well as feeder (shipped for fattening) and slaughter (shipped for immediate slaughter) steer.

Second, live transport is stressful for animals, with concomitant health risks to consumers. There are no international regulatory standards for live export. What industry standards exist for the design of oceangoing vessels for live transport are not evidence based, that is, they do not represent the outcome of any kind of controlled observation of the effects on the animals of varying design parameters (for example, ambient temperature, number of animals per stall, depth of straw or other underfoot matting). Travel times range up to five weeks, with some animals remaining on board an additional week before unloading. Onboard stressors are many. As you might expect, ammonia concentrations rise over the course of the voyage, irritating the mucosa of the animals' lungs and breathing passages; for sheep, 50 percent of deaths in transit where cause of death has been identified come from respiratory infections. Disease transmission is also a risk, and salmonellosis accounts for another big part of deaths in transit. Wet-bulb temperature in the hold can run to 34°C (93°F), so heat stress, electrolyte depletion, and acidosis run high too. Especially among sheep and goats, inanition—loss of appetite—is a problem: after months of pasturage, they do not adapt well to pellet feeding. This may be partly due to how transport interrupts the animals' seasonal behavior rhythm—animals fattened in the austral autumn and winter and then loaded for delivery in the boreal spring and summer are not able to switch quickly to restricted food intake and reliance on fat stores. Motion sickness may play a role in inanition too, along with overstocking; in less densely stocked hospital stalls, sick animals recover their appetite. All of this information comes from rather limited autopsy data. For ships embarking in Australia, reportable mortality, the threshold of deaths beyond which shippers must submit an incident report to the Department of Agriculture and Water Resources, is 1 percent for voyages of longer than ten days.

In light of these facts, it might seem that live export by air would be less inhumane than by sea, though again, evidence is wanting on how transport affects the animals. Figures for live export by air go back just to 2015 but show Australian exporters seeking to experiment. The second half of 2015 saw thirty-two consignments of live air export of cattle comprising more than 5,000 animals, along with close to 30,000 sheep and 50,000 goats, not to say more than 1,000 alpacas. No cattle died in transit, though close to half a percent of the sheep did and a smaller number of goats. For all species, Malaysia represented the key market, accounting for more than 80 percent by number of animals. In 2016, the number of consignments increased, but the number of animals decreased pro rata, as did the number of destination markets and the number of exporting firms involved, suggesting either a shakeout following initial enthusiasm or rapid concentration in the exporter market or random year-over-year fluctuation.

A third thing that seems clear about the live export market is that live export, whether by design or happenstance, has come to represent a form of regulatory arbitrage on standards of slaughter. This is something animal protection activists in Australia have been alert to, with clandestine recordings of animal abuse at slaughtering facilities in Indonesia and Vietnam sparking public outrage about the shoddy treatment of Australian cattle. As a number of observers of globalization have pointed out, arbitrage on citizenship rights and labor standards has played a central role in both stimulating and constraining flows of people from one country to another. Perhaps we should extend the same analysis to animals.

Nutrient Cycles and Biome Turnover

So far, for all that we've refined our awareness of how animal metabolism on one part of the Earth's surface becomes linked to human metabolism on other parts, we've been operating with a fairly coarse-grained concept of coupling: animal bodies, human meals. In the prologue, we looked at the costs of livestock production in terms of land, energy, water, greenhouse gas emissions, nitrogenous pollution, and other factors. It would be great if we could incorporate these ways of measuring the degree of enclosure of livestock metabolism into our heat map. This would mean adding new channels to our map, with signals, say, for moles of nitrogen and water passing from the lithosphere, hydrosphere, and vegetative cover into animal bodies and, at length, out of human bodies and back into the lithosphere and hydrosphere. Essentially what we'd like to do is construct a virtual respirometer, calorimeter, and nitrogen flux meter, maybe one for phosphorus too, with measurement gates at the points where energy, water, air, and key nutrients enter animal bodies and exit human bodies.

If we're taking things this far, we might also like to see how long-distance coupling of animal and human metabolism is playing out in Earth's *biome structure,* that is, in the distribution of categories of land and water defined by modal vegetation and land cover: various types of woodland, rangelands, croplands, and those parts of Earth densely inhabited by humans or dedicated to industrial manufacturing. As this list suggests, a growing part of the earth's surface is taken up by *anthropogenic* biomes, and we might expect to see phase-coupling, say, between the expansion of cattle rangeland in Queensland and that of urban areas in Southeast Asia.

This kind of resolving power is beyond our current state of knowledge. As we'll see in the next chapter, it is difficult enough to figure out what people are eating in basic typological terms (cereals and rice, meat, dairy, eggs, fruits and vegetables), let alone how energy, water, and nutrients are cycling from the biosphere through the foods they eat and back into the earth. At an aggregate level, we can make estimates. But at the level of individuals and households, it gets tricky. This level of resolution, it turns out, is crucial for understanding the relationship between income and the consumption of particular foods. It is to the question of meat's income elasticity that we turn, at last, in the next chapter.

More Intimate Kinds of Coupling

Before we do, a few parting thoughts on the nature of animal–human economic coupling. In this chapter, we've been concerned mainly with phase coupling over horizons of seasons, years, and millennia, but phase-coupling phenomena can unfold over a much wider range of time horizons. Two in particular warrant mention, both arising, in different ways, from how the bodies of large animals serve as reservoirs for microorganisms.

The first concerns disease. In chapter 4, I mentioned that domestication exposed humans to novel patterns of endemic infectious disease once they entered into standing co-residence with animals that harbored those diseases or their precursors. Today, endemic zoonoses represent the single greatest contributor to human debility and death, with on the order of a billion episodes of illness annually, most concentrated in the poorer parts of the world. At the same time, highly virulent epizootic epidemics have come to pose a growing threat to consumers in affluent as well as less affluent places. Increased risk of the emergence of highly pathogenic zoonoses such as the A H5N1 strain of avian influenza is strongly correlated with both increased stocking densities and the reduced genetic diversity and physiological hardiness of livestock bred for high feed conversion under confinement. So here is another channel for our heat map: the relationship between stocking densities and diminished effective (that is, genomic) livestock population size on the one hand and infectious disease burden in humans on the other.

The second picks up the thread from the section "A Holobiont Perspective" in chapter 2. If, as recent experiments suggest, the taxonomic composition of the gut microbiome is linked to diet, with a distinct signal for an animal-rich diet, what kind of long-term relationship might we observe between the long-distance traffic in livestock products and the emergence of a uniform human *enterotype* or gut microbiota profile? Again, this is a question we're just now in a position to ask and not yet to answer. What we can say is that the coupling of human and animal physiology extends down to the most intimate dimensions of our own experience as living things. This is what food behavior comes down to: what happens when we put something in our mouths, at home or in the street.

8 The Street

Fried Chicken and Hope

We don't know his name, but we know that he is a single father, homeless, and that he works as a human billboard, holding up a sign advertising luxury homes at a busy intersection in Taipei, standing for hours at a stretch in the traffic and the monsoon. His children, a girl and a boy, perhaps nine and twelve, wander the city's margin and haunt an immense supermarket, subsisting on free samples. At length they attract the interest of a floor manager who lives alone in a ruined house in the same forest where father and kids have set up a makeshift home. At night, on her return from work, she feeds expired produce to the stray dogs that congregate in the shell of a neighboring building. She seems to know them well. She has names for them—President, Star—and knows how much they habitually eat.

To get from where they sleep to the city, father and kids must cross the Tamsui River in a punt they keep hidden in the marsh grass. One night the father, drunk, marches his children down to the punt in a monsoon downpour, intentions unclear. The woman, following, intervenes and prevents the father from taking the children out on the river. Later—or perhaps it is earlier—the four are gathered at her home. They celebrate his birthday. She helps the kids with their homework. He soaks in the tub in a state of near cataplexy. The adults circle one another, unable to connect, and when at last he reaches out, she rebuffs him.

This is the plot of Tsai Ming-liang's film *Stray Dogs* (郊遊 *Jiaoyou,* "Excursion," 2013). With its use of long takes—at 138 minutes, the film unfolds in fewer than eighty camera setups, most of them static—and in its casual attitude toward the conventions of continuity editing, *Stray Dogs* challenges the viewer to attend closely. Twice, the camera focuses on people eating meat, specifically fried chicken. At one point we see father and kids eating together at the end of his workday, at another just him, scarfing down chicken and rice on a work break.

These are not the scenes that have attracted critical attention. Those scenes come just before the climactic showdown at the punt, when the father savages a head of cabbage his daughter has made into a doll, and at the end, when the adults contemplate a mural of a rock wall in a wordless two-shot that runs fourteen minutes. The meat-eating scenes, by comparison, feel like so much connective tissue. They did not jump out at me on first viewing. And then, a couple days later, the image of Lee Kang-sheng, who plays the father, shoveling chicken and rice into his mouth from a low-density polyethylene tray came back to me, and it has not left me since. *This,* I thought, *is the face of meat today.*

What do we know about the relationship between meat eating and affluence in the urban centers of the emerging world? Not in the aggregate, but at the level of household and individual behavior: Who is eating meat, and under what circumstances?

This question, of the relationship between aggregate correlations, as between income and meat consumption, and the everyday habits of the people whose behavior forms the basis for these correlations, is key. In interviews, Tsai has said that he had been seeing people like the protagonist of *Stray Dogs* on the streets for about ten years when he made the film. He had found himself wondering about their coping strategies. In this respect, the story that the food scenes in *Stray Dogs* tell is very much at odds with what you read in the literature on urbanization, income, and demand for meat. That story is one of affluence and its consequences: humans crave meat, and rising affluence in the cities of the emerging world has created a new stratum of consumers with the purchasing power to satisfy that craving. Meat, that is, is income elastic. But for the people depicted in *Stray Dogs,* meat is a badge not of affluence but of precariousness—it's a food you can eat on the go, it kills hunger, it's quick to prepare. For these people, at least, to say that meat is income elastic seemed to get the story backward. It's not that meat is income elastic. Rather, it's that cheap meat has become an enabling factor in a form of capitalism that requires lots of people like the nameless protagonist of *Stray Dogs.*

When I started looking into the literature on meat and income elasticity, I found that evidence bridging aggregate correlations between incomes and meat eating and individual or household-level behavior is scarce. Often we don't have a clear picture of what things look like at street level.

This final chapter, then, is a history of ignorance, a story of all that we do not know about the facts on the ground. To end on a note of ignorance is to hold out the hope that meat need not be a sentence, that we are not fated to dedicate ever greater parts of the Earth's resources to satisfying a bottomless appetite for animal foods. I believe this is not our fate, at least as far as our evolutionary legacy is concerned. This is a theme we'll take up further in the epilogue.

The Imaginary Life of Income Elasticity

In September 2016 a paper by economist Paul Romer began circulating in manuscript form. In "The Trouble with Macroeconomics," Romer argues that in the preceding thirty years, macroeconomics had made no progress identifying the real-world causes of trends in the abstract measures that are the subfield's stock in trade. If anything, it had gone backward, with careers built on a proliferation of imaginary causes whose relationships to events in the world are rarely, if ever, unpacked. To highlight the made-up nature of these causes, Romer gives them new names, some inspired by the conjectural substances favored by physicists of an earlier era:

- Phlogiston[, which] increases the quantity of consumption goods produced by given inputs . . .
- A troll who makes random changes to the wages paid to all workers
- A gremlin who makes random changes to the price of output
- Aether, which increases the risk preference of investors
- Caloric, which makes people want less leisure

At the time "The Trouble with Macroeconomics" began making the rounds, Romer was incoming chief economist at the World Bank (he has since been awarded the Nobel Prize). He enjoyed a degree of professional autonomy that most researchers could only dream of, and his remarks were received with irritation in some quarters. But reading "The Trouble with Macroeconomics," I thought of meat. Here was another instance where relationships inferred from summary statistics about income and consumption were being attributed to a cause that bore at best an incomplete relationship to observable behavior. The income elasticity of meat could be a candidate for Romer's panel of imaginary causes:

- The Colonel, who makes people crave meat as incomes in their city (province, region, country) rise

By this point, I knew I was not alone in my skepticism. A small literature had started to open up on the limitations of elasticities as a way of describing how people get food for themselves and their families. The problem is not just that elasticities, of income or whatever else, are too coarse-grained for making sense of household-level behavior. It is that they make overly strong assumptions about the role that price plays in shaping people's decisions about how much animal-source food to eat. So maybe something that looks like income elasticity from 1,000 miles up looks different on the ground—or maybe income elasticity is part of the story, but not all of it. How might things look if we started at the opposite end of the telescope, with the events leading up to the moment when people put food in their mouths? What new kinds of evidence would we need in order to find out?

A New Empire of Meat?

To start thinking about how people living in precarious circumstances might be compelled to rely on meat, let's compare the two modern *regimes of coercion* we've seen.

In the first, that of the cattle stations, the coercion is overt and explicit. Indigenous cattle workers and their households lived in a state of legally sanctioned exploitation comparable, depending on where and when you look, to corvée, indenture, and chattel slavery. In some cases, they were physically restrained from leaving the station they were associated with, in that police patrols would track down those who walked off without permission from the white station manager. There was no doubt in the minds of anyone involved that what was going on was exploitative and that the Aboriginal participants had little choice in the matter. The stations, for their part, saw the management of Aboriginal labor as one of the key themes of their own dialogue with state, territory, and commonwealth authorities.

In the second type of situation, coercion is more covert and implicit. No one is forcing the nameless protagonist of *Stray Dogs* to work as a human billboard. The real estate developer has no legal claim to his body or person apart from that manifest in whatever employment contract they may have. This is guaranteed to be loose; indeed, in this case, a casual relationship is of far greater benefit to the employer than to the work seeker, and over the past 30 years, the casualization of all manner of service and manufacturing work (including, as we saw in chapter 5, meatpacking) has been a hallmark of labor markets in the most "advanced" (industrialized, rule-governed) capitalist economies no less than in the emerging world. For that matter, no one is forcing our protagonist to remain in Taipei or to make himself available for work of this type. He receives wages in cash, and it is up to him to decide how to spend these cash wages, among other things, on food for his children and himself, shelter, and alcohol. Developers, along with others who depend on casual unskilled labor, may lobby the government to enact law that favors their continued access to the labor pools that make their businesses possible. But by and large, they do not have specific populations in mind—they simply want to ensure that there are no barriers to hiring whoever turns up desperate for work.

Of course, these are approximations, and there are many instances in the contemporary world where exploitative working conditions look a lot more like the knowing extraction of value from a captive population than like a faceless, "structural" violence that inheres in the system of production and consumption without anyone's being responsible for it or knowingly desiring it. But we've identified two poles, one of explicit subjection, the other of implicit control, and the question is, What kinds of inferences are valid across the divide between these two poles? Is it meaningful to say that the protagonist of *Stray Dogs* is forced to rely on meat in a way at all comparable to how Aboriginal Australians in the mid-twentieth-century livestock industry were forced to rely on meat?

Another way to put it would be: Is the world we inhabit today comparable to what we saw in North America and Australia (chapters 5 and 6) in the role that meat consumption plays in mediating the extraction of value from marginalized people?

This may sound like a leading question, but actually I don't have an answer. I think it is reasonable to imagine *empires without centers,* large-scale systems of economic exploitation defined by a vast lumen of the dispossessed from whom resources (labor, expertise) get drawn off rather than by a particular "metropole" or center responsible for the drawing off. And I think it is important to keep in view the fact that the violence of a situation like that depicted in *Stray Dogs* is never quite as faceless, intrinsic, or structural as we might like to believe. The question of how to apportion responsibility for economic violence—and here I mean all violence that is roughly economic in origin, in whatever form it manifests, including coercion, physical violence, injury, and illness—is of course value laden. But so is behavior. Brutality is never simply about economic interest. There is always something more going on, be it race hatred or a "politics of sight" like that which political scientist Timothy Pachirat experienced in an Omaha slaughterhouse (chapter 5).

These questions—When is economic violence attributable *to someone?* Who, or what, counts as its victims?—serve as a backdrop to what follows.

Where Do the Data Come From?

To make assertions, whether at street level or in aggregate, about the relationship between what people earn and what they eat, we need data. Data on household provisioning come from two kinds of sources, food balance sheets and household surveys. Food balance sheets are derived from state statistics on food production. They are notoriously unreliable for a host of reasons, including deliberate obfuscation by the individuals and institutions asked to provide information. In 2008 an external commission convened by the Food and Agriculture Organization (FAO) concluded that the problem had been getting worse since the 1980s. For large parts of Africa and Asia, the food balance sheet data that form the basis for FAO statistics (which form the basis in turn for ecologists' and geographers' estimates of energy throughput, nitrogen balance, and so on) do not even come from national balance sheets. Rather, FAO infers them from other data and its own models in the absence of appropriate submissions from state statistics bureaus.

The problem appears to be especially acute in the case of data about livestock. In China, for instance, at least up through around 2000, village, township, county, and prefectural authorities were under pressure from above to show rapid development in the livestock sector, leading to gross overstatement of livestock production. At the same time, small pig farmers and traders sought to avoid health inspection fees and slaughter taxes, leading to underestimation of how much meat was entering the market, at least in parts of the country where backyard slaughter still predominated.

These opposing incentives did not cancel out: for 1999, meat consumption as estimated from food balance sheets was more than double that estimated from an annual household survey (roughly 100,000 respondents, a third from urban areas). Since then, hog production in China has seen dramatic consolidation, and China's livestock inspection system has become much more sophisticated. Still, it is important to be aware of the limitations of food balance sheets. States and their subordinate administrative units, to say nothing of private agricultural enterprises, often have incentives in the reporting of production and consumption that run counter to the interests of FAO and its peer organizations in forming an accurate picture of who is eating what where.

The other major type of source for estimates of household provisioning behavior is household surveys. In chapter 6, we looked at a series of household dietary and nutrition surveys conducted in different segments of the Indigenous population of Australia and New Guinea. These surveys had their logistical and practical difficulties. The populations of interest lived in inaccessible places spread out over great distances. Often they were under the coercive control of individuals and institutions that did not understand their own interests to be aligned with those of the survey. In some cases, language barriers obtruded. In at least one village in the 1947 New Guinea survey, the respondents interpreted the survey team's visit as cause for feasting, distorting the results. Despite these difficulties, the surveys we looked at in chapter 6 share one property that makes them relatively easy to reason about: they were all small in scale, with respondents in the tens to hundreds. In this chapter, we'll again be drawing on household survey data. But this time the surveys in question cover thousands to tens of thousands of respondents, in some cases spread out over the entirety of mainland China.

Most large-scale surveys of individual- and household-level economic behavior rely on some form of *retrospective recall*—asking people what they've purchased or consumed in the past day, week, or some longer frame of time. Sometimes respondents are asked to do a *freelisting* exercise, that is, simply to list the foods they've been eating. In other cases, they're given a questionnaire that prompts them to indicate how often they eat different types of foods, so the set of categories for grouping foods together is determined in advance by the investigators (ideally, it's been validated in small-scale studies before being used with a larger population). In-home observational studies, even for a subpanel of respondents, are the exception. Seven-day quantitative records, with every component of every meal weighed before consumption, are rarer still. The methods survey designers and fieldworkers use to approximate a longitudinal quantitative record vary from place to place and study to study, and the aggregation of results from different surveys necessarily entails a flattening-out of the data.

The language we use to talk about survey methodology—households, in-home, meals—points up their most serious limitation: they rarely capture the behavior of those whose access to food is most precarious and inconsistent, those who, like the family in *Stray Dogs,* do not have a fixed address where questionnaires or fieldworkers can find them, let alone stable mealtimes—those who, as far as the conventional apparatus of state surveillance goes, are invisible. I am not saying it is impossible to reach these people. It is simply more time-consuming, and it demands more seasoned fieldworkers.

It also opens up a new set of questions of study design. Say you're interested in the lives of migrants from rural areas to cities. In China, internal migrants make up a significant part of the less affluent strata of the major cities, and often they remain invisible to the municipal bureaucracy even when they've lived in the city for years. You're prepared to devote considerable resources to forming a high-resolution picture of migrants' lives. But you still need to impose boundaries on your field of inquiry. How should you draw those boundaries? By looking at what goes on in a particular street or district where a high concentration of migrants live? By following a small number of individuals on their daily circuits? By tracing individuals' social networks out to their home villages and observing how resources flow from city to countryside and the reverse? Survey designers never have the resources to do all of these at once, and different approaches provide different kinds of information about migrants' lives.

These considerations point up one final limitation of surveys: even if you conduct the survey repeatedly, say, every year or two, the panel of respondents is different every time, so it is difficult to identify how individuals' and households' circumstances change over time. Let's say household income survey data indicate that the proportion of households living in poverty has been declining year over year for twenty years. You might then ask, Is the poverty that remains endemic, or is it transient? In other words, is it more the case that certain households have been unable to escape poverty, or is it more the case that households from a broader stratum of society remain at risk of falling into poverty but spend less time on average in poverty before getting out? To answer questions of this type, you need to follow particular households over time; you need a *longitudinal panel study*. Longitudinal designs reveal more about the *path dependence* of individual and household behavior, that is, how behavior is conditioned by the series of events leading up to the present, than a survey design that treats every iteration of the survey as a new cut through the population. Like the community study designs I've described, longitudinal studies are more time-consuming, but they provide information that one-off surveys, even if repeated, cannot. (In the case of poverty, data for rural China suggest that poverty has become more transient, and the vulnerability of any one household to slipping into poverty has fallen, even as income inequality has grown.)

However imperfect the data that household surveys provide, they offer the best resource for forming a picture of individual eating behavior and its economic correlates. Let's look at how.

Once You've Got Data, What Do You Do with Them?

By itself, 100,000 points of self-report data, whether about income or the number of times people in the respondent's household ate meat in the past week, tell you little about the pattern of behavior in the population—just as, by itself, color and position values for every pixel in a photograph tell you little about what the photograph shows. To make survey data meaningful, we need to abstract away from the individual examples. Of course, abstraction strips away potentially useful information even as it reveals something new. The question of how to model large volumes of data about behavior comes down to where to make the cut between structure and texture, between that which is essential and that which is superficial. Again, we are dealing with a value-laden question: what is texture for an economist might be structure for a historian or anthropologist, and what is texture when the question is, *What is the trend in mean energy intake over the past 30 years?* might be structure when the question becomes, *How has the animal-source component of meals changed over the same period?*

Already we've seen how efforts to cut to the structure of a population-level relationship, that between income and meat consumption, risk misrepresenting the underlying causes of that relationship. Earlier I alluded to a small literature expressing misgivings about the way elasticities are imputed to behavior on the basis of abstract population data. One alternative proposed in this literature is to *simulate* street-level behavior—to run history over and over, at a high level of detail, in a computational process where every individual or household is represented by a distinct data structure. Within the simulation, time unfolds as a series of discrete steps. At each step of time, the simulated individuals take different actions with probabilities derived from real-world survey data and the current state of the simulated world, including such parameters as income, location, and level of education. We may never have complete information about household behavior out in the world, but within the simulation we do—and in this way, such *agent-based models* can help us refine the assumptions we make when we bridge the gap between aggregate correlations and how people get food to their mouths. Agent-based modeling represents one approach to ridding our high-level models of phlogiston, caloric, and colonels.

Simulation represents a way of following summary trends all the way down, as it were, to the ground. But models that include detailed representations of individual behavior are no substitute for either more abstract models that use "closed-form" expressions (that is, differential equations—elasticities are a kind of closed-form model) or for longitudinal studies that track the evolution of behavior in a panel of individuals over a period of years. These all play complementary roles. By itself, simulation offers no way around the hard problem of predicting how a complex system will evolve over time.

And for a simulation to be informative, the probability structure of the simulated individuals' behavior must be based on high-quality data about how real individuals behave. So we're back to the need for high-resolution survey data.

One more thing to consider: One of the goals of abstracting, of separating structure from texture, is to reduce the number of explanatory factors in your model, to say, *These are the factors that account for the greatest part of the variance in behavior, from place to place or over time—these are the key determinants of nutrition, health, life chances, and so forth.* Statisticians have a wide variety of tools at their disposal for factor analysis. But these are useful only if you can specify the factors precisely enough to measure them. So we are faced with the challenge of *operationalizing* complex phenomena.

Consider the question of how "developed" a market is. In East and Southeast Asia, confined poultry and pig operations tend to be located on the periphery of cities. So for urban markets, the meat commodity chain is shorter both geographically and topologically. Added to this is the fact that cities offer a greater density of points of sale—supermarkets and fast-food outlets alongside wet markets (open-air fresh meat and produce markets) and food stalls. Already we can see how these factors might offer an alternative explanation for patterns of meat consumption. If cash incomes are higher in cities—they are—but livestock products also have greater access to consumers, we would like to say what part of the variance, say, in rural versus urban meat consumption is accounted for by one or the other. To do that, we'd need a way of quantifying market development or urbanicity. Like income, market urbanicity feels salient and conceptually coherent. But unlike income, it feels complex, not something we could distill down to a single number. (Then again, income has its own complexities—we've simply grown accustomed to thinking of it in unitary terms.)

What Is a City?

Up to this point, I've been using *city, urban,* and *urbanization* as if these were self-evident terms, but in fact they merit some unpacking. Without a doubt, urbanization is one of the most significant phenomena of human behavior today, not to say the behavior of many other species. Sometime around ten years ago, at this writing, the population of urban areas surpassed that of rural areas for the first time in human history, and urban populations continue to grow at faster rates than rural. Trends in the mean size of the Earth's largest cities show convexity, or accelerating growth, over the past 200 years, as do trends in the number of cities of population above some arbitrary threshold (say, a million inhabitants). In the same period, the geographic distribution of both urban populations and large cities has shifted from the North Atlantic to Asia and the Pacific Rim. Once again, China offers an exemplary case.

But what it means for a city to grow has varied from place to place and over time. The cities that exemplify contemporary urban growth bear scant resemblance to the compact, sharp-boundaried metropoles of mid-twentieth-century science fiction, let alone to London, Edo (present-day

Tokyo), and Peking (present-day Beijing) as they were 250 years ago, when they were the world's sole cities of a million inhabitants. Contemporary large urban agglomerations are characterized by a mosaic or ribbon texture, with patches of low-density inhabitance, often agricultural, interspersed with higher-density areas and road and rail networks incorporating outlying villages into the urban periphery long before they are subsumed administratively. In other cases, a new agglomeration may appear as transport networks, denser residential and industrial space, and amenities fill in the spaces between what had been distinct cities, with administrative coordination trailing infrastructure. This is the case, for instance, in Jingjinji, the region that subsumes Beijing, Tianjin, and Hebei province in northern China.

In some parts of the world, growth at the margins of an urban core has been driven by informal (or, if you prefer, autonomous) construction, undertaken by migrants, with new neighborhoods struggling for recognition from the municipal government and the extension of amenities such as running water and bus service. This has been the case in many cities in Latin America and South Asia. In other places, notably China, urban construction has been driven by the state and its subordinate administrative units, with competition among provinces and municipalities driving a construction boom that has left large parts of the interior of China dotted with "ghost cities," high-density residential districts with vacancy rates of up to 90 percent. Overconstruction has been complemented by informal growth, with expansion into the agricultural mosaic leaving municipal governments struggling to reorder remaining agricultural land for efficiency and residential density. The result is that much urbanization is better characterized as *peri*urbanization, with the fringe appearing not just at the outer edge of the urban core but in its interior.

Arguably, the mosaic and fringe-like quality of contemporary urbanization is nothing new. Even today, when you walk through central London, you can see how the character of adjoining districts was shaped by their origins in distinct villages. It is simply that today, the mosaic pattern is more salient, in part because urbanization is unfolding faster than in the past and in part because satellite imaging and other technologies of remote sensing have given us the means to grasp the texture of a much greater part of the Earth's surface at a glance. What remote sensing has also made clear is how cities become sinks for the *ecosystem services* of the surrounding area, things like fresh water, clean air, and primary productivity in the form of agricultural land, drawing on the resources of a much larger area without experiencing short-term feedback from those draws. For a while at least, rapidly growing cities are able to *externalize* the environmental costs of growth. The result is what ecologists have termed *red loops* (as opposed to green loops)—vicious circles in which urban growth, driven by factors not constrained by the resources of the surrounding area, imposes an unsustainable burden on those surrounding areas and the people and other living things that live there.

One of the easiest ways to illustrate these dynamics is to ask how the human energy budgets of urban areas compare with those of less densely inhabited areas. A rough answer is that cities consume one to two orders of magnitude more food energy than other kinds of built space, in some cases upward of 100,000 kcal per square meter per year. Increasingly, these calories comes from meat and other livestock products.

Livestock on the Urban Periphery

In chapter 7 we looked at long-distance flows of livestock products into East and Southeast Asia. But changes in the scale and character of domestic and regional production are if anything more dramatic. We've alluded to these changes already: the rise of periurban hog operations and broiler batteries. China is not alone here. Thailand, for example, is home to some 7 million pigs and 250 million chickens. The poultry market is highly export oriented, with 70 percent of broilers raised for export. The past two decades have seen rapid industrialization and market concentration. All the strategies you find in industrial poultry production in the United States you find in Thailand and Vietnam too: contract farming, vertical integration, batteries with over 100,000 birds. At the same time, the curve matching "farm" size (that is, size of production facility, be it a farm in the conventional sense or a battery) to number of producers remains *long-tailed*. In Thailand, for example, as of 2008, two-thirds of birds raised as broilers or layers were in facilities of 10,000 birds or more, yet the vast majority of farms had fewer than 100 birds. In China, the world's largest poultry market, the five largest firms involved in poultry production in 2016, encompassing layers and broilers, controlled less than 10 percent of the market. But those large producers have been responsible for some of the most sophisticated innovations in the business, including the use of automation (in essence, remote sensing drones) to improve hygiene.

In the previous chapter, we saw that the consumption of pork, relative to other forms of animal protein, has been on the decline in China. Globally, we could characterize the rise of chicken, over the past forty years, to become the modal form of animal protein, especially in urban settings, as a kind of "small-stock revolution" (by analogy with the broad-spectrum or small-game revolution discussed in chapter 3). But pork remains an important form of meat, with approximately half the world's pork production and consumption happening in China. Here, in contrast to what we saw in the previous chapter, growth has been dominated by domestic industrialization, with market concentration and vertical integration following. In 2014 the WH Group, a Hong Kong–based multisectoral firm with majority ownership of the largest pork processor in China, acquired US-based Smithfield Foods to become the world's largest pork concern. It is not alone among large Chinese agricultural firms, particularly in the pork and feedstock industries, in extending its reach abroad.

In part, what we're seeing here is the other side of the land acquisition phenomenon described in chapter 7—demand for value-added agricultural products, especially those featuring animal protein, has provided Chinese firms with the capital to acquire land, suppliers, and competitors in other parts of the world. But from the domestic perspective, foreign land acquisition represents just a small component of a much broader, state-led push for agricultural intensification. Over the past twenty-five years, the Chinese central government has made it clear that consolidation and vertical integration are to play key roles in this effort. The central government has formulated a special designation for firms that demonstrate a willingness to assume the risks associated with technological innovation and market expansion. These so-called *dragon head* companies receive certain regulatory and financing advantages, but the designation also confers prestige. The emphasis, in assessing firms for dragon head status, is on their role as integrators, processors, and distributors, not primary producers. Feedstock components, soybeans in particular, remain the bottleneck for confined animal production, and feed milling has undergone consolidation and vertical integration too. China is responsible for around 20 percent of global feedstock production, much of it closely integrated with confined pig farming.

Milk provides a third example of intensification, and one where long-distance coupling and domestic growth have a more complicated relationship. The growth of fresh fluid milk consumption in China is of special interest for how it illustrates the roles of taste and ideology in shaping eating habits. Until recently China had no tradition of fluid milk consumption. Adult lactase persistence is rare in the gene pool, making frequent fresh milk drinking uncomfortable for many. Nonetheless, widespread association of milk consumption with modernity has supported rapid growth in the market. In 2008, a number of major dairy producers in China were found to have adulterated fluid milk with melamine, a cyanamide-rich compound used in thermoplastic resins, whose nitrogen content allows it to mimic milk protein in spectroscopic quality tests. More than 300,000 people, including 54,000 infants, were injured. A small number suffered acute kidney failure, and a handful died. In the years since, milk imports have more than doubled year over year. German producers send around 200,000 metric tons of liquid milk to China every year, Australian 60,000, New Zealand more than 50,000. In 2016 the Ningbo-based Moon Lake Investments bought the Van Diemen's Land Co., a major dairy cooperative in Tasmania, outright, with the intent of air-freighting fresh milk daily from Hobart to Ningbo, and eventually other cities in China, and selling it for A$10 to $15 per liter, ten times what it sells for in Australia. Within China, the dairy industry is undergoing rapid consolidation. For the moment, foreign firms retain a controlling stake in many of the key producers.

Market concentration—the degree to which a small number of firms control large segments of the market—has been a key theme in studies of the global food system over the past decade. With meat, concentration in feedstock production, especially soybeans, may matter as much as concentration in livestock. In the United States, the median size of soybean farms doubled between 1987 and 2007, while soybean and cereal processing is dominated globally by just four firms. The outcome has been regulatory capture, with soybean subsidies pushing down the cost of meat production—or, rather, pushing it away from producers and consumers and onto taxpayers. In China, the role of the state in consolidation and vertical integration has been different—a kind of reverse capture, with the state imposing its prerogatives on private firms—and market concentration is at an earlier stage. It is not clear that a concept such as price distortion has the same meaning in places where the state has played such a central role in making markets. What is clear is that enhancing consumption of animal protein, especially in urban areas, has been a priority for state and private institutions alike.

Income, Poverty, Health, and Migration

Before we turn to what people are eating and how they're getting it, I want to look at some of the factors that shape urban life, above all income and migration status. In places such as China where urbanization has been a focus of state development strategy, you would do well to wonder two things. First, are cities more affluent, in terms of their inhabitants' incomes? Second, if cities are more affluent, what effect has this had on the life chances, including nutritional status, of those who inhabit them and those who live in less densely populated outlying areas? Among economists there is broad consensus that incomes tend to be higher in cities. But it also appears that poverty itself is urbanizing: a greater proportion of the people living under whatever arbitrary income threshold one chooses to define poverty live in cities. The urbanization of poverty presents a challenge of definition, since while cash incomes tend to be higher in urban areas, the cost of living is higher too.

This could especially be the case for recent arrivals to the city, who have lost most of the noncash entitlements, including entitlements to food, they had in their home villages (by virtue, say, of having access to land where they could grow food, or kin ties that provided guarantees of support in times of nutritional stress) but have not yet formed social networks in the city to make up for this loss. Urban migrants face a distinctive form of precariousness, a new vulnerability to sudden, even if transient, loss of entitlements to shelter, food, and other basic necessities. Earlier, I mentioned that in China, rural poverty has shifted from an endemic phenomenon to a transient one. How does this square with the urbanization of poverty? Urbanization is reducing rural poverty through a combination of remittances, the transfer of skills and networks on the part of returning migrants, and simply reducing the number of poor people in the countryside. What urbanization is not doing is generating uniform affluence, or even consistent income, in urban areas. So let's first look at income inequality within cities and between cities and rural areas.

In chapter 7, I noted that income stratification is itself becoming a global phenomenon. That is, differences in purchasing power among strata that cut across state boundaries are becoming more significant than differences in purchasing power between rich and poor states. The economist Branko Milanovic has attributed most of this shift to income growth in China. What does the newer, higher-income kind of income inequality look like for people living there?

Overall, income inequality has been growing in China since the mid-1980s, when the central government began emphasizing urban growth. Data from a recurring national income survey, the China Household Income Project, indicate that common measures of income inequality (Gini and Theil indices) are now higher in China than in the world as a whole. Rural inequality has grown faster than urban. Geography matters in more ways than one: the east–west gradient accounts for 30 percent of overall income inequality, with wealth concentrated in the coastal cities. This was the case even before the central government made urban growth a key part of its development strategy, but the coastal–interior divide has grown worse. In part this is an unavoidable consequence of the fact that coastal cities enjoy better access to distant markets.

Within cities, things look different. State-awarded preferential administrative designations intended to accelerate growth in select cities have also had the effect of reducing inequality at the municipal level. This is because these designations—Special Economic Zones, Open Cities—not only make it easier for designated municipalities to take in foreign investment; they also grant some autonomy from central planning and the authority to experiment with social policy. The result is that preferentially designated cities have had greater success implementing policies of income redistribution, including minimum wages, income subsidies, and unemployment insurance, than the country at large. This has had the effect of damping, though not reversing, the common trend toward greater inequality in cities. The effects of urban income inequality are perhaps easiest to see with shelter, with the cost of housing as a proportion of income closely tracking income inequality (Gini) over the first decade of the present century.

What about how urbanization and income inequality affect people's health? Cities, broadly, are healthier than sparsely inhabited areas for a combination of reasons—higher incomes and better access to health care among them. But cities impose their own health penalties. Worldwide, urban residents are at higher risk of schizophrenia and other forms of serious mental illness. They also suffer the effects of air pollution. This is not a uniquely urban burden or one limited to people living in the emerging world. According to 2016 World Health Organization estimates, upward of 80 percent of the Earth's human urban residents are exposed, whether transiently or continuously, to harmful levels of airborne particulate matter. In China, premature mortality due to fine particulate grew more than 40 percent between 2000 and 2010, with 1.25 million deaths attributable to $PM_{2.5}$ exposure across all causes (stroke, chronic obstructive pulmonary disease, lung cancer, ischemic heart disease). Again in China, self-assessed health ("How would you describe your health compared to that of others your age? Excellent, Good, Fair, Poor") tends to be poorer in cities, and it tends to decline with age. It is shaped by income inequality but also by gender. Older women are more reliant on family support than their male coevals, even in cities, where cash pensions have, in principle, eclipsed kin networks as a source of income in the later phases of life. The effects, among the poor, include lower self-assessed health.

Income inequality affects practically every dimension of life, and I could go on: intergenerational transmission of health and education statuses, household carbon footprint. But across the literature on urbanization and life chances in China, one factor recurs more than any other: the *hukou,* the household civil registration status that determines where, that is, in which administrative locality, you are entitled to access all manner of public services, from education for your children to health care to help enforcing employment law. Even after thirty years of widespread rural-to-urban migration, it remains next to impossible to secure a hukou conversion in the major cities no matter how long you've lived there—unless you are very wealthy. Panel data from 2003 to 2006 show that when migrants to Beijing in that era first got to the city, they tended to be healthier than their urban contemporaries, but their advantage disappeared after a few years. Other data indicate long-term migrants have higher serum lipid levels than their rural counterparts, suggesting diet and "lifestyle"—how much physical activity they get over the course of the day—suffer in the brutalizing and discriminatory work environments those without a local hukou are constrained to accept.

The hukou is unique to China, but the loss of social networks and in-kind entitlements is a common experience among migrants to cities worldwide. These are the people who are making the world we live in: assembling the T-shirts and phone handsets, manufacturing the industrial coatings, building and cleaning the new homes they cannot afford to move into, packing the meat in abattoirs and serving it in fast food outlets, and, more and more, especially among women migrants, caring for the aging and the infirm.

How are they feeding themselves?

Hand to Mouth

Late in 2016, with the outcome of the US presidential election still setting in, the essayist Stephen Marche published an eloge to "the Obama years" in the *Los Angeles Review of Books*. I was struck by how Marche captures the way eating changed in these years, the new role that food had come to play in affluent people's lives.

> Over the Obama years, taste expanded and contracted, outward and inward, into ever greater elaboration, line-caught tuna helicoptered in from Pacific trawlers, hundred-course tasting menus with 60 sips of wine, shaved velvet from the antlers of reindeers served on a bed of scavenged moss, and then, as countercurrent, a long dive into the comforts of street food, perfected fried chicken, tripe sandwiches, tacos, ramen, roti, the bread remembered from a tiny village on the outskirts of Lucca, the treasured sustenance from the glamorized peasantry of the global back alleys.

President Obama himself became an emblem of street food mania when, in May 2016, he turned up at a bún chả joint in Hanoi to eat grilled pork, noodles, and spring rolls with chef turned journalist Anthony Bourdain. This was not the only way, in these years, that street food became political. In Mumbai, the Hindu nationalist front Shiv Sena adopted vada pav, a fried mashed potato patty wrapped in a sweet, soft bun, as an emblem of Hindu national identity (and a source of revenue). In other places, efforts to reimagine street food—as animal free, compassionate, lighter on the coronary arteries but every bit as comforting—served a different kind of project of imagining the future. In *Stray Dogs,* street food becomes an emblem of the pathos of life lived on the streets. Presented with a raw cabbage, the antithesis of street food, the protagonist devours it in a blind rage and remains unsatisfied.

Street food as class fetish, street food as tribal chest thumping, street food as alternative future, street food as social commentary. What about street food as a means of satisfying hunger? For that matter, what about fast food, or food from the wet market, the supermarket, or from a backyard garden or chicken coop or a cousin's farm on the outskirts of the city? Can we enumerate the venues where city dwellers, especially the poor, get food?

Let's start with those that involve growing or raising it yourself or getting it from family who maintain plots outside the city. State veterinary surveys tend to ignore urban backyard agriculture, but it is not difficult to imagine why city dwellers might keep a few chickens or a pig. Monogastrics—one-stomached animals, as opposed to ruminants—are efficient converters of organic waste to food, and they don't take up much space. Until recently, there was no consensus on who is involved in urban agriculture, the extent to which it represents a household food security buffer as opposed to a source of cash income, or its potential to bolster food security among the urban poor. Participation varies widely by country (as few as one in ten households in parts of Indonesia, as many as seven in ten in Vietnam). Most urban agriculture is oriented toward growing crops; livestock is not uncommon, but it does not predominate. A key limitation of the data available is that most surveys have not distinguished between agricultural activity happening in the city per se and that happening in outlying areas but with the involvement, in person or by remittances, of migrants. In most parts of the world, rural–urban support networks represent a key form of social capital among poor migrants, especially where food security is concerned. But more and more, noncash support is flowing in the opposite direction, from urban to rural. This is largely down to climate change: with more frequent crop failures, rural inhabitants find themselves more dependent on cash to meet their food needs. The greater density of distribution networks in cities means that if you're paying cash, food is often less expensive there than in the countryside (not to mention the fact that city dwellers tend to have higher cash incomes).

Recent models based on the urban land area available to sustain an urban population have been pessimistic about urban agriculture's potential to serve as a food security buffer. And a comprehensive review of urban agriculture surveys going back to 1980 found that urban agriculture seems to provide no consistent contributions to either household members' macronutritional status or dietary diversity and very modest contributions to household income. These findings raise the question of what cues practitioners of urban agriculture are responding to. (Could agriculture perhaps be playing some kind of signaling role, like the calorically risky but prestigious forms of hunting we looked at in chapter 3?) But the takeaway is that poor migrants to rapidly growing cities are not getting the bulk of their energy and protein, or even substantial micronutrition, by self-provisioning. (Though in certain cities in the interior of China, periurbanization could be creating a situation in which new arrivals come to rely on nearby farmers rather than broader distribution networks to meet part of their food needs.)

Next, let's consider retail points of sale. Globally, food retailing exhibits a pattern of market concentration similar to what we saw in livestock and feedstock production. Here too, China represents both the exemplary growth market and a unique challenge. On the supplier side, markets remain long-tailed even in sectors that are emblems of integration elsewhere, notably poultry, and the central government has not been shy about promoting its own vision of integration. On the consumer side, tastes, expectations, and incomes remain highly regional. One major foreign retailer went to considerable trouble to recreate the experience of an open-air wet market in the fresh fish display you encounter when you first enter the store, only to find that fresh fish did not resonate with consumers away from the coast. Nonetheless, as in the dairy industry, transnational retailers have made headway in China, especially since 2004 when the central government, in conformance with its accession to the World Trade Organization, relaxed rules of entry. That same year, the Japanese convenience store firm Seven & I opened the first 7-Eleven in Beijing. In some cases, transnationals have acquired stakes in domestic retailers; in others they have opened new outlets under their own brands. The rapid proliferation of retail formats caught state regulators by surprise. The kinds of questions they have been forced to address offer a sense of how radically indoor retailing at scale has changed the built environment of provisioning—for instance, How much retail surface area must an outlet offer to qualify as a supermarket? (6,000 square meters.)

In fast food, the story is more intriguing. Earlier, I proposed a Romer-style imaginary force for the income elasticity attributed to meat. I called it the Colonel in homage to the iconic fast food brand character of the same rank. But lately the Colonel has not been doing so well in China. The first Kentucky Fried Chicken opened in Beijing in 1987. At this writing (early 2017), Yum! Brands, the parent company of the since-rebranded KFC, controls around 7,500 outlets in China, mostly KFC but with a smattering of Pizza Hut and local brands Little Sheep and East Dawning. It's not the kind of market penetration they enjoy in the United States, but still respectable. In 2015, Yum! and McDonald's together controlled 38 percent of the fast food market in China. And yet they're hedging. In 2016 Yum! spun off its China operations into a new firm with its own listing on the New York Stock Exchange. The move was widely understood as a way of protecting the parent company from future revenue volatility in China. A few months later, McDonald's sold more than half the value of its local business to a Chinese state-backed firm, Citic, and unloaded another big chunk to the private equity firm Carlyle Group. The reasons are many: Chinese- and Taiwanese-owned chains understand the market better in terms of both the foods people want and how they want to pay (above all, with WeChat); younger, more affluent urban consumers have more sophisticated tastes, while an aging population has less interest in fast food; the novelty of American fast food has worn off. But there's a further cause that appears in all the news coverage of fast food in China: foreign fast food brands are no longer immune to food safety scandals. Meat is at the center of the fast food menu, and it has been at the center of safety concerns. KFC in particular suffered a loss of consumer confidence in 2012 when it transpired that one supplier in Shanxi was aggressively dosing broilers with nontherapeutic antibiotics to meet a forty-five-day grow-out schedule. Two years later in Shanghai, another supplier was found to be repackaging meat that had expired unsold.

These kinds of supply-chain problems provide a vivid illustration of the difficulties of getting animal-source foods to market. But from an epidemiological perspective, adulteration and spoilage represent secondary concerns; it is mainly the fact that fast food emphasizes fatty cuts of meat and other foods high in animal fats, as opposed to fresh fruits and vegetables, that makes it a danger to well-being. Recently, epidemiological studies of the provisioning landscape of the type that have been so resonant in North America—think of news reports of urban "food deserts"—have started to appear in China. One study of this type surveyed 948 neighborhoods encompassing 225 square kilometers across twelve major cities. Its key findings were that three in four retail outlets offered no fruits and vegetables of any kind, but close to two-thirds of large outlets did. These large indoor retailers were nearly twice as common in cities that were more "developed" or "urbanized"—higher per capita household expenditure and disposable income, better transit system, more universities, and so on. But these same more developed cities also had more than twice as many Western-style fast food outlets as their less affluent, less populous counterparts.

Which is to say that in China at present, fast food remains a commodity of affluence. It would be instructive to know *how much* of the new meat consumption over the past twenty years has gone to fast food. If rising meat consumption generated by rising income affluence actually represents consumption of meat that is newly cheap because it is produced under confinement in periurban facilities close to the final point of sale and retailed by large transnationals willing to spend a lot to establish a foothold in China, then maybe the Colonel's mysterious demand-generating activity has more to do with the *price* elasticity of the meat supply than with an intrinsic human craving for meat.

Finally, wet markets, the global back alleys glamorized in vegan cookbooks and *Crazy Rich Asians*. Here I offer anecdote rather than evidence. In spring 2018, when I was revising this book, I spent three months in Pudong, on the southern fringe of Shanghai, trying out parts of the argument on Chinese university students. They were unimpressed, and I spent a lot of time walking the neighborhood rewriting in my head. By luck, not five minutes from my home stood a large wet market, perhaps one of the last of its kind in Shanghai. I took to spending time there every day. Stall keepers speculated on my nationality. A scallion pancake vendor harangued me for not sampling his product. A colleague assured me the place was much seedier than what you'd find out in the country. My students were consistently mystified to run into me there: Did I not prefer the Tesco down the road?

This strange holdover, a source of irritation to municipal authorities, expanded my understanding of the making and selling of meat. Here, pig carcasses were dressed on a band saw, the trotters and livers laid out on plywood trestle tables in the heat and flies. Tilapia flopped about in shallow tubs, occasionally landing on the cement, where they'd continue to flop, their breathing labored. Frogs were ranged in tight ranks under netting. Geese stood in tall cages, waiting. One day toward the end of my time there, on my way home from running errands, I took a shortcut through the market, entering at its northern end. It was four in the afternoon.

Ordinarily the market would be packed with pedestrians and motorbikes. Instead it was quiet, many of the stalls shuttered, vendors squatting out front. Was this some kind of holiday? I got halfway down to find police cordoning off the main laneway. On the far side of the police tape, a man was at work with a plasma torch, taking apart the entrance to a stall. *Yes,* the same colleague said—*just like that.* Apparently, the city had been trying to close it for years on the pretext of putting in a road. But a few months later, I learned the market was not quite done; it had simply shifted south, spilling out onto the undeveloped lots that bordered the highway.

We are still faced with the problem of accounting for the eating habits of the "floating population," those without local hukou and, more broadly, all those whom poverty renders invisible to epidemiological surveillance. Here we have more questions than answers. Let's imagine we were designing an agent-based model to simulate the eating habits of the urban poor. What would we need to know to properly set the parameters of our simulation? Among the things we'd want to know more about is *who* is buying and preparing food, and where they are preparing it, and with what implements. In many parts of the world, provisioning and food preparation have long been women's work. As women enter waged labor outside the home, particularly in large cities where they must commute between home and work, they face a new burden of *time and space poverty,* especially for food preparation and other kinds of work that can only be done at home. It is here where we start to see the practical advantages of meat. It takes a lot more energy, water, and other inputs to produce meat, calorie for calorie, than rice-, cereal-, legume-, or storage organ–based foods, but it often requires less time, space, equipment, and effort to prepare it. You don't even need a cooking vessel—an improvised charcoal brazier will do. Depending on how marginal your living situation is, the fact that meat is perishable may not matter; if you don't have a place to store food, daily procurement is your only option anyway. Meat's material properties—a heat-stable gel that offers a concentrated source of energy, protein, and micronutrients—turns out to be a good fit with the precariousness that defines so many people's lives in emerging urban environments. Meat condenses the long-distance coupling of biomes specialized for feedstocks, animal bodies, and human bodies into something you can hold in your hand and eat on the go, something that is immensely satiating in the immediate term, if not sustaining in the longer term.

We understand less about niche construction—the bidirectional flow of selection cues between a community and its environment—in urban space than we do about analogous phenomena, say, in the peri-Holocene Mediterranean or the dry grasslands of the Western Desert of Australia (recall chapter 3). Nowhere is this ignorance clearer than when it comes to how poor people in urban environments feed themselves.

What is clear is that it is premature to ascribe all or even most of the rise in aggregate meat consumption under urbanization and rising incomes to an intrinsic demand elasticity conditioned by evolution. Indeed, the fact that cities are now where people spend the balance of their time underscores something we saw way back in chapters 1 and 2: versatility, not specialization, has been the key to human flourishing.

Nutrition and Inequality

Poverty is not the unique province of newly urbanizing regions, nor is food insecurity. A 2016 study found that not having enough food was common among adolescents from low-income households in the United States. Respondents in every community canvassed reported knowing someone who had resorted to transactional dating to get food. Not long after, the US Department of Agriculture reported that energy-dense soft drinks and snack foods are overrepresented in the food-buying habits of recipients of supplemental nutrition assistance (SNAP)—though the more interesting finding was that SNAP recipients' purchases were not that far out of line with those of other US consumers.

Findings such as this bring us to the question of how to define malnutrition. In chapter 6, we saw two kinds of malnutrition: undernutrition (energy deficiency) and micronutrient deficiency. A third type, overnutrition, appeared briefly in the Pilbara mining camps where people ate huge volumes of damper (camp bread) and sugared tea and practically nothing else. Today it is overnutrition that gets all the press. Even in less affluent areas, energy overnutrition and obesity, compounded by micronutrient deficiencies, is eclipsing undernutrition as the modal nutrition-related risk to health. For perspective, it is important to note that one in three children in low- and middle-income countries remain at risk of stunting.

The strongest evidence of an elasticity-type relationship between income and a particular kind of food, derived from a large (over 130,000 respondents) survey that asked specifically about both income and eating habits, suggests that it is fruits and vegetables whose consumption is sensitive to income. The price of meat and other foods derived from livestock has been socialized, through feedstock subsidies, trade policy, and patterns of urban growth that favor widely distributed confined animal operations. The price of fruits and vegetables has not been socialized in this way.

Whether their lives unfold in close proximity or on opposite sides of the Earth, livestock and humans, above all cash-poor humans, find themselves locked in an accelerating cycle of extraction and suffering. The animals get eaten by the humans. The humans get eaten by the circumstances in which they live and work. The challenge posed by the Meat Question is less one of affluence than of inequality. Until we recognize that marginalized humans and animals raised under industrial conditions occupy coordinate roles in a single system of economic violence, we will make no progress unworking meat's power.

Epilogue: The End of Meat?

> "I don't eat meat," she said, slightly louder this time.
>
> "My word, so you're one of those 'vegetarians,' are you?" my boss asked. "Well, I knew that some people in other countries are strict vegetarians, of course. And even here, you know, it does seem that attitudes are beginning to change a little. Now and then there'll be someone claiming that eating meat is bad . . . after all, I suppose giving up meat in order to live a long life isn't all that unreasonable, is it?"
>
> "But surely it isn't possible to live without eating meat?" his wife asked with a smile.

> Is it true that human beings are fundamentally cruel? Is the experience of cruelty the one thing we share as a species? Is the dignity that we cling to nothing but self-delusion, masking from ourselves this single truth: that each one of us is capable of being reduced to an insect, a ravening beast, a lump of meat? To be degraded, damaged, slaughtered—is this the essential fate of humankind, one which history has confirmed as inevitable?

This is a long book, but it's impossible to cover everything. I have said nothing about aquaculture; nothing about the role of umami, the savory or gamey quality for which meat is so often prized, in stimulating satiety; nothing about cultured meat, meat grown in bioreactors from minute quantities of muscle tissue harvested from living animals. Some in the tissue culture communities harbor the dream that cultured meat will someday eclipse that taken from living animals. There are causes for doubt. The physiology of tissue growth imposes limits on the efficiency with which organic matter can be converted to muscle, whether on a range, in a confined grow-out facility, or in the controlled environment of a bioreactor, and the proof-of-concept cultured-meat fabrication plants that have attracted so much attention have yet to demonstrate that what is unsustainable in the first two can be made sustainable in the third. For the time being, cultured meat remains on the margin of the meat economy.

Perhaps the biggest omission is biodiversity. Livestock species are not the only animals to suffer genome loss under intensive agriculture. The seven months it took me to write this book saw a steady stream of reports offering new, more pessimistic estimates of the species health of a range of animals not raised for meat, from giraffes to cheetahs to most of the order Primates apart from humans. The expansion of agriculture accounts for the single greatest threat to wild animal species, well ahead of hunting and fishing and rivaled only by logging and urbanization. There is no consensus on how to price biodiversity loss, and it is difficult to compare it to conventional dimensions of the cost of growing food such as energy, water, or pollution. But it is real nonetheless.

So for all that I've tried to make this book comprehensive, it offers just a single perspective on the Meat Question. This perspective is centered on my conviction that the economic violence of meat has less to do with who can and cannot afford it than with how meat serves to prop up a system of asymmetric benefits from all forms of economic activity, not just that related to food. Growing demand for meat is not simply an outcome of growing affluence. It is a symptom of the inequality and oppression that have accompanied that affluence.

But perhaps I have not made my perspective clear enough. From the outset I wanted this book to have a certain deadpan quality. I wanted the experiences that formed the sources of my own interest in the topic to remain outside the frame. I did not want to alienate readers who came to the theme with a perspective different from my own. As we saw in chapter 6, what we eat is among the most intimate facts about us, and there is something uniquely unnerving about having our eating behavior observed. When it comes to eating, surveillance just about always entails judgment. No other dimension of behavior is fraught in this way, not even sex, for in contrast to sex, and more than sleeping or handling money, eating is something we do in the presence of others. Vegetarians feel judged by meat eaters, and meat eaters, even when they form the overwhelming majority, often feel put on the defensive in the presence of vegetarians, as the passage quoted in the first epigraph, from the Korean novelist Han Kang's *The Vegetarian,* makes exquisitely clear. I did not want anyone to come to this book in a defensive state of mind, not least because this book began not with conviction but with doubt.

With a handful of exceptions, I have kept a vegetarian diet for more than twenty-five years and a vegan or plant-based diet for more than nineteen. When I first stopped eating meat, I could not have said why, save that it seemed like a worthwhile experiment. When I gave up eating other kinds of animal source foods, my reasons were clear. Today you'd describe them in terms of footprint, but at the time I thought of it in terms of fairness: I wanted to limit my claim on the Earth's resources to levels that would allow the largest number of people to enjoy the quality of life that I took for granted. I wanted my own way of living to represent a vote for a *K*-selected, as opposed to an *r*-selected, humanity.

My thinking about the relationship between my own choices and the life chances of people in distant parts of the world was confused, but I was clear about one thing: I was not getting into this out of concern for animal liberation. Indeed, animal liberationists drove me a bit crazy. Their vision of the world seemed limited in its refusal to take contextual environmental and economic factors into account. Perhaps, I thought, in some circumstances the most ethical thing to do, if by *ethical* you meant minimizing resource depletion and maximizing the life chances of all living things, was for humans to eat animals. Veganism made sense for me, living an urban life, but it might not make sense in places, say, with an ample supply of fish and little arable land. (The example I sometimes gave was Norway. Later, when I'd worked on a goat dairy on the coast of Norway and when I'd come to understand that the cost of transporting food from one place to another is not always the dominant term in its total cost, I had to revise this view.) Animal liberationists, I felt, missed this. Their vision struck me as arrogant in its universalist pretensions. The fact that my own reasoning bore the imprint of the same coarse-grained consequentialism as theirs escaped my attention.

Time passed. I learned how to cook and got smart about protein and B_{12}. Veganism became the defining fact of my adult life, affecting every decision I made about how to feed, clothe, and care for myself. And then something curious happened. When I'd been keeping an animal-free diet for about ten years, I realized that I was no longer certain why I was doing it. I mean that in two senses. First, I was no longer certain my old reasons were valid. Second, I was no longer certain my old reasons were still my reasons. At some point along the way, I had become more realistic about the weight my own actions carried, or failed to carry, in nudging humanity toward a more inclusive form of fairness. At the same time, in the intervening years I had become something of an animal liberationist; at the very least, I was committed to a much broader understanding of the interests of other-than-human animals.

By then I was aware of the role played by livestock in the colonization of Australia. This was not a new theme in the history of empire. But historians had mainly treated livestock as factors in *environmental* history, that is, in the transformation of the human-inhabited biome of the Americas, Africa, Asia, and the Pacific Islands into landscapes congenial to food production. This is a phenomenon that has played out everywhere farmers and herders have displaced foragers. You see it in Australia, but you see something else too: not just livestock remaking the land but livestock remaking the lives of the people. And these were not just any people. These were the models for Man the Hunter. For human behavioral ecologists, the indigenous foragers of the north and west of Australia represented, in the discipline's early years, the closest living thing to a type specimen, a society that within living memory had been getting its living, so the hypothesis went, in much the same way as it had since the late Pleistocene.

Here, I thought, was a book waiting to be written: about livestock intensification and the dispossession of the people whose habits have been the basis for so many specious claims about the role of meat in the history of humanity, about how meat became a global commodity and what that has meant for dispossessed people everywhere. It did not hurt that Australia is among the world's leading exporters of livestock products or that its livestock economy was dealing with the effects of a seventeen-year drought. I could clarify my own sense of the relationships between environmental justice, animal welfare, and economic constraints on human action and maybe help others think critically about these things. This book began, then, as an effort to find out two things. On a personal level, I wanted to see if I still had valid reasons for being vegan. But more than that, I wanted to see if I could provide an enriched basis for reasoning about the relationship between humans and other vertebrates, one that went beyond the emancipationist arguments common in the animal liberation literature to take into account the differentiated economic and ethical roles that different kinds of animals, humans included, play in our world. To say that animals are "just like us" in certain key respects did not, I felt, go far enough: I wanted to show that animals and marginalized humans have been made to play coordinate roles in a single system of economic violence. Animals and humans have been played against one another, their interests made mutually exclusive, so that in championing the interests of the one—to living space, a good diet, and freedom from oppression—we end up trampling those of the other.

At the same time, I wanted to show that arguments, as the boss's wife says to Yeong-hye in *The Vegetarian*, that it isn't possible to live without meat—implicitly, because of the role that meat played in human evolution—dramatically misapprehend the relationship between biology and destiny. If anything, the strategic flexibility that earlier humans showed toward meat demonstrates exactly why we should be neither quick to assume that the present-day surge in meat eating represents demand elasticity unleashed by rising incomes nor that a world without meat could never come to pass. No one frets over how to convert the emerging urban areas that are to be the setting for so much meat eating into something like the Plio-Pleistocene savanna. Evolutionary conditioning is not fate in the narrow sense that past behavior dictates future behavior but in the broader sense that we come to new environments with a repertoire of faculties and liabilities born of our past experiences of fashioning niches out of the materials at hand. In the case of the human nutritional niche, these faculties include a remarkable capacity for dietary breadth. The liabilities include a tendency toward niche entrenchment—digging a channel for behavior so deep that it comes to maladaptively constrain the horizon of possibilities of future behavior. In the limit, entrenchment can make it impossible to imagine a new channel, a new niche, when the conditions that made the existing one productive no longer hold.

There is no question that the dynamic landscape in which humans have constructed their niche is shifting, and shifting at a rate that will make it difficult, if not impossible, to establish a new niche before we have exhausted the present one. If this is a crisis, it is a crisis not just of "the environment" but of capitalism, which has proved impervious to signals of impending niche exhaustion.

The meat economy is just part of what is driving the series of crises that seem to define global capitalism today. But it is a bigger part than we tend to think. One recent effort to explore the environmental and health implications of different scenarios for the future of human diet concluded that only under a strict vegan scenario—worldwide abandonment of animal-source foods—could food production and distribution contribute to climate stabilization to a degree in line with the proportion of greenhouse gas emissions currently linked to food.

The same study found that the priced benefits of reducing meat consumption related to human health would be greater than those related to emissions linked to climate change. For both kinds of benefit, health related and environmental, the benefits of adopting a diet lower in meat and other animal-source foods would be greater in aggregate in less-affluent parts of the world but greater per capita in the affluent world. That is, at a population level, poor and emerging countries stand to benefit more, but at an individual or household level, consumers in rich countries have greater incentive to overcome the entrenchment, economic and cultural, that shapes their own dietary habits.

The finding that the "health-related" benefits of reducing meat consumption outweigh the "environmental" benefits, and that per capita benefits are greater in the affluent than in the poor and emerging worlds, would seem to lend credence to the belief that what drives behavior change is self-interest, not interest in the flourishing of socially distant others. In the prologue, I pointed out that not so long ago it was possible to imagine that consumers in affluent countries *would* change their food behavior for the benefit of distant others—or at least that they would adopt an understanding of self-interest broad enough to encompass the benefits that would accrue to them from the flourishing of people they would never meet. Today, a world in which people give up anything, let alone a favored kind of food, for the benefit of distant others feels very far away. But it would be a mistake to assume, simply because self-interest is the tool we have at hand, that self-interest is enough to bring about the kind of change needed to avoid niche depletion.

The crisis of meat, like the larger crises of which it forms one part, is not a crisis of consumer behavior. Indeed, the reduction of political responsibility to choices one makes as a consumer is part of the problem. A personal decision to give up animal-source foods will not have an appreciable effect on the circumstances that condemn humans and animals to oppression in the parts of the world responsible for most of the growth in animal consumption. It may have other valuable effects—for instance, reducing your carbon footprint and your complicity in animal suffering. If enacted by a large enough part of the population in the affluent world, it might make confined animal production, in your own country or elsewhere, modestly less profitable. But if, as I've argued, the road to the global meat economy was paved not with insatiable demand but rather with a ratcheting of production constrained loosely, if at all, by prior demand, why should we expect a tide of changing consumer preferences to rein in production now? Via feedstock subsidies and the externalization of pollution costs, not to say an elongation and obfuscation of value chains that makes the brutality of livestock production invisible to all but a handful of people, the cost of meat has been socialized and its price at the consumer point of sale reduced to historic lows. Giving up meat has many benefits, but we need to recognize the limits of consumer activism. Your giving up meat will not change the circumstances that lead a person such as the protagonist of *Stray Dogs*, or any of the 800 million people in the world who live in extreme poverty, to make the decisions they do about how to feed themselves and their families. Recall the Chatham House study cited in the prologue: household-level demand elasticity for meat, where it was found at all, was found in the affluent world. As I argued in the previous chapter, the causes of apparent aggregate demand elasticity are too complex to be reduced to innate craving.

There is a danger, in speaking of crisis, be it the crisis of capitalism, of climate change, or of growing demand for meat, that we will allow ourselves to acquiesce in the foreshortened horizon of the future that has led us to the present. It would be folly to offer a detailed scenario for the next hundred years. But I am convinced that if humanity survives to 2119, there is a chance that the society of that time will be one where consuming animals is uncommon, perhaps unheard of. For that to happen, the pressures of niche depletion must certainly play a role. But these pressures alone will not be enough. It will also take an awareness that the violence done to animals raised for food is economic violence, in fact, is of a piece with the violence done to a large segment of humanity in the name of unconstrained accumulation.

Notice that in the foraging societies we looked at in chapter 3, meat was, and is, an index of egalitarianism. In contrast, in the societies we looked at in part II, whether you subscribe to the income elasticity thesis or the alternative I've proposed, meat has become an index of inequality. It is when we start to see the ethical significance of foreswearing meat in terms of the role meat plays in making possible a regime of economic violence that affects animals and humans *together* that we begin to imagine how meat will end.

A few months after my trip to V Street, I was in Laos. After a few weeks of travel, subsisting mainly on green papaya salads, I found I could no longer function properly. It began to seem inevitable that I would eat meat. I had imagined this possibility in advance and was surprised at how upsetting I found it in the event—as I said, my reasons for keeping a vegan diet have changed over the years. My girlfriend and I went to an open-air stall near where we were staying in Vientiane, roofed but with no walls, the kitchen at the front, a fridge with bottled water and the ubiquitous Beerlao at the back, rows of plastic tables and chairs. We ordered a fish, most likely a mud carp. It arrived, breaded and charred on the outside, a bundle of lemongrass in its mouth. The physiological relief it provided was virtually instant. I was full of sorrow but also gratitude. I did not think this fish had given itself to me as a gift. But I was grateful to it nonetheless, even as I recognized that my gratitude was self-serving: the fish had had no say in the matter. It is easy to say in retrospect that I had been careless, that with better preparation I might have avoided having to eat meat. But the truth is, I had been both careful and committed, trawling the aisles of the convenience stores in the frontier town of Phonsavan for oatmeal and roasted almonds, letting myself get to the point where I was in danger of falling over in the street. The fish may not have been a gift, but the capacity to thrive on a wide range of foods certainly is. For that too I was grateful—grateful that I could incorporate the fish's body into my own and feel restored.

To imagine a world in which humans no longer get any part of their subsistence from animals is to imagine a world where the bond of economic necessity, of precariousness, between humans and animals has been succeeded by a bond of mutual regard, among humans and on the part of humans for other living things. This is a more radical vision than that which underlies arguments for the cessation of meat eating on grounds of health, or carbon footprint, or animal sentience. But the history of our own species is one of radical divergences from niches past—from alloparenting and cooperative child rearing to dietary diversification to reflexivity to domestication to urbanization. The basic political question of our time, as Han suggests in the passage from *Human Acts* quoted in the second epigraph above, is whether human beings are fundamentally cruel, condemned to reduce one another to lumps of meat. To answer that question in the negative will require a divergence, in diet among other things, as radical as any we have experienced before.

Notes

Prologue. Breakfast at the End of Empire

Page 1 *Australia–China cattle trade*: Sedgman 2015; Heath and Petrie 2016.

Page 1 *Melbourne–Chongqing flight*: Whitley 2015.

Page 1 *Australian live export*: Wright and Muzzatti 2003; Phillips and Santurtun 2013; Ferguson 2011; and Thomas, Robinson, and Armitage 2016.

Page 2 *Different tokens of exchange*: Guyer 2004; Graeber 2011.

Carnivore Planet

Page 3 *Demand for meat, costs of confined production generally*: Foley et al. 2011; Herrero and Thornton 2013; Pelletier and Tyedmers 2013; Thornton 2010; Kearney 2010; Steinfeld et al. 2006.

Page 3 *2014 Queensland cattle cull*: Weise 2015.

Page 4 *Water footprint*: Mekonnen and Hoekstra 2012.

Page 4 *Greenhouse gas emissions*: Gerber et al. 2013; Vermeulen Campbell, and Ingram 2012.

Page 5 *Reactive nitrogen species*: Pelletier and Tyedmers 2013.

Page 5 *Declining marginal yield gains*: Foley et al. 2011; Bajželj et al. 2014; Bailey, Froggat, and Wellesley 2014.

Income and Evolution

Page 6 *Poverty and urbanization*: Samman 2013; Ravallion, Chen, and Sangraula 2007.

Page 6 *"There is absolutely no doubt"*: Smil 2014, 67.

Page 7 *Chatham House survey*: Wellesley, Harper, and Froggat 2015.

Man the Hunter

Page 8 *"Hunting is the master behavior pattern"*: Laughlin 1968, 304.

Page 8 *"despite the fact that the majority of peoples"*: Lee and DeVore 1968, 4, emphasis in the original.

Page 9 *"hunting is so universal"*: Lee and DeVore 1968, 7.

Page 9 *"The diet is primarily vegetarian"*: Gould 1980, 62.

Page 9 *"Men's hunting activities"*: Hamilton 1980, 11.

Page 10 *Dispossession of foragers*: White 1983; Rowse 1998.

Page 10 *Child removal, residential schools*: Attwood 2005; Niezen 2017.

Page 10 *Limited autonomy*: Austin-Broos 2009.

Page 10 *Debility in Indigenous communities*: Smith 2016; Webster 2016.

Affluence

Page 11 *Sahlins on affluence*: Sahlins [1972] 2000, 95.

Page 12 *Yolngu foraging*: Sahlins [1972] 2000, 109–114, citing McCarthy and McArthur 1960.

Page 13 *"At all settlements rations are distributed"*: McArthur 1960, 14–17.

Page 15 *Yolngu population densities*: Keen 2006.

The Paleolithic Diet

Page 15 *Index sources*: Eaton and Konner 1985; Eaton, Eaton, and Konner 1997; Cordain et al. 2000.

Page 17 *"The range and content of foods they consume"*: Eaton and Konner 1985, 283–285, my emphasis.

Page 17 *Other estimates of forager dietary ratios*: For example, Ströhle and Hahn 2011.

Page 17 *History of ethnographic atlases*: Hardy 2010; Berson 2017.

Page 18 *Meat and masculinity*: Adams [1990] 2015.

Page 18 *"Eat less processed food and less fatty meat" (paraphrasing)*: Katz and Meller 2014.

Carrying Capacity

Page 19 *"a crisis of lifestyle"*: Pollan 2009, 171.

Page 20 *"competition for foods of the meat–fish–poultry–eggs group"*: Sherman 1950, 138.

Page 20 *Demand-side mitigation out of the question*: Bailey et al. 2014.

Violence

Page 21 *Politics of sight*: Pachirat 2011; compare Bulliet 2007.

Chapter 1. Humans

A Day at the Beach

Page 27 *Conversation slows and grows more abstract*: Wiessner 2014.

Page 29 *Coprolites*: Ungar and Sponheimer 2013.

Page 30 *Paleosols*: Potts 2012b.

Page 30 *Stable-isotope ratios*: Ungar and Sponheimer 2013.

Page 30 *Skeletal cut marks*: Braun 2013.

Ethnographic Analogies

Page 32 *Chimpanzee model untenable*: Sayers, Raghanti, and Lovejoy 2012.

Page 32 *Behavioral ecology's racist past*: Berson 2014.

Page 32 *Forager studies done sensitively*: Bliege Bird and Bird 2008.

An Early Hominin Chronology

Page 34 *The hominins are a clade*: Villmoare et al. 2015; Antón and Snodgrass 2012; Schwartz 2012; Neubauer and Hublin 2012.

Page 35 *Projecting patterns of life history on skeletal remains*: Dean 2016; Schwartz 2012.

Page 36 *Developmental plasticity*: Antón and Snodgrass 2012.

Page 36 *Cooperative breeding*: Hrdy 2012; Hawkes 2012; Rosenberg 2012.

Equifinality

Page 38 *Domesticity*: Wilson 1988.

Page 38 *Niches*: Braun 2013; Fuentes 2016.

Stone Tools

Page 38 *The earliest evidence*: Lewis and Harmand 2016; Potts 2012a; Braun 2013; Dennell and Roebroeks 2005; Liu, Hu, and Wei 2013.

Page 39 *Débitage*: Pelegrin 2009; Braun 2013.

Page 39 *Oldowan and Acheulean*: For caveats on lithic technology chronologies, Shea 2011.

Faunal Assemblages

Page 40 *Taphonomy and butchery*: Braun 2013.

Page 40 *"Meat made us human"*: Bunn 2007.

Teeth and Versatility

Page 41 *Functional adaptivity*: Ungar, Grine, and Teaford 2006.

Page 42 *Microwear*: Ungar and Sponheimer 2011, 2013.

Page 42 *"The most obvious conclusion we can draw"*: Ungar 2012, S325.

Page 42 *Other tissues possibly*: Walker, Zimmerman, and Leakey 1982.

Chapter 2. Hunting

Improved Diet

Page 45 *Bioavailability*: Leonard, Zimmerman, and Leakey 2007.

Page 46 *Nutrition transition*: Foley et al. 2011; Tilman and Clark 2014, 519:

> Relative to the average global diet of 2009, the 2050 global-average per capita income-dependent diet would have 15% more total calories and 11% more total protein, with dietary composition shifting to having 61% more empty calories ["calories from refined fats, refined sugars, alcohols and oils"], 18% fewer servings of fruits and vegetables, 2.7% less plant protein, 23% more pork and poultry, 31% more ruminant meat, 58% more dairy and egg and 82% more fish and seafood.

Page 47 *Relishes*: Mintz 1985.

Page 47 *Metabolic niche construction*: O'Brien and Laland 2012; Ungar and Sponheimer 2013; Fumagalli et al. 2015.

Page 47 *Amino acid roles*: Layman et al. 2015.

Page 48 *Working memory, episodic memory, and imagination*: Nowell 2010.

Enter Hunting

Page 48 *Million-year interval*: Foley et al. 2016

Page 48 *The Acheulean industries*: Gamble, Gowlett, and Dunbar 2011; Kuhn 2013.

Page 49 *Metapopulation*: Roebroeks and Soressi 2016.

Page 49 *At least two distinct social–technical horizons*: But see Gao et al. 2013.

Middle Paleolithic Eurasia

Page 49 *Dating the Middle Paleolithic*: Stiner 2013

Page 50 *Use of fire*: Attwell, Kovarovic, and Kendal 2015. The earliest proposed ash deposits come from Wonderwerk Cave, South Africa (1.7 Ma), and Koobi Fora, Kenya (1.6 Ma). The first unmistakable evidence of hearth construction comes from Gesher Benot Ya'aqov, Israel, c.790–690 ka.

Page 50 *Levallois technique*: Pelegrin 2009; Kuhn 2013; Roebroeks and Soressi 2016.

Page 50 *Uses of stone artifacts in Europe*: Stiner 2013; Conard et al. 2015.

Page 50 *Resins and adhesives*: Roebroeks and Soressi 2016.

Page 50 *Operative chains*: Haidle 2010.

Page 50 *"It is safe to say that MP people were dedicated large game hunters"*: Stiner 2013, S290.

Page 51 *"The finds from the Horse Butchery Site"*: Conard et al. 2015, 14.

Page 51 *Faunal assemblage analysis*: Clark and Kandel 2013; Fiorenza et al. 2015.

Page 51 *Neanderthals relied extensively on plant foods*: Naito et al. 2016; Hardy 2010.

Page 52 *Practically no meat*: Henry et al. 2014; Weyrich et al. 2017.

Page 52 *Protein toxicity*: a.k.a. hyperaminoacidemia, "rabbit starvation." See Layman et al. 2015.

Page 52 *Inuit diet*: Fiorenza et al. 2015.

Middle Stone Age Africa

Page 53 *Still Bay and Howiesons Poort industries*: Wurz 2013; Clark and Kandel 2013.

Page 54 *Effective population*: "The size of an idealized [i.e., panmictic] population that would show the same amount of genetic diversity as the population of interest" (Ellegren and Galtier 2016, 422). Effective population underestimates actual population by up to an order of magnitude.

Page 54 *Effective population of* H. sapiens, *genetic swamping*: Pearson 2013; Roebroeks and Soressi 2016.

Page 54 *Maladaptive technology loss, treadmill theory*: Collard, Buchanan, and O'Brien 2013; Andersson and Read 2016.

The Physiological Legacy of Dietary Versatility

Page 55 *Both*: Tip of the hat to Emily Pawley.

Page 55 *Social precocity*: Hrdy 2012; Rosenberg 2012; Phillips-Silver and Keller 2012; Tomasello 2008, chap. 4.

Encephalization

Page 56 *Cognitive buffering*: Isler and Van Schaik 2014.

Page 56 *This has often been taken to mean meat*: For instance, Finch and Stanford 2004, 11, citing Milton 1999.

Page 57 *"animal products, nuts, or underground tubers"*: Aiello and Wheeler 1995, 211. Wrangham's proposal (Wrangham et al. 1999) that cooking played the decisive role in the development of human life history has attracted a lot of attention. In essence: only cooked underground storage organs, not meat, could meet *H. erectus*'s energetic needs during lean seasons, cooking increases the risk of food theft by concentrating food resources in one place, *ergo* women needed to retain large males as hearth guards. The story rests on sketchy evidence for controlled use of fire at 1.6 Ma, overly strong assumptions about the sexual division of labor, and rather free speculation about the origins of human pair-bonding—and it does not jibe with new evidence about mid-Pleistocene plant consumption (Henry, Brooks, and Piperno 2014).

Page 57 *Brain–*X *tradeoffs*: Navarrete, van Schaik, and Isler 2011.

Page 57 *Allocation trade-offs*: Isler and Van Schaik 2014.

Page 57 *As diet improved*: Leonard, Snodgrass, and Robertson 2007.

Dietary Quality Revisited

Page 58 *No reason to imagine earlier hominins were* less *efficient at DHA synthesis than we*: Carlson and Kingston 2007; Cunnane and Crawford 2014.

Adiposity

Page 59 *Bipedalism*: Niemitz 2010; Roberts and Thorpe 2014.

Page 59 *Compared to other mammals*: For this paragraph and the following, see Kuzawa 1998; Kuzawa et al. 2014.

Page 59 *Physiological buffering*: The role of diet in ectopic adipogenesis—the growth of fat in places where it does not serve a structurally or physiologically essential purpose—is a topic of ongoing research. Excess sugar intake has been implicated, as has excess consumption of saturated fats. See Ma et al. 2015; Fekete et al. 2015.

Physical Activity

Page 60 *Total energy expenditure*: Pontzer et al. 2014. How do you measure energy expenditure in circumstances that approximate normal everyday physical activity? The current gold standard uses *doubly-labeled water* (DLW), water containing enriched levels of rare stable isotopes of both hydrogen (^{2}H) and oxygen (^{18}O). Study participants drink a dose of doubly-labeled water. Over ten to fourteen days, the labeled moieties leave the body via excretion, perspiration, and respiration. Urine contains both hydrogen and oxygen, while expired carbon dioxide contains just oxygen. Daily urine sampling allows you to estimate the rate at which carbon dioxide is being expired: labeled oxygen will disappear from the urine faster than labeled hydrogen relative to its molar abundance in water, and the rate divergence indicates how much labeled oxygen is being lost through respiration. DLW has been validated to within 2 to 3 percent of laboratory respirometric estimates of energy expenditure. See Leonard 2012 and Pontzer 2015.

Page 60 *TEE grade shift tracks the shift to a slower life history*: That is, the TEE:rate-of-growth regression lines for all eutherians and that for the order Primates run parallel, with that for Primates shifted to the left.

Page 60 *Adaptation to food scarcity*: Pontzer 2012.

Page 60 *Gains in TEE plateau rapidly*: Pontzer 2015.

Page 61 *Cursorial hunting*: Bramble and Lieberman 2004; Pontzer 2012; Raichlen and Polk 2013.

A Holobiont Perspective

Page 62 *"a large interdependent and symbiotic community"*: Warinner and Lewis 2015, 740.

Page 62 *Taxonomic diversity*: Karasov, Martínez del Rio, and Caviedes-Vidal 2011.

Page 62 *Rapid remodeling*: David et al. 2014.

Page 63 Bacteroides *prevalence*: Moeller et al. 2014.

Page 63 *Loss of treponemes*: Obregon-Tito et al. 2015; Warinner and Lewis 2015.

The Roots of Versatility

Page 65 *Long-term climate periodicity*: Maslin and Christensen 2007; Potts 2012a, 2012b. Regional climate does not always track global trends (Behrensmeyer 2006; Blome et al. 2012).

Page 65 *Periods of high volatility correspond best*: Potts 2012b.

Chapter 3. Modernity

Fire Sticks and Planning

Page 67 *Human life history varies considerably*: Kuzawa and Bragg 2012.

Page 68 *"Martu use a five-tiered seral classification"*: Bird et al. 2016.

Page 69 *"nurturing, feeding, giving it room to grow"*: Bird et al. 2016, S71.

The Problem with Modernity

Page 72 *Problems with behavioral modernity*: Shea 2011.

Page 72 *Australia as a counterexample*: Habgood and Franklin 2008. Mitochondrial phylogenies indicate Sahul was colonized in a single migration event at 50 ka (Tobler et al. 2017); optical dating of artifact assemblages suggests an earlier date (Clarkson et al. 2017).

Diet in the Upper Paleolithic

Page 73 H. sapiens *dispersals*: Hublin 2015; Blome et al. 2012.

Page 74 *Brief windows of overlap*: Roussel, Soressi, and Hublin 2016.

Page 74 *Relying more on fast-moving small prey*: Stiner et al. 2000.

Page 75 *Faster-moving animals faster to reproduce*: Compare Fisher, Blomberg, and Owens 2002 for Australia.

Page 75 *Farther west at the same latitude*: For this paragraph and the two that follow, Dias, Detry, and Bicho 2016.

Page 76 *Trend in dental microwear*: For these paragraphs, see El Zaatari and Hublin 2014; El Zaatari et al. 2016.

Page 78 *Genetic mutation as the cause of enhanced working memory*: Wynn and Coolidge 2010. These hypotheses underestimate the functional anatomical complexity of working memory (Jin and Maren 2015).

Megafauna Extinctions

Page 80 *Overkill*: The first five paragraphs of this discussion draw on Meltzer 2015.

Page 82 *Indexical value of redistributing large game*: Bird et al. 2013.

Page 82 *Colonization accounted for roughly 60 percent of the variation*: Bartlett et al. 2016.

Page 82 *Nowhere near understanding*: The same can be said of megafauna—Malhi et al. 2016.

Page 83 *Megafauna extinctions in Sahul*: Johnson et al. 2016; contrast Wroe et al. 2013.

Subsistence Strategy and Social Structure

Page 84 *Intensification in other domains*: For instance, Vallverdú et al. 2010.

Page 84 *Hunting sand monitors*: Bird et al. 2016. Without burning, the expected yield is 35 kcal/hour, a net energy loss. With burning, it is over 1,500 kcal/hour.

Page 85 *Absence of longer-term motivation*: Bliege Bird 2015.

Page 85 *Sharing of unpredictable resources*: Bliege Bird 2015.

Page 85 *Immediate-return*: Woodburn 1982.

Page 85 *Aversion to selfishness among the Martu*: Bliege Bird and Bird 2008.

Page 85 *Demand sharing*: Austin-Broos 2009.

Page 86 *Saturation utility*: Jones et al. 2013.

Page 88 *"In a sense, it is the dependable efforts of the women"*: Gould 1980, 62.

Page 88 *Women's emphasis on low-variance resources*: Bliege Bird 2015, 251.

Page 89 *If your sole object were to ensure you were adequately fed*: Bliege Bird and Bird 2008.

Chapter 4. Domestication

Page 91 *Register boundaries*: Guyer 2004.

What Is Domestication?

Page 93 *Living tools*: Shipman 2010.

Page 94 *Niche construction*: Zeder 2016; McClure 2015.

Pathways to Domestication

Page 94 *Three pathways*: Zeder 2012.

Page 95 *Dogs*: Shannon et al. 2015.

Page 95 *Cattle in the Jordan*: Marom and Bar-Oz 2013.

Page 96 *Horses*: Outram et al. 2009.

What Caused Domestication?

Page 97 *Residential mobility*: Stiner et al. 2000, 2009; Dias, Detry, and Bicho 2016.

Lines of Evidence

Page 99 *Cyprus*: Vigne 2015.

Page 99 *Domestication of humans*: Leach 2003.

Page 100 *Problems with genetic evidence*: Larson 2011.

Page 101 *Neolithic livestock domestications*: Larson and Fuller 2014; Cucchi et al. 2011; Mengoni Goñalons 2008.

Scenes of Domestication

Southwest Asia

Page 103 *Gods and bulls in Southwest Asia*: Cauvin 2001.

Page 103 *Stored in households*: Bliege Bird 2015, 250.

Page 104 *Use of domesticates for feasts*: Asouti and Fuller 2013.

China

Page 104 *Neolithization in China*: Cohen 2011; Jing, Flad, and Yunbing 2008; Chi and Hung 2013; Zhuang 2015; Cucchi et al. 2011.

Page 105 *Jiahu flutes*: Zhang et al. 1999.

Diffusion

Page 107 *Mesolithic population replacement in Iberia*: McClure et al. 2008.

Page108 *Seaweed foddering in the Orkneys*: Tresset and Vigne 2011.

Domestication Syndrome

Page 108 *Morphological markers of domestication*: Leach 2003.

Page 108 *Belyaev's foxes*: Trut, Oskina, and Kharlamova 2009.

A Landscape, Not a Membrane

Page 110 *Domestication continuum*: Smith 2001.

Page 110 *Immediate- and delayed-return foraging*: Woodburn 1982.

Page 111 *"Over the last 150 years"*: Terrell et al. 2003, 340.

Page 111 *Southeast Asia*: Scott 2009.

Page 112 *Mobility waxed and waned*: Honeychurch 2014.

Domestication and Nutrition

Page 112 *Stable-isotope analysis:* Fontanals-Coll et al. 2016.

Page 113 *Anemia*: Ascorbic acid facilitates the gut absorption of the non-heme-bound iron common in plant-source foods. It also plays a broader, poorly understood role in iron metabolism. See Beck et al. 2014; Lane and Richardson 2014.

Page 114 *Zoonoses*: Karesh et al. 2012; Muehlenbein 2016.

Page 114 *Jomon and Yayoi*: Temple 2010; Nakajima, Nakajima, and Yamazaki 2010.

Empire

Page 116 *Pasturage made the steppe productive*: Honeychurch 2014; Honeychurch and Makarewicz 2016.

Page 117 *Livestock as currency*: Guyer 2004; Hutchinson 1996.

Chapter 5. Enclosures

Page 125 *Remarkably quiet*: At the height of the iron boom, in 2010, the population of greater Port Hedland was about 14,000.

Page 126 *Wittenoom Gorge*: Today the Banyjima are recognized as part of the Martu nation, discussed in chapter 3.

Page 126 *Iron boom*: Bradsher 2016.

Page 127 *The Pilbara*: The Pilbara is a region of dry tropical desert and scrub of approximately 508,000 square kilometers extending in a narrow band from the De Grey River north to the Ashburton River and from the Indian Ocean coast inland east approximately 720 kilometers (450 miles) . It is flat, with an average elevation of 990 meters above sea level. The climate is monsoonal. This is the hottest part of Australia: wet season daytime temperatures at Marble Bar often top 49°C (120°F), with 40°C (104°F) common throughout the region. It is rare for daytime readings to fall below 14°C (57°F) in the coolest part of the dry season, July and August, though in some places, overnight dry season temperatures do get below freezing. Rainfall varies more than 40 percent year to year, with an annual precipitation of 200 to 350 millimeters (8 to 14 inches), most of it in the form of summer cyclones.

Page 127 *The same could be said of petroleum*: Mitchell 2011.

A Metabolic View of Colonization

Page 128 *Intensification and modernization*: Boserup 1965; Leach 1999; Cullather 2010.

Grazing

Page 130 *As early as 7 ka*: Honeychurch and Makarewicz 2016; Dunne et al. 2012. On the Bantu expansion, Macholdt et al. 2014.

Page 131 *Grazing thrived in those places*: Dye and La Croix 2013.

Southeast Australia

Page 131 *Van Diemen's Land*: Boyce 2010.

Page 131 *Transport and assignment*: Foxhall 2011; Reid 2003.

Page 131 *War in Tasmania*: Ryan 2013.

Page 132 *Squatting*: Weaver 1996; Alston, Harris, and Mueller 2012.

Page 133 *"Imagine you have lived your life"*: Kenny 2007, 167; cf. Paterson 2010.

Western North America

Page 133 *Dry grasslands*: For the next two paragraphs, Zappia 2016; Sheridan 2007.

Page 134 *Bison-centered niche*: Isenberg 2000. Prior to the introduction of horses, Plains communities had hunted bison by driving them toward bluffs and precipitating a stampede.

Page 134 *Railroads . . . Chicago*: Cronon 1991.

Page 135 *"die-offs of Biblical proportions"*: Sheridan 2007, 125.

Page 135 *Taylor Grazing Act*: Skillen 2008.

Page 135 *"low, patchy, and unpredictable"*: Sheridan 2007, 126. Part of what makes rangelands patchy and unpredictable is that they remain dependent on rainfall.

Page 136 *Engender different corporate structures*: Mitchell 2011.

Milking and Shearing

Page 137 *Secondary products*: The secondary productions formulation is commonly attributed to archaeologist Andrew Sherratt. What follows draws on Greenfield

2010; Vigne and Helmer 2007; Evershed et al. 2008; and Honeychurch and Makarewicz 2016.

Page 137 *Largely dairy in nature*: Fontanals-Coll et al. 2016.

From Persons to Property

Page 138 This section draws on Nadasdy 2007, 2016; Pedersen 2001; Willerslev, Vitebsky, and Alekseyev 2016; Ingold 2000.

Page 140 *Bronze Age Scandinavia*: Armstrong Oma 2010.

Page 141 *Under the right combination*: For example, Isenberg 2000. In the case of bison, the ecological pressures included a series of smallpox epidemics that made village life untenable.

Page 141 *Lakota Ghost Dance*: For this paragraph, Ostler 1996, 2001; DeMallie 1982; Biolsi 1995. The testimony of Louise Weasel Bear was first brought to wide attention by Dee Brown [1970] 1991.

Industrialization and Confinement

Breeding

Page 142 *This story repeated*: On Texas Longhorns, see Specht 2016; on pigs, White 2011; on chickens, Boyd 2001.

Page 144 *Subtherapeutic doses*: In 2013 the US Food and Drug Administration announced a policy of encouraging pharmaceuticals vendors and livestock producers to voluntarily phase out prophylactic and growth-promoting use of antimicrobials. European countries have been more proactive in banning the practice, though not uniformly.

Feeding

Page 144 *CAFOs*: Pew Commission 2008.

Page 145 *Feedlots*: Wagner, Archibeque, and Feuz 2014.

Page 146 *"Some finishing diets"*: Wagner, Archibeque, and Feuz 2014, 547.

Page 146 *"In regard to water-quality issues"*: Wagner, Archibeque, and Feuz 2014, 551.

Page 146 *Soybean subsidies*: Starmer and Wise 2007.

Page 147 *Environmental zeitgebers*: Berson 2015.

Killing

Page 147 *Slaughterhouses*: Fitzgerald 2010; Cronon 1991.

Page 147 *"Some balk when prodded up the chute"*: Pachirat 2011, 39.

Page 148 *Chain speed*: Workers at other plants have reported mandated chain speeds of 400 per hour, an increase of more than 100 percent since the 1970s. In Europe chain speeds are considerably lower. See Fitzgerald 2010.

The Law

Page 148 *R. v. Mow-watty*: Ford and Salter 2008.

Page 149 *Jurisdiction*: On its evolution, Sassen 2006.

Page 149 *Law of the interface, Cherokee cases*: Ford 2011.

Page 149 Terra nullius: The source of the *terra nullius* story is the High Court of Australia's decision in *Mabo v. Queensland* (1992), which established the basis for the system of Native Title alluded to above. See Berson 2014.

Page 150 *What liberalism demands of its subjects*: On liberalism and empire, Pitts 2005.

Page 150 *Property as performance*: Rose 1994.

Chapter 6. Assimilation

Slaughter and Civilization

Page 154 *Casualization of meatpacking in New Zealand*: Gewertz and Errington 2010, 38–44.

Page 155 *Pilbara people had not suffered the same pressures*: Compare Tonkinson 1974.

The Station Era

Page 155 *Sheep and cattle were introduced into South Australia and Queensland*: Paterson 2010.

Page 156 *A series of such contacts*: Compare Beck and Sieber 2010. On the Bantu expansions, Macholdt et al. 2014.

Page 156 *By the 1860s, Aboriginal people living near sheep stations*: For the paragraphs that follow, Berndt and Berndt 1952.

Page 156 *Dry rations became essential*: Rowse 1998.

Page 157 *United Aborigines' Mission*: Berndt and Berndt 1952, 111.

Page 157 *Disease*: Not all introduced disease was sexually transmitted. Berndt and Berndt (1952, 114) note that station life had led to a sharp increase in colds, flus, pneumonia, and other respiratory infections as Aboriginal people on mission and stock stations were required to wear clothes without being made aware of the need to dry clothes that had been dampened by rain. This is just one example of how indoor living was imposed on Australians in an incoherent and piecemeal fashion.

Page 157 *Gerontocracy of Aboriginal Law*: Keen 2006.

Page 158 *The Dreaming*: Berson 2014.

Page 158 *Three grades of interaction with white society*: Berndt and Berndt 1952, 145–148.

Page 159 *Adopted by white families*: This form of adoption has since come to be understood as one aspect of a policy of Indigenous child removal that extended into the 1970s. See Read 2003.

Page 159 *Stock raids*: In Australia, stock raids were generally acts of bravado or retaliation. In contrast to what we saw with the Comanche in chapter 5, no indigenous tradition of herding developed in Australia, though former stock workers periodically established Aboriginal-owned stock operations.

Page 159 *Massacres at Forrest River and Coniston*: Ngabidj and Shaw 1981; Rose 1992.

Page 159 *"It was the tail-end of a disastrous period"*: Stanner [1966] 1978, 253. For the rest of this paragraph, see Stevens 1974; Kelly 1963, 1971.

Page 160 *Cattlemen sanguine*: Stevens 1974, 34.

Page 160 *Dependent on coerced Aboriginal labor*: Most Aboriginal men in the cattle industry (upward of 70 percent) worked as stockmen, managing cattle on the range, performing castrations, breaking horses, and so on. Others worked as mechanics, boundary riders, and gardeners (Stevens 1974, 44).

Page 161 *Wards and dependents*: Stevens 1974, 27. Including female family members performing unpaid domestic labor, the number of non-Aboriginal workers on cattle stations in the Northern Territory in this period was roughly between 1,000 and 1,600.

Page 161 *Not until 1967*: In a 1967 referendum, white Australians voted nine to one to amend the Commonwealth constitution to grant the central government power to make law for Indigenous people and to have the Indigenous population counted in the apportionment of legislative representation. The Commonwealth had come into existence in 1901 through a merger of the Crown colonies of New South Wales, Queensland, Victoria, Tasmania, South Australia (then responsible for the Northern Territory), and Western Australia.

Page 162 *Award wage arbitration*: Stanner [1966] 1978.

Page 162 *"The working natives were virtually peons"*: Stanner [1966] 1978, 253. He is referring to the treatment of Indigenous people in the gold mines as well as on the stock stations. Compare Berndt and Berndt 1986, 7, quoting testimony before an 1899 South Australia Select Committee on native labor: "No person can live in the Northern Territory without knowing that the natives employed in the back blocks are treated, in many cases, just as any other chattel would be."

Page 162 *"absolutely dependent upon the blacks"*: Quoted in Berndt and Berndt 1986, 9.

Page 163 *"Most of the men"*: Berndt and Berndt 1986, 60. Wave Hill lies approximately 900 kilometers (560 miles) south of Darwin. By the mid-1960s, the station encompassed 12,000 square kilometers. In 1967, it became the site of one of the first Aboriginal land rights actions when its mainly Gurindji Aboriginal population, some 50 workers and 200 dependents, walked off. Their demands escalated from wage parity to the transfer of 1,300 square kilometers of the land under pastoral lease to Gurindji title. A standoff ensued. It dragged on until 1975, when the Commonwealth finally awarded the Gurindji a lease over 5 percent of the land they had claimed. By this time, a separate case involving Yolngu at Yirrkala to the north had led to the establishment of an Aboriginal land claims process in the territory. On these events, see Merlan 2005; Berson 2014.

Page 163 *Underwear*: Berndt and Berndt 1986, 82; Stevens 1974, 186.

Page 163 *Men were denied . . . "The authority of European men"*: Berndt and Berndt 1986, 124; Stevens 1974, 186–188.

Page 163 *Nowhere was the misery clearer*: For this paragraph and the next, Stevens 1974; Berndt and Berndt 1986.

Page 164 *Nigger farming*: Stevens 1974, 85–91.

Page 164 *Managers estimated meat consumption*: Berndt and Berndt 1986, 72–75; Stevens 1974, 90. At Wave Hill, the Berndts were told that the meat consumed by Aboriginal staff and dependents over the first six months of 1945 represented the yield of 164 head of cattle.

Page 165 *Northern Territory Aboriginal dietary survey*: For the next four paragraphs, Wilson 1951a. I am indebted to Smith and Smith 1999 for bringing Wilson's work to my attention.

Page 165 *Victoria River Downs*: Owned by Bovril, the station encompassed close to 19,000 square kilometers and was situated 1,200 kilometers (745 miles) north and east of Alice Springs.

Page 166 *"The natives collected the meal from the kitchen"*: Wilson 1951a, 36. Generally dry stores were freighted to the remote stations from the south by a combination of air, rail, and road transport twice a year, at the beginning and end of the wet season. Outstations and stock camps at remote points on a station were resupplied every four to six weeks. Milk sometimes came from herds of dairy cattle and goats, but the milk consumed by Aboriginal workers and their dependents was mainly powdered. Fresh fruit and vegetables were sometimes supplied by air freight; not every station had a working garden.

Page 166 *National Archives of Australia*: For what follows, see National Archives of Australia [hereafter, NAA] A1658 4/1/6.

Page 167 *Over the protests . . . too complicated*: NAA A1658 4/1/6, 148 and 154. The memo from the Department of Health explains,

> As baldly stated, without specification of suitable components or suggestion of alternatives, the diet is likely to become a standardised and monotonous minimum not materially superior to the old salt beef and damper, tea and sugar, supplement, the abuse of which by the uninformed and the unscrupulous has necessitated promulgation of a detailed diet scale," and goes on to stress that assimilation must include the "inculcat[ion] in the native [of] a diversified range of dietary wants and tastes" and "the means for their gratification.

Weet-Bix Empire

Page 169 *Drinking tea with A*: Out of deference to Aboriginal protocols of respect, I have elected not to give my interlocutor's full name lest its appearance cause pain to her kin when she is gone.

Page 170 *The government are fooling themselves*: A has been proved right; see Branley and Hermant 2014. The BasicsCard was introduced in the Northern Territory as part of a package of measures hastily assembled by the central government in 2007 following the publication of a report suggesting an epidemic of child sexual abuse in remote Indigenous communities in the Territory; see Altman and Hinkson 2007.

Page 170 *The first black labor action*: Merlan 2005; Hess 1994. The strike encompassed cattle and sheep stations and was timed to coincide with the onset of shearing and roundup early in the dry season (May). In contrast to the later Gurindji strike of 1966–1975, strikers did not seek to establish a stock operation of their own, though they did establish a mining collective when participants were dismissed from the stations. After a three-year standoff, the strikers were partly successful in gaining wage concessions and improved working conditions, aided by the Port Hedland longshoremen, who refused to load wool from noncompliant stations.

Page 171 *"Natives in the town"*: Wilson 1951b, 27.

The View from New Guinea

Page 175 *First contact with police patrols*: Schieffelin and Crittenden 1991.

Page 175 *"principally on native foods."*: Hipsley 1950, 13.

Page 176 *Busama a "battle-ground" etc.*: Hipsley 1950, 101, 109, 25–6.

Page 176 *"signs of gross inadequacy of protein"*: Hipsley 1950, 25.

Page 176 *Basic knowledge about the protein content*: Hipsley 1950, 110. Compare Waterlow 1986.

Page 177 *Rickets*: Clements 1942. In the 1942 study, the 47 percent consisted predominantly of transient cases that resolved within the year. By this standard, the 1947 New Guinea survey may have underestimated incidence of transient mild rickets.

Page 177 *Micronutrient status . . . enlarged thyroid*: Hipsley 1950, 25–27, 152–156.

Page 177 *"Wherever practicable, great nutritional value . . . "*: Hipsley 1950, 28.

Hunger

Page 177 *"Over the past few months I have been concerned"*: NAA E51 1971/1881, 198–199.

Page 178 *The first Indigenous land rights case*: The case in question, *Milirrpum v. Nabalco Pty Ltd,* grew enormously technical, and the petitioners ultimately lost. But it paved the way for 1976 Aboriginal Land Rights (Northern Territory) Act, which established commissions to hear claims of what came to be called traditional ownership.

Page 179 *It opted not to intervene*: NAA A1658 4/1/6, 14: "In the best interests of the native it is important that we should not permit spontaneous impulses of charity and compassion, to lead us into courses of action which may operate to his irremediable harm." These lines formed part of a response by the director of the Commonwealth Department of Health to reports from Mount Margaret Mission (Great Victoria Desert, southern aspect of the Western Desert) on the emaciation of the foragers living in the bush.

Page 179 *"meals should consist"*: NAA E51 1971/1881, 177.

Page 179 *Hipsley argued*: NAA E51 1971/1881, 150–156, citing Mason et al. 1974 on Ethiopia. High-protein supplementation carries a risk of dehydration because under starvation, protein is catabolized for energy, producing urea, which must be excreted.

Page 179 *Subsequent correspondence suggests*: NAA E51 1971/1881, 228, 169.

Page 180 *By practically any measure*: Brewster and Morris 2015; Cairney and Dingwall 2010; Smith 2016.

Page 180 *When all you've got*: Lee et al. (2016) evaluated the nutritional life chances of people living in remote Aboriginal settlements in the southeastern Western Desert. A "typical basket" of healthy foods cost 35 percent more than a comparable basket in Alice Springs. The availability of fresh fruits and vegetables and fresh animal-source produce had improved markedly since the 1980s, and the cost of a "healthy diet" had declined from 80 percent of mean family income in 1998 to 50 percent. But reliance on energy-dense convenience foods had also increased, with discretionary foods (those chosen without an eye toward nutritional value) accounting for more than 40 percent of the diet.

Intermezzo: Race and the Science of Starvation

Page 181 *Wilson quotes Sherman*: Wilson 1951b, 3, citing Sherman 1950, 6.

Page 182 *Oscar refused to manifest*: Howe, Mattill, and Hawk 1912. For the fasting literature, see Lusk 1906; Kleiber [1961] 1975.

Page 182 *Fasting gained popularity*: Griffith 2000. Energy intake restriction continues to find favor as a technique of life extension. Clinical evidence for the effectiveness of drastic calorie restriction is mixed. But intermittent fasting has gained strong clinical support as a means of slowing the aging process. See Martens and Seals 2016.

Page 182 *Controlled trials of calorie restriction*: Benedict 1918.

Page 182 *Relationship between body size and basal metabolic rate*: Price et al. 2012.

Page 183 *Chittenden undertook clinical studies*: Chittenden 1904.

Page 183 *Not especially healthy*: Lunch for the soldiers for one week in November 1903 included hamburgers, macaroni and cheese, clam chowder, bean porridge, and beef stew.

Page 183 *Praise for Chittenden's work*: Benedict 1906; Sherman 1950, 185.

Page 183 *"Before the emancipation of the Japanese"*: McCay 1912, 25.

Page 183 *"There is little doubt that the evidence"*: McCay 1912, 102.

Page 184 *"Do we know, for example, how far"*: Adolph 1944, 3.

Chapter 7. Coupling

A Great Uncoupling?

Page 185 *Hanjin*: Kim and Park 2016.

Page 186 *The Great Uncoupling*: Appelbaum 2016; Campbell and Kennedy 2017.

Page 186 *Globalization of inequality*: Milanovic 2016.

Page 186 *Return on capital*: Piketty 2014.

Page 186 *V Street*: Landau and Jacoby 2016.

Page 187 *Meat consumption in China*: Kearny 2010. Weis 2013 offers a divergent and higher estimate.

A Heat Map Thought Experiment

Page 192 *Boxed beef*: Horowitz 2006; Pachirat 2011.

Page 192 *One-child policy*: Greenhalgh 2008.

Page 192 *Famine in North Korea*: Haggard and Noland 2009; Demick 2009.

Value Chains and Topologies

Page 194 *Often topological distances matter more than physical distances*: Hillier 2007.

Page 194 *Twenty-five percent of food traded internationally*: Clapp 2016, 77.

Infrastructures of Coupling

Legal Infrastructure: Free Trade Agreements

Page 194 This section draws on Clapp 2016, chap. 3.

Page 195 *Food aid*: Cullather 2010.

Page 196 *Dumping had the corollary effect*: Murphy 2009.

Page 196 *Over the ten-year period 2006–2015*: Heath and Petrie 2016.

Page 196 *Overall Chinese beef imports*: Gale, Hansen, and Jewison 2015.

Page 196 *In 2016 China resumed imports from the United States*: Mulvaney and Skerritt 2016. The United States has shown remarkable intransigence on BSE, refusing either to ban meat and bonemeal in ruminant feedstocks or to bring its audit trail up to the standards used in Canada, Europe, Japan, and Australia. See Weiss, Thurbon, and Mathews 2006.

Page 196 *The same year, Brazil and Uruguay overtook Australia*: On the beef export market, Rabobank's Global Beef Index represents a key source: rabobank-food-agri business-research.pr.co.

Page 196 *ChAFTA*: Sedgman 2015.

Page 196 *Demand for pork in China*: Schneider 2017; Yuan 2016; Whitley 2015; Bloomberg News 2015.

Page 196 *Poultry in China*: Ho 2017.

Page 197 *Japan's use of trade agreements to bolster strategic relationships*: Capling 2008.

Financial Infrastructures: Derivatives and Land Investments

Page 198 *Commodity futures in nineteenth-century Chicago*: Cronon 1991.

Page 198 *Shanghai Containerized Freight Index*: Yang 2016.

Page 198 *Three-fifths of the capitalization came from noncommercial traders*: Clapp 2016, 176–178; Schneyer 2011; Vander Stichele 2012.

Page 199 *A large proportion of food crop yield goes to feedstocks*: Weis 2013.

Page 199 *"South Korea has signed deals"*: Sassen 2013, 30–31. Compare Clapp 2016, 184–189.

Page 200 *Absence of formal title may serve foreign investors*: Li 2015.

Page 200 *Macquarie Group's pitch for land investment*: Larder, Sippel, and Lawrence 2015.

Page 200 *Chinese investment in Australian livestock*: Whitley 2016; Stringer 2016; Scott 2016.

Logistics: The Cold Chain and Live Transport

Page 201 *The cold chain refers to the ensemble of artifacts*: The next four paragraphs draw on a sampling of recent technical literature in cold-chain logistics for fresh food: Defraeye et al. 2015; Guillier et al. 2016; Aung and Chang 2014; Bruckner et al. 2012; Mack et al. 2014; Kuo and Chen 2010.

Page 201 *Ice cream . . . "exotic chill"*: Aung and Chang 2014.

Page 202 *The energy flushed away . . . tremendous headroom*: Zilio 2014; International Institute of Refrigeration 2009; Food and Agriculture Organization 2011, 16, 26. Figures such as these should be taken with a grain of salt, as they represent the conclusions of studies published as much as fifteen years earlier.

Page 203 *Most of the cost of maintaining cold-chain capacity*: Food and Agriculture Organization 2011, 9. Ideally, an assessment of the opportunity costs of refrigeration would also operationalize food loss in a higher-resolution way, for instance, distinguishing between losses due to spoilage and those due to retail marketing standards. See FLW Protocol Steering Committee 2016.

Page 203 *Australia is its most enthusiastic proponent*: Between 1995 and 2012, Australia exported some 13 million cattle in 6,447 shipments (Moore et al. 2014).

Page 203 *Live transport is stressful*: Moore et al. 2014; Phillips and Santurtun 2013; Appleby et al. 2008.

Page 204 *Live export by air*: Department of Agriculture and Water Resources ongoing.

Page 204 *Arbitrage on citizenship rights*: Biao, Yeoh, and Toyota 2013.

Page 204 *Legal status of animals*: Tatoian 2015.

Nutrient Cycles and Biome Turnover

Page 205 *Beyond our current state of knowledge*: But see Cumming et al. 2014; Ellis 2015; Herrero et al. 2015.

More Intimate Kinds of Coupling

Page 206 *Zoonoses*: Karesh et al. 2012; Muehlenbein 2016.

Page 206 *Coupling extends down to the most intimate dimensions*: Provenza, Meuret, and Gregorini 2015.

Chapter 8. The Street

Fried Chicken and Hope

Page 207 Stray Dogs: Tsai 2013. For another reading, see Weigel 2016.

The Imaginary Life of Income Elasticity

Page 209 *"The Trouble with Macroeconomics"*: Romer 2016.

Page 210 *Limitations of elasticities*: Baker and Enohoro 2014; Van Wijk 2014.

Where Do the Data Come From?

Page 212 *FAO infers them from other data and its own models*: Hawkesworth et al. 2010.

Page 213 *Estimates from balance sheets versus those from household surveys*: Ke 2002, 2–4.

Page 213 *China's livestock inspection system*: Schneider 2017.

Page 215 *Transience of rural poverty in China*: Ward 2016.

Once You've Got Data, What Do You Do with Them?

Page 217 *Quantifying market development*: On the complexity of income, Milanovic 2016.

What Is a City?

Page 217 For the first two paragraphs, see Sattherthwaite 2007.

Page 218 *Ghost cities*: He, Mol, and, Lu 2016; Yao, Luo, and Wang 2014; Bloomberg News 2016c.

Page 218 *Periurbanization*: Abramson 2016.

Page 218 *Origins in distinct villages*: Compare Hillier 2007.

Page 219 *Red loops and green loops*: Cumming et al. 2014.

Page 219 *Urban energy budgets*: Downey 2016.

Livestock on the Urban Periphery

Page 219 *Poultry in Thailand*: Herrero et al. 2013, Supporting information, 44; Ahuja 2012; NaRanong 2007; Padungtod, Kadohira, and Hill 2008.

Page 219 *Poultry in China*: Ho 2017.

Page 220 *Dragon head companies*: Schneider 2017.

Page 220 *Feedstock in China*: Yuan 2016.

Page 221 *Milk in China*: Wiley 2007; Scott 2016; Gopalan 2017.

Page 221 *Concentration in feedstock*: Howard 2016, 105–106.

Income, Poverty, Health, and Migration

Page 222 *Urbanization of poverty*: Ravallion et al. 2007; Samman 2013; Tacoli 2013. Migrants tend to self-select for traits that make them more like those in cities, for example, younger, better educated, and with fewer dependents (Wang, Wan, and Yang 2014).

Page 223 *Milanovic has attributed most of this shift*: Milanovic 2016.

Page 223 *Income inequality in China*: Wang et al. 2014.

Page 223 *Special Economic Zones and Open Cities*: Valerio Mendoza 2016.

Page 223 *Income inequality and housing costs*: Zhang 2015.

Page 224 *Mortality from $PM_{2.5}$ exposure*: Xie et al. 2016.

Page 224 *Self-assessed health and aging*: Baeten, Wan, and Yang 2013.

Page 224 *Income inequality affects practically every dimension of life*: Eriksson, Pan, and Qin 2014; Yang and Qiu 2016; Xu, Han, and Lu 2016.

Page 224 *Rural-to-urban migrants' health status*: Song and Sun 2016. Elevated serum lipid levels might also indicate a greater reliance on fatty meat.

Page 225 *Making the world we live in*: On occupational segregation by migration and hukou status in China, see Zhang and Wu 2017; Fitzgerald et al. 2013.

Page 225 *Care labor*: Biao, Yeoh, and Toyota 2013.

Hand to Mouth

Page 225 *"The Obama Years"*: Marche 2016.

Page 225 *Shiv Sena and vada pav*: Solomon 2015.

Page 226 *State veterinary surveys tend to ignore*: Herrero et al. 2013, Supporting Information, 43.

Page 226 *Participation varies widely*: Zezza and Tasciotti 2010.

Page 226 *Reversing the flow of in-kind support*: Tacoli, Bukhari, and Fisher 2013, 17–18.

Page 226 *Recent models*: Badami and Ramankutty 2015.

Page 226 *Comprehensive metareview*: Poulsen et al. 2015.

Page 227 *Periurbanization and provisioning*: Abramson 2016.

Page 227 *Recreating the wet market experience*: Tacconelli and Wrigley 2009. On retail concentration globally, Howard 2016, 34–40.

Page 227 *7-Eleven*: Wang 2011; compare Howard 2016, 40.

Page 227 *Retail formats*: Wang 2011.

Page 228 *Fast food*: Bloomberg News 2016a, 2016b, 2017; Minter 2015; Kaiman 2013.

Page 228 *Provisioning landscape*: Liao et al. 2016.

Page 230 *Time and space poverty*: Tacoli, Bukhari, and Fisher 2013, 18.

Page 231 *Urban nutritional niche construction*: Downey 2016.

Nutrition and Inequality

Page 231 *Transactional dating in the United States*: Popkin, Scott, and, Galvez 2016.

Page 231 *SNAP recipients' food-buying habits*: O'Connor 2017.

Page 231 *Malnutrition*: Lu, Black, and Richter 2016; Black et al. 2013; NCD Risk Factor Collaboration 2016; Global BMI Mortality Collaboration 2016.

Page 232 *Income elasticity of fruits and vegetables*: Miller et al. 2016.

Epilogue: The End of Meat?

Page 233 *Epigraphs*: Han 2015, 22–23; Han 2016, 140.

Page 233 *Aquaculture*: Bostock et al. 2010.

Page 233 *Satiety*: Hayes et al. 2014.

Page 233 *Cultured meat*: Wurgaft 2019.

Page 234 *Threats to wild animal species*: Maxwell et al. 2016; Estrada et al. 2017.

Page 237 *Niche entrenchment*: The term *entrenchment* comes from the work of philosopher William Wimsatt. See Caporael, Griesemer, and Wimsatt 2013.

Page 237 *Crisis of capitalism*: Streeck 2016.

Page 238 *One recent effort to explore the environmental and health implications*: Springmann et al. 2016.

Sources

Abramson, D. 2016. "Periurbanization and the Politics of Development-as-City-Building in China." *Cities* 53:156–162.

Adams, C. (1990) 2015. *The Sexual Politics of Meat: A Feminist Vegetarian Critical Theory*. London: Bloomsbury.

Adolph, W. 1944. "The Protein Problem of China." *Science* 100:1–4.

Ahuja, V., ed. 2012. *Asian Livestock: Challenges and Opportunities*. Rome: Food and Agriculture Organization.

Aiello, L., and P. Wheeler. 1995. "The Expensive-Tissue Hypothesis: The Brain and Digestive System in Human and Primate Evolution." *Current Anthropology* 36:199–221.

Alston, L., E. Harris, and B. Mueller. 2012. "The Development of Property Rights on Frontiers: Endowments, Norms, and Politics." *Journal of Economic History* 72:741–770.

Altman J., and M. Hinkson, eds. 2007. *Coercive Reconciliation: Stabilise, Normalise, Exit Aboriginal Australia*. Melbourne: Arena.

Andersson, C., and D. Read. 2016. "The Evolution of Cultural Complexity: Not by the Treadmill Alone." *Current Anthropology* 57:261–286.

Antón, S., and J. Snodgrass. 2012. "Origins and Evolution of Genus *Homo*: New Perspectives." *Current Anthropology* 53:S479–S496.

Appelbaum, B. 2016. "A Little-Noticed Fact about Trade: It's No Longer Rising." *New York Times,* October 30. www.nytimes.com/2016/10/31/upshot/a-little-noticed-fact-about-trade-its-no-longer-rising.html.

Appleby, M., V. Cussen, L. Garcés, L. Lambert, and J. Turner. 2008. *Long Distance Transport and Welfare of Farm Animals*. Wallingford, UK: CABI.

Asouti, E., and D. Fuller. 2013. "A Contextual Approach to the Emergence of Agriculture in Southwest Asia: Reconstructing Early Neolithic Plant-Food Production." *Current Anthropology* 54:299–345.

Attwell, L., K. Kovarovic, and J. Kendal. 2015. "Fire in the Plio-Pleistocene: The Functions of Hominin Fire Use, and the Mechanistic, Developmental and Evolutionary Consequences." *Journal of Anthropological Sciences* 93:1–20.

Attwood, B. 2005. *Telling the Truth about Aboriginal History*. Sydney: Allen & Unwin.

Aung M., and Y. Chang. 2014. "Temperature Management for the Quality Assurance of a Perishable Food Supply Chain." *Food Control* 40:198–207.

Austin-Broos, D. 2009. *Arrernte Present, Arrernte Past: Invasion, Violence, and Imagination in Indigenous Central Australia*. Chicago: University of Chicago Press.

Badami M., and N. Ramankutty N. 2015. "Urban Agriculture and Food Security: A Critique Based on an Assessment of Urban Land Constraints." *Global Food Security* 4:8–15.

Baeten, S., T. Van Ourti, and E. van Doorslaer. 2013. "Rising Inequalities in Income and Health in China: Who Is Left Behind?" *Journal of Health Economics* 32:1214–1229.

Bailey, R., A. Froggat, and L. Wellesley. 2014. *Livestock—Climate Change's Forgotten Sector: Global Public Opinion on Meat and Dairy Consumption*. London: Chatham House.

Bajželj, B., K. Richards, J. Allwood, P. Smith, J. Dennis, E. Curmi, and C. Gilligan. 2014. "Importance of Food-Demand Management for Climate Mitigation." *Nature Climate Change* 4:924–929.

Baker, D., and E. Enahoro. 2014. "Policy Analysis and Advocacy for Livestock-Based Development: The Gap between Household-Level Analysis and Higher-Level Models." *Food Policy* 49:361–364.

Bartlett, L., D. Williams, G. Prescott, A. Balmford, R. Green, A. Eriksson, P. Valdes, J. Singarayer, and A. Manica. 2016. "Robustness Despite Uncertainty: Regional Climate Data Reveal the Dominant Role of Humans in Explaining Global Extinctions of Late Quaternary Megafauna." *Ecography* 39:152–161.

Beck, J., and S. Sieber. 2010. "Is the Spatial Distribution of Mankind's Most Basic Economic Traits Determined by Climate and Soil Alone?" *PLoS One* 5(5):e10416.

Beck, K., C. Conlon, R. Kruger, and J. Coad. 2014. "Dietary Determinants of and Possible Solutions to Iron Deficiency in Young Women Living in Industrialized Countries: A Review." *Nutrients* 6:3747–3776.

Behrensmeyer, A. 2006. "Climate Change and Human Evolution." *Science* 311:476–478.

Benedict, F. 1906. "The Nutritive Requirements of the Body." *American Journal of Physiology* 16:409–439.

Benedict, F. 1918. "Physiological Effects of a Prolonged Reduction in Diet on Twenty-Five Men." *Proceedings of the American Physiological Society* 57:479–490.

Berndt, R., and C. Berndt. 1952. *From Black to White in South Australia.* Melbourne: Cheshire.

Berndt, R., and C. Berndt. 1986. *End of an Era: Aboriginal Labour in the Northern Territory.* Canberra: Australian Institute of Aboriginal Studies.

Berson, J. 2014. "The Dialectal Tribe and the Doctrine of Continuity." *Comparative Studies in Society and History* 56:381–418.

Berson, J. 2015. *Computable Bodies: Instrumented Life and the Human Somatic Niche.* London: Bloomsbury.

Berson, J. 2017. "The Topology of Endangered Languages." *Signs and Society* 5:96–123.

Biao, X., B. Yeoh, and M. Toyota, eds. 2013. *Return: Nationalizing Transnational Mobility in Asia.* Durham, NC: Duke University Press.

Biolsi T. 1995. "The Birth of the Reservation: Making the Modern Individual among the Lakota." *American Ethnologist* 22:28–53.

Bird, D., R. Bliege Bird, B. Codding, and N. Taylor. 2016. "A Landscape Architecture of Fire: Cultural Emergence and Ecological Pyrodiversity in Australia's Western Desert." *Current Anthropology* 57:S65–S79.

Bird, D., B. Codding, R. Bliege Bird, D. Zeanah, and C. Taylor. 2013. "Megafauna in a Continent of Small Game: Archaeological Implications of Martu Camel Hunting in Australia's Western Desert." *Quaternary International* 297:155–166.

Black, R., C. Victora, S. Walker, Z. Bhutta, P. Christian, M. de Onis, M. Ezzati, et al. 2013. "Maternal and Child Undernutrition and Overweight in Low-Income and Middle-Income Countries." *Lancet* 382:427–451.

Bliege Bird, R. 2015. "Disturbance, Complexity, Scale: New Approaches to the Study of Human–Environment Interactions." *Annual Review of Anthropology* 44:241–257.

Bliege Bird R., and D. Bird. 2008. "Why Women Hunt: Risk and Contemporary Foraging in a Western Desert Aboriginal Community." *Current Anthropology* 49:655–693.

Bloomberg News. 2015. "China Pork Price Jump Seen Faltering as Big Farms Boost Output." *Bloomberg News,* September 2. www.bloomberg.com/news/articles/2015-09-02/china-pork-price-jump-seen-faltering-as-big-farms-boost-output.

Bloomberg News. 2016a. "China Starts to Lose Its Taste for McDonald's and KFC." *Bloomberg News,* August 3. www.bloomberg.com/news/articles/2016-08-03/china-starts-to-loses-its-taste-for-mcdonald-s-and-kfc.

Bloomberg News. 2016b. "Has Yum Worked Out How Fast-Food Firms Can Crack China?" *Bloomberg News*, October 31. www.bloomberg.com/news/articles/2016-10-31/yum-s-spinoff-offers-roadmap-for-western-brands-in-china-market.

Bloomberg News. 2016c. "Easing China's Housing Bubble Has Unintended Side Effects." *Bloomberg News*, December 29. www.bloomberg.com/news/articles/2016-12-29/china-s-megacity-housing-bubble-cure-has-small-town-side-effects.

Bloomberg News. 2017. "McDonald's Sells Control of China Business to Citic, Carlyle." *Bloomberg News*, January 9. www.bloomberg.com/news/articles/2017-01-09/mcdonald-s-sells-control-of-china-business-to-citic-carlyle.

Blome, M., A. Cohen, C. Tryon, A. Brooks, and J. Russell. 2012. "The Environmental Context for the Origins of Modern Human Diversity: A Synthesis of Regional Variability in African Climate 150,000–30,000 Years Ago." *Journal of Human Evolution* 62:563–592.

Boserup, E. 1965. *The Conditions of Agricultural Growth: The Economics of Agrarian Change under Population Pressure*. London: Allen & Unwin.

Bostock, J., B. McAndrew, R. Richards, K. Jauncey, T. Telfer , K. Lorenzen, D. Little, et al. 2010. "Aquaculture: Global Status and Trends." *Philosophical Transactions of the Royal Society B* 365:2897–2912.

Boyce, J. 2010. *Van Diemen's Land*. Melbourne: Black.

Boyd, W. 2001. "Making Meat: Science, Technology, and American Poultry Production." *Technology and Culture* 42:631–664.

Bradsher, K. 2016. "In Australia, China's Appetite Shifts from Rocks to Real Estate." *New York Times*, September 24. www.nytimes.com/2016/09/25/business/international/australia-china-mining-port-hedland.html.

Bramble, D., and D. Lieberman. 2004. "Endurance Running and the Evolution of *Homo*." *Nature* 432:345–352.

Branley, A., and N. Hermant. 2014. "BasicsCard Users Buying Banned Cigarette with Welfare, Bartering Groceries for Cash and Alcohol." *ABC News*, September 1. www.abc.net.au/news/2014-08-31/welfare-recipients-skirting-around-income-management-rules/5708012.

Braun, D. 2013. "The Behavior of Plio-Pleistocene Hominins: Archaeological Perspectives." In *Early Hominin Paleoecology*, edited by M. Sponheimer, J. Lee-Thorp, K. Reed, and P. Ungar, 325–351. Boulder: University of Colorado Press.

Brewster, D., and P. Morris. 2015. "Indigenous Child Health: Are We Making Progress?" *Journal of Paediatrics and Child Health* 51:40–47.

Brown, D. (1970) 1991. *Bury My Heart at Wounded Knee: An Indian History of the American West.* London: Vintage.

Bruckner, S., A. Albrecht, B. Petersen, and J. Kreyenschmidt. 2012. "Influence of Cold Chain Interruptions on the Shelf Life of Fresh Pork and Poultry." *International Journal of Food Science and Technology* 47:1639–1646.

Bulliet, R. 2007. *Hunters, Herders, and Hamburgers: The Past and Future of Human–Animal Relationships.* New York: Columbia University Press.

Bunn, H. 2007. "Meat Made Us Human." In *Evolution of the Human Diet: The Known, the Unknown, and the Unknowable,* edited by P. Ungar, 191–201. Oxford: Oxford University Press.

Cairney, S., and K. Dingwall. 2010. *Journal of Paediatrics and Child Health* 46:510–515.

Calcagno, J., and A. Fuentes, eds. 2012. "What Makes Us Human? Answers from Evolutionary Anthropology." *Evolutionary Anthropology* 21:182–194.

Capling, A. 2008. "Preferential Trade Agreements as Instruments of Foreign Policy: An Australia–Japan Free Trade Agreement and Its Implications for the Asia Pacific Region." *Pacific Review* 21:27–43.

Caporael, L., J. Griesemer, and W. Wimsatt, eds. 2013. *Developing Scaffolds in Evolution, Culture, and Cognition.* Cambridge, MA: MIT Press.

Carlson, B., and J. Kingston 2007. "Docosahexaenoic Acid Biosynthesis and Dietary Contingency: Encephalization without Aquatic Constraint." *American Journal of Human Biology* 19:585–588.

Campbell, M., and S. Kennedy. 2017. "Davos Wonders If It's Part of the Problem." *Bloomberg Businessweek,* January 13. www.bloomberg.com/politics/articles/2017-01-13/davos-wonders-if-it-s-part-of-the-problem.

Cauvin, J. 2001. *The Birth of the Gods and the Origins of Agriculture.* Translated by T. Watkins. Cambridge: Cambridge University Press.

Chi, Z., and H. Hung. 2013. "Jiahu 1: Earliest Farmers beyond the Yangtze River." *Antiquity* 87:46–63.

Chittenden, R. 1904. *Physiological Economy in Nutrition.* New York: Stokes.

Clapp, S. 2016. *Food,* 2nd ed. London: Polity.

Clark, J., and A. Kandel. 2013. "The Evolutionary Implications of Variation in Human Hunting Strategies and Diet Breadth during the Middle Stone Age of Southern Africa." *Current Anthropology* 54:S269–S287.

Clarkson, C., Z. Jacobs, B. Marwick, R. Fullagar, L. Wallis, M. Smith, R. Roberts, et al. 2017. "Human Occupation of Northern Australia by 65,000 Years Ago." *Nature* 547:306–310.

Clements, F. 1942. "Rickets in Infants Aged under One Year: The Incidence in an Australian Community and a Consideration of the Aetiological Factors." *Medical Journal of Australia*, March 21:336–346.

Cleveland, D. 2013. *Balancing on a Planet: The Future of Food and Agriculture*. Berkeley: University of California Press.

Cohen, D. 2011. "The Beginnings of Agriculture in China: A Multiregional View." *Current Anthropology* 52:S273–S293.

Cohen, J. 1995. *How Many People Can the Earth Support?* New York: Norton.

Collard, M., B. Buchanan, and M. O'Brien. 2013. "Population Size as an Explanation for Patterns in the Paleolithic Archaeological Record: More Caution Is Needed." *Current Anthropology* 54:S388–396.

Conard, N., J. Serangeli, U. Böhner, B. Starkovich, C. Miller, B. Urban, and T. Van Kolfschoten. 2015. "Excavations at Schöningen and Paradigm Shifts in Human Evolution." *Journal of Human Evolution* 89:1–17.

Cordain, J. , L., Miller, S. Eaton, N. Mann, S. Holt, and J. Speth. 2000. "Plant–Animal Subsistence Ratios and Macronutrient Energy Estimations in Worldwide Hunter-Gatherer Diets." *American Journal of Clinical Nutrition* 71:682–692.

Cronon, W. 1991. *Nature's Metropolis: Chicago and the Great West*. New York: Norton.

Cucchi, T., A. Hulme-Beaman, J. Yuan, and K. Dobney. 2011. "Early Neolithic Pig Domestication at Jiahu, Henan Province, China: Clues from Molar Shape Analyses Using Geometric Morphometric Approaches." *Journal of Archaeological Science* 38:11–12.

Cullather, N. 2010. *The Hungry World: America's Cold War Battle against Poverty in Asia*. Cambridge, MA: Harvard University Press.

Cumming, G., A. Buerkert, E. Hoffmann, E. Schlecht, S. von Cramon-Taubadel, and T. Tscharntke. 2014. "Implications of Agricultural Transitions and Urbanization for Ecosystem Services." *Nature* 515:50–57.

Cunnane, S., and M. Crawford. 2014. "Energetic and Nutritional Constraints on Infant Brain Development: Implications for Brain Expansion during Human Evolution." *Journal of Human Evolution* 77:88–98.

David, L., C. Maurice, R. Carmody, D. Gootenberg, J. Button, B. Wolfe, A. Ling, et al. 2014. "Diet Rapidly and Reproducibly Alters the Human Gut Microbiome." *Nature* 505:559–563.

Dean, M. 2016. "Measures of Maturation in Early Fossil Hominins: Events at the First Transition from Australopiths to Early *Homo*." *Philosophical Transactions of the Royal Society B* 371:20150234.

Defraeye, T., P. Cronjé, T. Berry, U. Opara, A. East, M. Hertog, P. Verboven, and B. Nicolai. 2015. "Towards Integrated Performance Evaluation of Future Packaging for Fresh Produce in the Cold Chain." *Food Science and Technology* 44:201–225.

DeMallie, R. 1982. "The Lakota Ghost Dance: An Ethnohistorical Account." *Pacific Historical Review* 51:385–405.

Demick, B. 2009. *Nothing to Envy: Ordinary Lives in North Korea*. New York: Spiegel and Grau.

Dennell, R., and W. Roebroeks. 2005. "An Asian Perspective on Early Human Dispersal from Africa." *Nature* 438:1099–1104.

Department of Agriculture and Water Resources. Ongoing. "Livestock Exports by Air." www.agriculture.gov.au/export/controlled-goods/live-animals/live-animal-export-statistics/livestock-exports-by-air.

Dias, R., C. Detry, and N. Bicho. 2016. "Changes in the Exploitation Dynamics of Small Terrestrial Vertebrates and Fish during the Pleistocene–Holocene Transition in the SW Iberia: A Review." *Holocene* 26:964–984.

Domínguez-Rodrigo, M., and C. Musiba. 2010. "How Accurate Are Paleoecological Reconstructions of Early Paleontological and Archaeological Sites?" *Evolutionary Biology* 37:128–140.

Downey, G. 2016. "Being Human in Cities: Phenotypic Bias from Urban Niche Construction." *Current Anthropology* 57:S52–S64.

Dunne, J., R. Evershed, M. Salque, L. Cramp, S. Bruni, K. Ryan, S. Biagetti, and S. di Lernia. 2012. "First Dairying in Green Saharan Africa in the Fifth Millennium BC." *Nature* 486:390–394.

Dye, A., and S. La Croix. 2013. "The Political Economy of Land Privatization in Argentina and Australia, 1810–1850: A Puzzle." *Journal of Economic History* 73:901–936.

Eaton, S., and M. Konner. 1985. "Paleolithic Nutrition: A Consideration of Its Nature and Current Implications." *New England Journal of Medicine* 312:283–289.

Eaton, S., S. Eaton III, and M. Konner. 1997. "Paleolithic Nutrition Revisited: A Twelve-Year Retrospective on Its Nature and Implications." *European Journal of Clinical Nutrition* 51:207–216.

Ellegren, H., and N. Galtier. 2016. "Determinants of Genetic Diversity." *Nature Reviews Genetics* 17:422–433.

Ellis, E. 2015. "Ecology in an Anthropogenic Biosphere." *Ecological Monographs* 85:287–331.

El Zaatari, S., F. Grine, P. Ungar, and J-J. Hublin. 2016. "Neandertal versus Modern Human Dietary Responses to Climatic Fluctuations." *PLoS One* 11(4):e0153277.

El Zaatari, S., and J-J. Hublin. 2014. "Diet of Upper Paleolithic Modern Humans: Evidence from Microwear Texture Analysis." *American Journal of Physical Anthropology* 153:570–581.

Eriksson, T., J. Pan, and X. Qin. 2014. "The Intergenerational Inequality of Health in China." *China Economic Review* 31:392–409.

Estrada, A., P. Garber, A. Rylands, C. Roos, E. Fernandez-Duque, A. Di Fiore, K. Nekaris, et al. 2017. "Impending Extinction Crisis of the World's Primates: Why Primates Matter." *Science Advances* 3e1600946.

Evershed, R., S. Payne, A. Sherratt, M. Copley, J. Coolidge, D. Urem-Kotsu, K. Kotsakis, et al. 2008. "Earliest Date for Milk Use in the Near East and Southeastern Europe Linked to Cattle Herding." *Nature* 455:528–531.

Fekete, K., E. Györei, S. Lohner, E. Verduci, C. Agostini, and T. Decsi. 2015. "Long-Chain Polyunsaturated Fatty Acid Status in Obesity: A Systematic Review and Meta-Analysis." *Obesity Reviews* 16:488–497.

Ferguson, S. 2011. "A Bloody Business." *Four Corners*. ABC, May 30. www.abc.net.au/4corners/special_eds/20110530/cattle/.

Finch, C., and C. Stanford. 2004. "Meat-Adaptive Genes and the Evolution of Slower Aging in Humans." *Quarterly Review of Biology* 79:3–50.

Fiorenza, L., S. Benazzi, A. Henry, D. Salazar-García, R. Blasco, A. Picin, S. Wroe, and O. Kullmer. 2015. "To Meat or Not to Meat? New Perspectives on Neanderthal Ecology." *Yearbook of Physical Anthropology* 156:43–71.

Fisher, D., S. Blomberg, and I. Owens. 2002. "Convergent Maternal Care Strategies in Ungulates and Macropods." *Evolution* 56:167–176.

Fitzgerald, A. 2010. "A Social History of the Slaughterhouse: From Inception to Contemporary Implications." *Research in Human Ecology* 17:58–69.

Fitzgerald, S., X. Chen, H. Qu, and M. Sheff. 2013. "Occupational Injury amongst Migrant Workers in China: A Systematic Review." *Injury Prevention* 19:348–354.

FLW Protocol Steering Committee. 2016. *Food Loss and Waste Accounting and Reporting Standard*. Washington, DC: World Resources Institute.

Foley, J., N. Ramankutty, K. Brauman, E. Cassidy, J. Gerber, M. Johnston, N. Mueller, et al. 2011. "Solutions for a Cultivated Planet." *Nature* 478:337–342.

Foley, R. 2016. "Mosaic Evolution and the Pattern of Transitions in the Hominin Lineage." *Philosophical Transactions of the Royal Society B* 371:20150244.

Foley, R., L. Martin, M. Mirazón Lahr, and C. Stringer. 2016. "Major Transitions in Human Evolution." *Philosophical Transactions of the Royal Society B* 371:20150229.

Fontanals-Coll, M., M. Eulàlia Subirà, M. Díaz-Zorita Bonilla, and J. Gibaja. 2016. "First Insights into the Neolithic Subsistence Economy in the North-East Iberian Peninsula: Paleodietary Reconstruction through Stable Isotopes." *American Journal of Physical Anthropology* 2016:1–15.

Food and Agriculture Organization. 2011. *"Energy-Smart" Food for People and Climate.* Rome: Food and Agriculture Organization.

Ford, L. 2011. *Settler Sovereignty: Jurisdiction and Indigenous People in America and Australia, 1788–1836*. Cambridge, MA: Harvard University Press.

Ford, L., and B. Salter. 2008. "From Pluralism to Territorial Sovereignty: The 1816 Trial of Mow-watty in the Superior Court of New South Wales." *Indigenous Law Journal* 7:67–86.

Foxhall, K. 2011. "From Convicts to Colonists: The Health of Prisoners and the Voyage to Australia, 1823–53." *Journal of Imperial and Commonwealth History* 39:1–19.

Fuentes, A. 2016. "The Extended Evolutionary Synthesis, Ethnography, and the Human Niche: Toward an Integrated Anthropology." *Current Anthropology* 57:S13–S26.

Fuentes, A., and P. Wiessner. 2016. "Reintegrating Anthropology: From Inside Out." *Current Anthropology* 57:S3–S12.

Fumagalli, M., I. Moltke, N. Grarup, F. Racimo, P. Bjerregaard, M. Jørgensen, T. Korneliussen, et al. 2015. "Greenlandic Inuit Show Genetic Signatures of Diet and Climate Adaptation." *Science* 349:1343–1347.

Gale, F., J. Hansen, and M. Jewison. 2015. "China's Demand for Agricultural Imports." USDA Economic Information Bulletin No. (EIB-136) 39, February. Washington, DC: US Department of Agriculture.

Gamble, C., J. Gowlett, and R. Dunbar. 2011. "The Social Brain and the Shape of the Paleolithic." *Cambridge Archaeological Journal* 21:115–135.

Gao, X. 2013." Paleolithic Cultures in China: Uniqueness and Divergence." *Current Anthropology* 54: S358–S370.

Gerber, P., H. Steinfeld, B. Henderson, A. Mottet, C. Opio, J. Dijkman, A. Falcucci, and G. Tempio. 2013. *Tackling Climate Change through Livestock: A Global Assessment of Emissions and Mitigation Options*. Rome: Food and Agriculture Organization.

Gewertz, D., and J. Errington J. 2010. *Cheap Meat: Flap Food Nations in the Pacific Islands*. Berkeley: University of California Press.

Global BMI Mortality Collaboration. 2016. "Body-Mass Index and All-Cause Mortality: Individual-Participant-Data Meta-Analysis of 239 Prospective Studies in Four Continents." *Lancet* 388:776–786.

Gopalan, N. 2017. "Mengniu Should Have Gone Organic." *Bloomberg News,* January 5. www.bloomberg.com/gadfly/articles/2017-01-05/china-mengniu-should-have-gone-organic.

Gould, R. 1980. *Living Archaeology*. Cambridge: Cambridge University Press.

Graeber, D. 2011. *Debt: The First 5,000 Years*. New York: Melville House.

Greenfield, H. 2010. "The Secondary Products Revolution: The Past, the Present, and the Future." *World Archaeology* 42:29–54.

Greenhalgh, S. 2008. *Just One Child: Science and Policy in Deng's China*. Berkeley: University of California Press.

Griffith, M. 2000. "Apostles of Abstinence: Fasting and Masculinity during the Progressive Era." *American Quarterly* 52:599–638.

Guillier, L., S. Duret, H.-M. Hoang, D. Flick, and L. Onrawee. 2016. "Is Food Safety Compatible with Food Waste Prevention and Sustainability of the Food Chain?" *Procedia Food Science* 7:125–128.

Guyer, J. 2004. *Marginal Gains: Monetary Transactions in Atlantic Africa*. Chicago: University of Chicago Press.

Habgood, P., and N. Franklin. 2008. "The Revolution That Didn't Arrive: A Review of Pleistocene Sahul." *Journal of Human Evolution* 55:187–222.

Haggard, S., and M. Noland. 2009. *Famine in North Korea: Markets, Aid, and Reform*. New York: Columbia University Press.

Haidle, M. 2010. "Working-Memory Capacity and the Evolution of Modern Cognitive Potential: Implications from Animal and Early Human Tool Use." *Current Anthropology* 51:S149–S166.

Hamilton, A. 1980. "Dual Social Systems, Technology, Labour and Women's Secret Rites in the Eastern Western Desert of Australia." *Oceania* 51:4–19.

Han, K. 2015. *The Vegetarian*. Translated by D. Smith. London: Portobello.

Han, K. 2016. *Human Acts*. Translated by D. Smith. London: Portobello.

Hardy, B. 2010. "Climatic Variability and Plant Food Distribution in Pleistocene Europe: Implications for Neanderthal Diet and Subsistence." *Quaternary Science Reviews* 29:662–679.

Hawkes, K. 2012. "Grandmothers and Their Consequences." *Evolutionary Anthropology* 21:189.

Hawkesworth, S., A. Dangour, D. Johnston, K. Lock, N. Poole, J. Rushton, R. Uauy, and J. Waage. 2010. "Feeding the World Healthily: The Challenge of Measuring the Effects of Agriculture on Health." *Philosophical Transactions of the Royal Society B* 365:3083–3097.

Hayes, M., E. Mietlicki-Baase, S. Kanoski, and B. De Jonghe. 2014. "Incretins and Amylin: Neuroendocrine Communication between the Gut, Pancreas and Brain in Control of Food Intake and Blood Glucose." *Annual Review of Nutrition* 34:237–260.

He, G., A. Mol, and Y. Lu. 2016. "Wasted Cities in Urbanizing China." *Environmental Development* 18:2–13.

Heath, M., and D. Petrie. 2016. "China's Economic Revolution Is Showing Up All over Australia." *Bloomberg News,* March 27. www.bloomberg.com/news/articles/2016-03-27/view-4-000-miles-from-china-shows-economic-revolution-underway.

Henry, A., A. Brooks, and D. Piperno. 2014. "Plant Foods and the Dietary Ecology of Neanderthals and Early Modern Humans." *Journal of Human Evolution* 69:44–54.

Herrero, M., and P. Thornton. 2013. "Livestock and Global Food Change: Emerging Issues for Sustainable Food Systems." *Proceedings of the National Academy of Sciences USA* 110:20878–20881.

Herrero, M., P. Havlik, H. Valin, A. Notenbaert, M. Rufino, P. Thornon, M. Blümmel, F. Weiss, D. Grace, and M. Obersteiner. 2013. "Biomass Use, Production, Feed Efficiencies, and Greenhouse Gas Emissions from Global Livestock Systems." *Proceedings of the National Academy of Sciences USA* 110:20888–20893.

Herrero, M., S. Wirsenius, B. Henderson, C. Rigolot, P. Thornton, P. Havlík, I. de Boer, and P. Gerber. 2015. "Livestock and the Environment: What Have We Learned in the Past Decade?" *Annual Review of Environment and Resources* 40:177–202.

Hess, M. 1994. "Black and Red: The Pilbara Pastoral Workers' Strike, 1946." *Aboriginal History* 18:65–83.

Hillier, B. 2007. *Space Is the Machine: A Configurational Theory of Architecture.* London: Space Syntax.

Hipsley, E., ed. 1950. *Report of the New Guinea Nutrition Survey Expedition 1947.* Canberra: Commonwealth Department of External Territories.

Ho, P. 2017. "Robot Nannies Look After 3 Million Chickens in Coops of the Future." *Bloomberg News,* January 12. www.bloomberg.com/news/articles/2017-01-12/china-tries-nanny-robots-to-keep-chickens-healthy.

Honeychurch, W. 2014. "Alternative Complexities: The Archaeology of Pastoral Nomadic States." *Journal of Archaeological Research* 22:277–326.

Honeychurch, W., and C. Makarewicz. 2016. "The Archaeology of Pastoral Nomadism." *Annual Review of Anthropology* 45:341–359.

Horowitz, R. 2006. *Putting Meat on the American Table: Taste, Technology, Transformation.* Baltimore: Johns Hopkins University Press.

Howard, P. 2016. *Concentration and Power in the Food System: Who Controls What We Eat?* London: Bloomsbury.

Howe, P., H. Mattill, and P. Hawk. 1912. "Fasting Studies: VI. Distribution of Nitrogen during a Fast of One Hundred and Seventeen Days." *Journal of Biological Chemistry* 11:103–127.

Hrdy, S. 2012. Comes the Child before the Man: Development's Role in Producing Selectable Variation." *Evolutionary Anthropology* 21:188.

Hublin, J-J. 2015. "The Modern Human Colonization of Western Eurasia: When and Where?" *Quaternary Science Reviews* 118:194–210.

Hutchinson, S. 1996. *Nuer Dilemmas: Coping with Money, War and the State.* Berkeley: University of California Press.

Ingold, T. 2000. *The Perception of the Environment: Essays on Livelihood, Dwelling and Skill.* London: Routledge.

International Institute of Refrigeration. 2009. "The Role of Refrigeration in Worldwide Nutrition." www.iifiir.org/userfiles/file/publications/notes/NoteFood_05_EN.pdf.

Isenberg, A. 2000. *The Destruction of the Bison: An Environmental History, 1750–1920.* Cambridge: Cambridge University Press.

Isler, K., and C. Van Schaik. 2014. "How Humans Evolved Large Brains: Comparative Evidence." *Evolutionary Anthropology* 23:65–75.

Jin, J., and S. Maren. 2015. "Prefrontal–Hippocampal Interactions in Memory and Emotion." *Frontiers in Systems Neuroscience* 9:170.

Jing, Y., R. Flad, and L. Yunbing. 2008. "Meat-Acquisition Patterns in the Neolithic Yangzi River Valley, China." *Antiquity* 82:351–366.

Johnson, C., S. Rule, S. Haberle, A. Kershaw, G. Merna McKenzie, and B. Brook. 2015. "Geographic Variation in the Ecological Effects of Extinction of Australia's Pleistocene Megafauna." *Ecography* 39:109–116.

Jones, J., R. Bliege Bird, and D. Bird. 2013. "To Kill a Kangaroo: Understanding the Decision to Pursue High-Risk/High-Gain Resources." *Proceedings of the Royal Society B* 280:20131210.

Kaiman, J. 2013. "China's Fast-Food Pioneer Struggles to Keep Customers Saying 'YUM!'" *Guardian*, January 4. www.theguardian.com/world/2013/jan/04/china-fast-food-pioneer.

Karasov, W., C. Martínez del Rio, and E. Caviedes-Vidal. 2011. "Ecological Physiology of Diet and Digestive Systems." *Annual Review of Physiology* 73:69–93.

Karesh, W., A. Dobson, J. Lloyd-Smith, J. Lubroth, M. Dixon, M. Bennett, S. Aldrich, et al. 2012. "Ecology of Zoonoses: Natural and Unnatural Histories." *Lancet* 380:1936–1945.

Katz, D., and S. Meller. 2014. "Can We Say What Diet Is Best for Health?" *Annual Review of Public Health* 35:83–103.

Ke, B. 2002. *Perspectives and Strategies for the Livestock Sector in China over the Next Three Decades*. Livestock Policy Discussion Paper No. 7. Rome: Food and Agriculture Organization.

Kearney, J. 2010. "Food Consumption Trends and Drivers." *Philosophical Transactions of the Royal Society B* 365:2793–2807.

Keen, I. 2006. "Constraints on the Development of Enduring Inequalities in late Holocene Australia." *Current Anthropology* 47:7–38.

Kelly, J. 1963. "The Transport of Cattle in Northern Australia." *Australian Quarterly* 35:16–31.

Kelly, J. 1971. *Beef in Northern Australia*. Canberra: Australian National University Press.

Kelso, J. 2010. "Metastable Mind." In *Cognitive Architecture: From Biopolitics to Noopolitics*, edited by D. Hauptmann and W. Neidich, 117–138. Rotterdam: 010.

Kenny, R. 2007. *The Lamb Enters the Dreaming: Nathanael Pepper and the Ruptured World*. Melbourne: Scribe.

Kim, S., and K. Park. 2016. "Hanjin Shipping Files for Court Protection after Revamp Rejected." *Bloomberg News*, August 31. www.bloomberg.com/news/articles/2016-08-31/hanjin-shipping-files-for-court-protection-after-revamp-rejected-isinaafe.

Kleiber, M. (1961) 1975. *The Fire of Life: An Introduction to Animal Energetics*. Huntington, NY: Krieger.

Kuhn, S. 2013. "Roots of the Middle Paleolithic in Eurasia." *Current Anthropology* 54: S255–S268.

Kuo, J-C., and M-C. Chen. 2010. "Developing an Advanced Multi-Temperature Joint Distribution System for the Food Cold Chain." *Food Control* 21:559–566.

Kuzawa, C. 1998. "Adipose Tissue in Infancy and Childhood: An Evolutionary Perspective." *Yearbook of Physical Anthropology* 41:177–209.

Kuzawa, C., and J. Bragg. 2012. "Plasticity in Human Life History Strategy: Implications for Contemporary Human Variation and the Evolution of the Genus *Homo*." *Current Anthropology* 53: S369–S382.

Kuzawa, C., H. Chugani, L. Grossman, L. Lipovich, O. Muzik, P. Hof, D. Wildman, C. Sherwood, W. Leonard, and N. Lange. 2014. "Metabolic Costs and Evolutionary Implications of Human Brain Development." *Proceedings of the National Academy of Sciences USA* 111:13010–13015.

Landau, R., and K. Jacoby. 2016. *V Street: 100 Globe-Hopping Plates on the Cutting Edge of Vegetable Cooking*. San Francisco: Morrow.

Lane, D., and D. Richardson. 2014. "The Active Role of Vitamin C in Mammalian Iron Metabolism: Much More Than Just Enhanced Iron Absorption!" *Free Radical Biology and Medicine* 75:69–83.

Larder, N., S. Sippel, and G. Lawrence. 2015. "Finance Capital, Food Security Narratives and Australian Agricultural Land." *Journal of Agrarian Change* 15:492–603.

Larson, G. 2011. "Genetics and Domestication: Important Questions for New Answers." *Current Anthropology* 52:S485–S495.

Larson, G., and D. Fuller. 2014. "The Evolution of Animal Domestication." *Annual Review of Ecology, Evolution, and Systematics* 45:115–136.

Laughlin, W. 1968. "Hunting: An Integrated Biobehavior System and Its Evolutionary Importance." In *Man the Hunter*, edited by R. Lee and I. DeVore, 304–320. Chicago: Aldine.

Layman, D., T. Anthony, B. Rasmussen, S. Adams, C. Lynch, G. Brinkworth, and T. Davis. 2015. "Defining Meal Requirements for Protein to Optimize Metabolic Roles of Amino Acids." *American Journal of Clinical Nutrition* 101:1330S–1338S.

Leach, H. 1999. "Intensification in the Pacific: A Critique of the Archaeological Criteria and Their Application." *Current Anthropology* 40:311–339.

Leach, H. 2003. "Human Domestication Reconsidered." *Current Anthropology* 44:349–368.

Leonard, W. 2012. "Laboratory and Field Methods for Measuring Human Energy Expenditure." *American Journal of Human Biology* 24:372–384.

Leonard, W., J. Snodgrass, and M. Robertson. 2007. "Effects of Brain Evolution on Human Nutrition and Metabolism." *Annual Review of Anthropology* 27:311–327.

Lee, A., S. Rainow, J. Tregenza, L. Tregenza, L. Balmer, S. Bryce, M. Paddy, J. Sheard, and D. Schomburgk. 2016. "Nutrition in Remote Aboriginal Communities: Lessons from Mai Wiru and the Anangu Pitjantjatjara Yankutjatjara Lands." *Australia New Zealand Journal of Public Health* 40:S81–S88.

Lee, R., and I. DeVore. 1968. "Problems in the Study of Hunter-Gatherers." In *Man the Hunter*, edited by R. Lee and I. DeVore, 3–12. Chicago: Aldine.

Lewis, J., and S. Harmand. 2016. "An Earlier Transition for Stone Tool Making: Implications for Cognitive Evolution and the Transition to *Homo*." *Philosophical Transactions of the Royal Society B* 371:20150233.

Li, T. 2015. Transnational Farmland Investment: A Risky Business." *Journal of Agrarian Change* 15:560–568.

Liao, C., Y. Tan, C. Wu, S. Wang, C. Yu, W. Cao, W. Gao, J. J. Lv, and L. Li. 2016. "City Level of Income and Urbanization and Availability of Food Stores and Food Service Places in China." *PLoS One* 11(3):e0148745.

Liu, Y., Y. Hu, and Q. Wei. 2013. "Early to Late Pleistocene Human Settlements and the Evolution of lithic Technology in the Nihewan Basin, North China: A Macroscopic Perspective." *Quaternary International* 295:204–214.

Lu, C., M. Black, and L. Richter. 2016. "Risk of Poor Development in Young Children in Low-Income and Middle-Income Countries: An Estimation and Analysis at the Global, Regional, and Country Level." *Lancet Global Health* 4:e916–e922.

Lusk, G. 1906. *The Elements of the Science of Nutrition*. Philadelphia: Saunders.

Ma, J., M. Karlsen, M. Chung, P. Jacques, R. Saltzman, C. Smith, C. Fox, and N. McKeown. 2016. "Potential Link between Excess Added Sugar Intake and Ectopic Fat: A Systematic Review of Randomized Controlled Trials." *Nutrition Reviews* 74:18–32.

McArthur, M. 1960. "Food Consumption and Dietary Levels of the Aborigines at the Settlements." In *Records of the American–Australian Scientific Expedition to Arnhem Land*, vol. 2, *Anthropology and Nutrition*, edited by C. Mountford, 14–26. Melbourne: Melbourne University Press.

McCarthy, F., and M. McArthur. 1960. "The Food Quest and the Time Factor in Aboriginal Economic Life." In *Records of the American–Australian Scientific Expedition to Arnhem Land*, vol. 2, *Anthropology and Nutrition*, edited by C. Mountford, 145–194. Melbourne: Melbourne University Press.

McCay, D. 1912. *The Protein Element in Nutrition*. London: Edward Arnold.

McClure, S. 2015. "The Pastoral Effect: Niche Construction, Domestic Animals, and the Spread of Farming in Europe." *Current Anthropology* 56:901–910.

McClure, S., L. Molina Balaguer, and J. Bernabeu Auban. 2008. "Neolithic Rock Art in Context: Landscape History and the Transition to Agriculture in Mediterranean Spain." *Journal of Anthropological Archaeology* 27:326–337.

Macholdt, E., V. Lede, C. Barbieri, S. Mpoloka, H. Chen, M. Slatkin, B. Pakendorf, and M. Stoneking. 2014. "Tracing Pastoralist Migrations to Southern Africa with Lactase Persistence Alleles." *Current Biology* 24:875–879.

Mack, M., P. Dittmer, M. Veigt, M. Kus, U. Nehmiz, and J. Kreyenschmidt. 2014. "Quality Tracing in Meat Supply Chains." *Philosophical Transactions of the Royal Society A* 372:20130308.

Malhi, Y., C. Doughty,M. Galetti, F. Smith, J-C. Svenning, and J. Terborgh. 2016. "Megafauna and Ecosystem Function from the Pleistocene to the Anthropocene." *Proceedings of the National Academy of Sciences USA* 113:838–846.

Marche, S. 2016. "The Obama Years." *Los Angeles Review of Books,* November 30. lareviewofbooks.org/article/the-obama-years/.

Marom, N., and G. Bar-Oz. 2013. "The Prey Pathway: A Regional History of Cattle (*Bos taurus*) and Pig (*Sus scrofa)* Domestication in the Northern Jordan Valley, Israel." *PLoS One* 8(2): e55958.

Martens, C., and D. Seals. 2016. "Practical Alternatives to Chronic Calorie Restriction for Optimizing Vascular Function with Ageing." *Journal of Physiology* 594:7177–7195.

Maslin, M., and B. Christensen B. 2007. "Tectonics, Orbital Forcing, Global Climate Change, and Human Evolution in Africa." *Journal of Human Evolution* 53:443–464.

Mason, J., R. Hay, J. Holt, J. Seaman, and M. Bowden. 1974. "Nutritional Lessons from the Ethiopian Drought." *Nature* 248:647–650.

Maxwell, S., R. Fuller, T. Brooks, and J. Watson. 2016. "The Ravages of Guns, Nets and Bulldozers." *Nature* 536:143–145.

Mekonnen, M., and A. Hoekstra. 2012. "A Global Assessment of the Water Footprint of Farm Animal Products." *Ecosystems* 15:401–415.

Meltzer, D. 2015. "Pleistocene Overkill and North American Mammalian Extinctions." *Annual Review of Anthropology* 44:33–53.

Mengoni Goñalons, G. 2008. "Camelids in Ancient Andean Societies: A Review of the Zooarchaeological Evidence." *Quaternary International* 185:59–68.

Merlan, F. 2005. "Indigenous Movements in Australia." *Annual Review of Anthropology* 34:473–494.

Milanovic, B. 2016. *Global Inequality: A New Approach for the Age of Globalization.* Cambridge, MA: Harvard University Press.

Miller, V., S. Yusuf, C. Chow, M. Dehghan, D. Corsi, K. Lock, B. Popkin, et al. 2016. "Availability, Affordability, and Consumption of Fruits and Vegetables in 18 Countries across Income Levels: Findings from the Prospective Urban Rural Epidemiology (PURE) Study." *Lancet Global Health* 4:e695–e703.

Milton, K. 1999. " Hypothesis to Explain the Role of Meat-Eating in Human Evolution." *Evolutionary Anthropology* 8:11–21.

Minter, A. 2015. "Fast Food Loses Its Sizzle in China." *Bloomberg News,* October 22. www.bloomberg.com/view/articles/2015-10-22/u-s-fast-food-chains-lose-their-sizzle-in-china.

Mintz, S. 1985. *Sweetness and Power: The Place of Sugar in Modern History.* New York: Penguin.

Mitchell, T. 2011. *Carbon Democracy: Political Power in the Age of Oil.* London: Verso.

Moeller, A., Y. Li, E. Ngole, S. Ahuka-Mundeke, E. Lonsdorf, A. Pusey, M. Peeters, B. Hahn, and H. Ochman. 2014. "Rapid Changes in the Gut Microbiome during Human Evolution." *Proceedings of the National Academy of Sciences USA* 111:16431–16435.

Moore, S., M. O'Dea, N. Perkins, A. Barnes, and A. O'Hara. 2014. "Mortality of Live Export Cattle on Long-Haul Voyages: Pathologic Changes and Pathogens." *Journal of Veterinary Diagnostic Investigations* 26:252–265.

Muehlenbein, M. 2016. "Disease and Human/Animal Interactions." *Annual Review of Anthropology* 45:395–416.

Mulvaney, L., and J. Skerritt. 2016. "China May Purchase U.S. Beef in 2016 after 12-Year Ban." *Bloomberg News,* January 29. www.bloomberg.com/news/articles/2016-01-29/china-may-resume-u-s-beef-imports-in-2016-ending-12-year-ban.

Murdock, G. 1967. "Ethnographic Atlas: A Summary." *Ethnology* 6:109–236.

Murphy, S. 2009. "Free Trade in Agriculture: A Bad Idea Who's Time Is Done." *Monthly Review* 61(3). monthlyreview.org/2009/07/01/free-trade-in-agriculture-a-bad-idea-whose-time-is-done/.

Nadasdy, P. 2007. The Gift in the Animal: The Ontology of Hunting and Human–Animal Sociality." *American Ethnologist* 34:25–43.

Nadasdy, P. 2016. "First Nations, Citizenship and Animals, or Why Northern Indigenous People Might Not Want to Live in Zoopolis." *Comparative Studies in Society and History* 49:1–20.

Naito, Y., Y. Chikaraishi, D. Drucker, N. Ohkouchi, P. Semal, C. Wißing, and H. Bocherens. 2016. "Ecological Niche of Neanderthals from Spy Cave Revealed by Nitrogen Isotopes of Individual Amino Acids in Collagen." *Journal of Human Evolution* 93:82–90.

Nakajima, T., M. Nakajima, and T. Yamazaki. 2010. "Evidence for Fish Cultivation during the Yayoi Period in Western Japan." *International Journal of Osteoarchaeology* 20:127–134.

NaRanong, V. 2007. "Structural Changes in Thailand's Poultry Sector and Its Social Implications." In *Poultry in the 21st Century: Avian Influenza and Beyond.* Rome: Food and Agriculture Organization.

National Archives of Australia. A1658 4/1/6. "Aboriginals—General Dietary Survey—Aboriginal Settlements."

National Archives of Australia. E51 1971/1881. "Meetings on Nutrition of Aboriginal Infants and Preschool Children."

Navarrete, A., C. van Schaik, and K. Isler. 2011. "Energetics and the Evolution of Human Brain Size." *Nature* 480:91–93.

NCD Risk Factor Collaboration. 2016. "Trends in Adult Body-Mass Index in 200 Countries from 1975 to 2014: A Pooled Analysis of 1698 Population-Based Measurement Studies with 19.2 Million Participants." *Lancet* 387:1377–1396.

Neubauer, S., and J-J. Hublin. 2012. "The Evolution of Human Brain Development." *Evolutionary Biology* 39:568–586.

Ngabidj, G., and B. Shaw. 1981. *My Country of the Pelican Dreaming: The Life of an Australian Aborigine of the Gadjerong, Grant Ngabidj, 1904–1977 As Told to Bruce Shaw.* Canberra: Australian Institute of Aboriginal Studies.

Niemitz, C. 2010. "The Evolution of the Upright Posture and Gait: A Review and a New Synthesis." *Naturwissenschaften* 97:241–263.

Niezen, R. 2017. *Truth and Indignation: Canada's Truth and Reconciliation Commission on Indian Residential Schools*, 2nd ed. Toronto: University of Toronto Press.

Nowell, A. 2010. "Working Memory and the Speed of Life." *Current Anthropology* 51:S121–S133.

O'Brien, M., and K. Laland. 2012. "Genes, Culture, and Agriculture: An Example of Human Niche Construction." *Current Anthropology* 53:434–470.

Obregon-Tito, A., R. Tito, J. Metcalf , K. Sankaranarayanan, J. Clemente, L. Ursell, Z. Xu, et al. 2015. "Subsistence Strategies in Traditional Societies Distinguish Gut Microbiomes." *Nature Communications* 6:6505.

O'Connor, A. 2017. "In the Shopping Cart of a Food Stamp Household: Lots of Soda." *New York Times,* January 13. www.nytimes.com/2017/01/13/well/eat/food-stamp-snap-soda.html.

Oma Armstrong, K. 2010. "Between Trust and Dominance: Social Contracts between Humans and Animals." *World Archaeology* 42:175–187.

Ostler, J. 1996. "Conquest and the State: Why the United States Employed Massive Military Force to Suppress the Lakota Ghost Dance." *Pacific Historical Review* 65:217–248.

Ostler, J. 2001. "'The Last Buffalo Hunt' and Beyond: Plains Sioux Economic Strategies in the Early Reservation Period." *Great Plains Quarterly* 21:115–130.

Outram, A., N. Stear, R. Bendrey, S. Olsen, A. Kasparov, V. Zaibert, N. Thorpe, and R. Evershed. 2009. "The Earliest Horse Harnessing and Milking." *Science* 323:1332–1335.

Padungtod, P., M. Kadohira, and G. Hill. 2008. "Livestock Production and Foodborne Diseases from Food Animals in Thailand." *Journal of Veterinary Medicine and Science* 70:873–879.

Pachirat, T. 2011. *Every Twelve Seconds: Industrialized Slaughter and the Politics of Sight.* New Haven: Yale University Press.

Paterson, A. 2010. "Hunter-Gatherer Interactions with Sheep and Cattle Pastoralists from the Australian Arid Zone." In *Desert Peoples: Archaeological Perspectives*, edited by P. Veth, M. Smith, and P. Hiscock, 276–292. London: Wiley.

Pearson, O. 2013. "Hominin Evolution in the Middle–Late Paleolithic." *Current Anthropology* 54:S221–S233.

Pedersen, M. 2001. "Totemism, Animism, and North Asian Indigenous Ontologies." *Journal of the Royal Anthropological Institute* n.s. 7:411–427.

Pelegrin, J. 2009. "Cognition and the Emergence of Language: A Contribution from Lithic Technology." In *Cognitive Archaeology and Human Evolution*, edited by S. de Beaune, F. Coolidge, and T. Wynn, 95–108. Cambridge: Cambridge University Press.

Pelletier, N., and P. Tyedmers. 2010. "Forecasting Potential Global Environmental Costs of Livestock Production 2000–2050." *Proceedings of the National Academy of Sciences USA* 107:18371–18374.

Pew Commission on Industrial Farm Animal Production. 2008. *Putting Meat on the Table: Industrial Farm Animal Production in America.* Philadelphia: Pew Charitable Trusts.

Phillips, C., and E. Santurtun. 2013. "The Welfare of Livestock Transported by Ship." *Veterinary Journal* 196:309–314.

Phillips-Silver, J., and P. Keller. 2012. "Searching for Roots of Entrainment and Joint Action in Early Musical Interactions." *Frontiers in Human Neuroscience* 6:26.

Piketty, T. 2014. *Capital in the Twenty-First Century.* Translated by A. Goldhammer. Cambridge, MA: Harvard University Press.

Pitts, J. 2005. *A Turn to Empire: The Rise of Imperial Liberalism in Britain and France.* Princeton: Princeton University Press.

Pollan, M. 2009. "Why Bother?" In *Food, Inc.: How Industrial Food Is Making Us Sicker, Fatter and Poorer—and What You Can Do about It*, edited by K. Weber, 169–177. New York: Public Affairs.

Pontzer, H. 2012. "Ecological Energetics in Early *Homo.*" *Current Anthropology* 53: S346–S358.

Pontzer, H. 2015. "Energy Expenditure in Humans and other Primates: A New Synthesis." *Annual Review of Anthropology* 44:169–178.

Pontzer, H., D. Raichlen, A. Gordon, K. Schroepfer-Walker, B. Hare, M. O'Neill, K. Muldoon, et al. 2014. "Primate Energy Expenditure and Life History." *Proceedings of the National Academy of Sciences USA* 111:1433–1437.

Popkin, S., M. Scott, and M. Galvez. 2016. *Impossible Choices: Teens and Food Insecurity in America.* Washington, DC: Urban Institute.

Potts, R. 2012a. "Environmental and Behavioral Evidence Pertaining to the Evolution of Early *Homo.*" *Current Anthropology* 53:S299–S317.

Potts, R. 2012b. "Evolution and Environmental Change in Early Human Prehistory." *Annual Review of Anthropology* 41:151–167.

Poulsen, M., P. McNab, M. Clayton, and R. Neff. 2015. "A Systematic Review of Urban Agriculture and Food Security Impacts in Low-Income Countries." *Food Policy* 55:131–146.

Price, C., J. Weitz, V. Savage, J. Stegen, A. Clarke, D. Coomes, P. Dodds, et al. 2012. "Testing the Metabolic Theory of Ecology." *Ecology Letters* 15:1465–1474.

Provenza, F., M. Meuret, and P. Gregorini. 2015. "Our Landscapes, Our Livestock, Ourselves: Restoring Broken Linkages among Plants, Herbivores, and Humans with Diets That Nourish and Satiate." *Appetite* 95:500–519.

Raichlen, D., and J. Polk. 2013. "Linking Brains and Brawn: Exercise and the Evolution of Human Neurobiology." *Proceedings of the Royal Society B* 280:20122250.

Ravallion, M., S. Chen, and P. Sangraula. 2007. "The Urbanization of Global Poverty." *World Bank Research Digest* 1(4): 1, 8.

Read, P. 2003. "How Many Separated Aboriginal Children?" *Australian Journal of Politics and History* 49:155–163.

Reid, K. 2003. "Setting Women to Work: The Assignment System and Female Convict Labor in Van Diemen's Land, 1820–1839." *Australian Historical Studies* 34:1–25.

Roberts, A., and S. Thorpe. 2014. "Challenges to Human Uniqueness: Bipedalism, Birth and Brains." *Journal of Zoology* 292:281–289.

Roebroeks, W., and M. Soressi. 2016. "Neandertals Revised." *Proceedings of the National Academy of Sciences USA* 113:6372–6379.

Romer, P. 2016. "Trouble with Macroeconomics, Update [blog post], September 21. paulromer.net/trouble-with-macroeconomics-update/.

Rose, C. 1994. *Property and Persuasion: Essays on the History, Theory, and Rhetoric of Ownership*. Boulder, CO: Westview.

Rose, D. 1992. *Dingo Made Us Human: Life and Land in an Australian Aboriginal Culture*. Cambridge: Cambridge University Press.

Rosenberg, K. 2012. "How We Give Birth Contributes to the Rich Social Fabric That Underlies Human Society." *Evolutionary Anthropology* 21:190.

Roussel, M., M. Soressi, and J-J. Hublin. 2016. "The Châtelperronian Conundrum: Blade and Bladlet Lithic Technologies from Quinçay, France." *Journal of Human Evolution* 95:13–32.

Rowse, T. 1998. *White Flour, White Power: From Rations to Citizenship in Central Australia*. Cambridge: Cambridge University Press.

Ryan, L. 2013. "The Black Line in Van Diemen's Land: Success or Failure?" *Journal of Australian Studies* 37:1–8.

Sahlins, M. (1972) 2000. *Culture in Practice: Selected Essays*. New York: Zone.

Samman, E., ed. 2013. "Eradicating Global Poverty: A Noble Goal, But How Do We Measure It?" *Development Progress* [newsletter], June 1. London: Overseas Development Institute.

Sassen, S. 2006. *Territory, Authority, Rights: From Medieval to Global Assemblages*. Princeton: Princeton University Press.

Sassen, S. 2013. "Land Grabs Today: Feeding the Disassembling of National Territory." *Globalizations* 10:25–46.

Sattherthwaite, D. 2007. *The Transition to a Predominantly Urban World and Its Underpinnings*. London: International Institute for Environment and Development.

Sayers, K., M. Raghanti, and C. Lovejoy. 2012. "Human Evolution and the Chimpanzee Referential Doctrine." *Annual Review of Anthropology* 41:119–138.

Schieffelin, E., and R. Crittenden, eds. 1991. *Like People You See in a Dream: First Contact in Six Papuan Societies*. Stanford: Stanford University Press.

Schneider, M. 2017. "Dragon Head Enterprises and the State of Agribusiness in China." *Journal of Agrarian Change* 17:3–21.

Schneyer, J. 2011. "Commodity Traders: The Trillion Dollar Club." *Reuters*, October 28. www.reuters.com/article/us-commodities-houses-idUSTRE79R4S320111028.

Schwartz, G. 2012. "Growth, Development, and Life History throughout the Evolution of *Homo*." *Current Anthropology* 53:S395–S408.

Scott, J. 2009. *The Art of Not Being Governed: An Anarchist History of Upland Southeast Asia*. New Haven: Yale University Press.

Scott, J. 2016. "Tasmania to Get First Direct Flight to China (But Only for Milk)." *Bloomberg News,* October 26. www.bloomberg.com/news/articles/2016-10-26/tasmania-to-get-first-direct-flight-to-china-but-only-for-milk.

Sedgman, P. 2015. "Australia Signs Agreement to Feed China's Surging Cattle Demand." *Bloomberg News,* July 20. www.bloomberg.com/news/articles/2015-07-20/australia-signs-agreement-to-feed-china-s-surging-cattle-demand.

Sen, A. 1981. *Poverty and Famines: An Essay on Entitlement and Deprivation.* Oxford: Oxford University Press.

Shannon, L., R. Boyko, M. Castelhano, E. Corey, J. Hayward, C. McLean, M. White, et al. 2015. "Genetic Structure of Village Dogs Reveals a Central Asia Domestication Origin." *Proceedings of the National Academy of Sciences USA* 112:13639–13644.

Shea J. 2011. "*Homo sapiens* Is as *Homo sapiens* Was: Behavioral Variability Versus `Behavioral Modernity' in Paleolithic Archaeology." *Current Anthropology* 52:1–35.

Sheridan, T. 2007. "Embattled Ranchers, Endangered Species, and Urban Sprawl: The Political Ecology of the New American West." *Annual Review of Anthropology* 36:121–138.

Sherman, H. 1950. *The Nutritional Improvement of Life.* New York: Columbia University Press.

Shipman, P. 2010. "The Animal Connection and Human Evolution." *Current Anthropology* 51:519–538.

Skillen, J. 2008. "Closing the Public Lands Frontier: The Bureau of Land Management, 1961–1969." *Journal of Policy History* 20:419–445.

Smil, V. 2014. "Eating Meat: Constants and Changes." *Global Food Security* 3: 67–71.

Smith, B. 2001. "Low-Level Food Production." *Journal of Archaeological Research* 9:1–43.

Smith, P. 2016. "Suicide Crisis among Indigenous Australians Tests Rural Services." *British Medical Journal* 354:4652.

Smith, P., and R. Smith. 1999. "Diets in Transition: Hunter-Gatherer to Station Diet and Station Diet to the Self-Select Store Diet." *Human Ecology* 27:115–133.

Solomon, H. 2015. "`The Taste No Chef Can Give': Processing Street Food in Mumbai." *Cultural Anthropology* 30:65–90.

Song, Y., and W. Sun. 2016. "Health Consequences of Rural-to-Urban Migration: Evidence from Panel Data in China." *Health Economics* 25:1252–1267.

Specht, J. 2016. "The Rise, Fall, and Rebirth of the Texas Longhorn: An Evolutionary History." *Environmental History* 21:43–363.

Springmann, M., H. Godfray, M. Rayner, and P. Scarborough. 2016. "Analysis and Valuation of the Health and Climate Change Cobenefits of Dietary Change." *Proceedings of the National Academy of Sciences USA* 113:4146–4151.

Stanner, W. (1966) 1978. *White Man Got No Dreaming: Essays 1938–1973.* Canberra: Australian National University Press.

Starmer, E., and T. Wise. 2007. "Feeding at the Trough: Industrial Livestock Firms Saved $35 Billion from Low Feed Prices." Policy Brief No. 07–03. Cambridge, MA: Global Development and Environment Institute, Tufts University. www.ase.tufts.edu/gdae/Pubs/rp/PB07-03FeedingAtTroughDec07.pdf

Steinfeld, H., P. Gerber, T. Wassenaar, V. Castel, M. Rosales, and C. de Haan. 2006. *Livestock's Long Shadow: Environmental Issues and Options.* Rome: Food and Agriculture Organization.

Stevens, F. 1974. *Aborigines in the Northern Territory Cattle Industry.* Canberra: Australian Institute of Aboriginal Studies.

Stiner, M. 2013. "An Unshakable Middle Paleolithic? Trends versus Conservatism in the Predatory Niche and Their Social Ramifications." *Current Anthropology* 54:S288–S304.

Stiner, M., R. Barkai, and A. Gopher. 2009. "Cooperative Hunting and Meat Sharing 400–200 kya at Qesem Cave, Israel." *Proceedings of the National Academy of Sciences USA* 106:13207–13212.

Stiner, M., N, Munro, and T. Surovell T. 2000. "The Tortoise and the Hare: Small-Game Use, the Broad-Spectrum Revolution, and Paleolithic Demography." *Current Anthropology* 41:39–79.

Streeck, W. 2016. *How Will Capitalism End?* London: Verso.

Stringer, D. 2016. "China May Have a Thing or Two to Teach Australia about Wool." *Bloomberg News,* May 23. www.bloomberg.com/news/articles/2016-05-23/china-tycoon-saves-australia-lambs-to-show-perks-of-foreign-cash.

Ströhle, A., and A. Hahn. 2011. "Diets of Modern Hunter-Gatherers Vary Substantially in Their Carbohydrate Content Depending on Ecoenvironment: Results from an Ethnographic Analysis." *Nutrition Research* 31:429–435.

Tacconelli, W., and N. Wrigley. 2009. "Organizational Challenges and Strategic Responses of Retail TNCs in Post–WTO-Entry China." *Economic Geography* 85:49–73.

Tacoli, C., B. Bukhari, and S. Fisher S. 2013. *Urban Poverty, Food Security and Climate Change.* London: International Institute for Environment and Development.

Tatoian, E. 2015. "Animals in the Law: Occupying a Space between Legal Personhood and Personal Property." *Journal of Environmental Law and Litigation* 31:147–166.

Temple, D. 2010. "Patterns of Systemic Stress during the Agricultural Transition in Prehistoric Japan." *American Journal of Physical Anthropology* 142:112–124.

Terrell, J., J. Hart, S. Barut, N. Cellinese, A. Curet, T. Denham, C. Kusimba, et al. 2003. "Domesticated Landscapes: The Subsistence Ecology of Plant and Animal Domestication." *Journal of Archaeological Method and Theory* 10:323–368.

Thomas, J., Robinson L, Armitage R. 2016. "'Australian Cattle' Being Bludgeoned to Death in Vietnam Sparks Government Investigation." *ABC News,* June 16. www.abc.net.au/news/2016-06-16/australian-cattle-bludgeoned-with-sledgehammer-in-vietnam/7516326.

Thornton, P. 2010. "Livestock Production: Recent Trends, Future Prospects." *Philosophical Transactions of the Royal Society B* 365:2853–2867.

Tilman, D., and M. Clark. 2014. "Global Diets Link Environmental Sustainability and Human Health." *Nature* 515:518–522.

Tobler, R., A. Rohrlach, J. Soubrier, P. Bover, B. Llamas, J. Tuke, N. Bean, et al. 2017. "Aboriginal Mitogenomes Reveal 50,000 Years of Regionalism in Australia." *Nature* 544:180–184.

Tomasello, M. 2008. *Origins of Human Communication.* Cambridge, MA: MIT Press.

Tonkinson, R. 1974. *Aboriginal Victors of the Desert Crusade.* Menlo Park, CA: Cummings.

Tresset, A., and J-D. Vigne. 2011. "Last Hunter-Gatherers and First Farmers of Europe." *Comptes Rendues Biologies* 334:182–189.

Trut, L., I. Oskina, and A. Kharlamova. 2009. "Animal Evolution during Domestication: The Domesticated Fox as a Model." *Bioessays* 31:349–360.

Tsai, M., director. 2013. *Stray Dogs [郊遊Jiaoyou].* Homegreen Films (Taiwan), digital video.

Ungar, P. 2012. "Dental Evidence for the Reconstruction of Diet in African Early *Homo.*" *Current Anthropology* 53:S318–S329.

Ungar, P., F. Grine, and M. Teaford. 2006. "Diet in Early *Homo*: A Review of the Evidence and a New Model of Adaptive Versatility." *Annual Review of Anthropology* 35:209–228.

Ungar, P., and M. Sponheimer. 2011. "The Diets of Early Hominins." *Science* 334:190–193.

Ungar, P., and M. Sponheimer. 2013. "Hominin Diets." In *A Companion to Paleoanthropology,* edited by D. Begun, 165–182. Hoboken, NJ: Wiley.

Valerio Mendoza, O. 2016. "Preferential Policies and Income Inequality: Evidence from Special Economic Zones and Open Cities in China." *China Economic Review* 40:228–240.

Vallverdú, J., M. Vaquero, I. Cáceres, E. Allué, J. Rosell, P. Saladié, G. Chacón, et al. 2010. "Sleeping Activity Area within the Site Structure of Archaic Human Groups: Evidence from Abric Romaní Level N Combustion Activity Areas." *Current Anthropology* 51:137–145.

Vander Stichele, M. 2012. "Challenges for Regulators: Financial Players in the (Food) Commodities Derivatives Markets." SOMO Briefing Paper, November. Amsterdam: Stichting Onderzoek Multinationale Ondernemingen (Centre for Research on Multinational Corporations).

Van Wijk, M. 2014. "From Global Economic Modeling to Household Level Analyses of Food Security and Sustainability: How Big Is the Gap and Can We Bridge It?" *Food Policy* 49:378–388.

Vermeulen, S., B. Campbell, and J. Ingram. 2012. "Climate Change and Food Systems." *Annual Review of Environment and Resources* 37:195–222.

Vigne, J-D. 2011. "The Origins of Animal Domestication and Husbandry: A Major Change in the History of Humanity and the Biosphere." *Comptes Rendues Biologies* 334:171–181.

Vigne, J-D. 2015. "Early Domestication and Farming: What Should We Know or Do for a Better Understanding?" *Anthropozoologica* 50:123–150.

Vigne, J-D., and D. Helmer. 2007. "Was Milk a 'Secondary Product' in the Old World Neolithisation Process? Its Role in the Domestication of Cattle, Sheep and Goats." *Anthropozoologica* 42:9–40.

Villmoare, B., W. Kimbel, C. Seyoum, C. Campisano, W. DiMaggio, J. Rowan, D. Braun, J. Arrowsmith, and K. Reed. 2015. "Early *Homo* at 2.8 Ma from Ledi-Geraru, Afar, Ethiopia." *Science* 347:1352–1355.

Wagner, J., S. Archibeque, and D. Feuz. 2014. "The Modern Feedlot for Finishing Cattle." *Annual Review of Animal Biosciences* 2:535–554.

Walker, A., M. Zimmerman, and R. Leakey. 1982. "A Possible Case of Hypervitaminosis A in *Homo erectus*." *Nature* 296:248–250.

Wang, C., G. Wan, and D. Yang. 2014. "Income Inequality in the People's Republic of China: Trends, Determinants, and Proposed Remedies." *Journal of Economic Surveys* 28:686–708.

Wang, E. 2011. "Understanding the 'Retail Revolution' in Urban China: A Survey of Retail Formats in Beijing." *Services Industry Journal* 31:169–194.

Ward, P. 2016. "Transient Poverty, Poverty Dynamics, and Vulnerability to Poverty: An Empirical Analysis Using a Balanced Panel from Rural China." *World Development* 78:541–553.

Warinner, C., and C. Lewis. 2015. "Microbiome and Health in Past and Present Human Populations." *American Anthropologist* 117:740–741.

Waterlow, J. 1986. "Metabolic Adaptation to Low Intakes of Energy and Protein." *Annual Review of Nutrition* 6:495–526.

Weaver, J. 1996. "Beyond the Fatal Shore: Pastoral Squatting and the Occupation of Australia, 1826 to 1852." *American Historical Review* 101:981–1007.

Webster, P. 2016. "Canada's Indigenous Suicide Crisis." *Lancet* 387:2494.

Weigel, M. 2016. "Slow Wars." *n+1* 25. nplusonemag.com/issue-25/essays/slow-wars/.

Weis, T. 2013. "The Meat of the Global Food Crisis." *Journal of Peasant Studies* 40:65–85.

Weise, K. 2015. "Inside Queensland's Brutal Cattle Cull." *Bloomberg News*. www.bloomberg.com/features/2015-global-drought-stories/#australia.

Weiss, L., E. Thurbon, and J. Mathews. 2006. "Free Trade in Mad Cows: How to Kill a Beef Industry." *Australian Journal of International Affairs* 60:376–399.

Wellesley, L., C. Happer, and A. Froggat. 2015. *Changing Climate, Changing Diets: Pathways to Lower Meat Consumption*. London: Chatham House.

Weyrich, L., S. Duchene, J. Soubrier, L. Arriola, B. Llamas, J. Breen, A. Morris, et al. 2017. "Neanderthal Behaviour, Diet, and Disease Inferred from Ancient DNA in Dental Calculus." *Nature* 544:357–361.

White, R. 1983. *The Roots of Dependency: Subsistence, Environment, and Social Change among the Choctaws, Pawnees, and Navajos*. Lincoln: University of Nebraska Press.

White, S. 2011. "From Globalized Pig Breeds to Capitalist Pigs: A Study in Animal Cultures and Evolutionary History." *Environmental History* 16:94–120.

Whitley, A. 2015. "The Real Cattle Class: Cows Fly to China on 747s." *Bloomberg News,* November 8. www.bloomberg.com/news/articles/2015-11-08/the-real-cattle-class-747-full-of-cows-feeds-china-beef-craving.

Whitley, A. 2016. "China's Money Could Help Kill Two Cows Every Minute in Australia." *Bloomberg News,* March 29. www.bloomberg.com/news/articles/2016-03-29/china-s-money-could-help-kill-two-cows-every-minute-in-australia.

Wiessner, P. 2014. "Embers of Society: Firelight Talk among the Ju/'hoansi Bushmen. *Proceedings of the National Academy of Sciences USA* 111:14027–14035.

Wild, R., and P. Anderson. 2007. *Ampe Akelyernemane Meke Mekarle: "Little Children Are Sacred."* Report of the Northern Territory Board Inquiry into the Protection of Aboriginal Children from Sexual Abuse. Darwin: Northern Territory Government.

Wiley, A. 2007. "The Globalization of Cow's Milk Production and Consumption: Biocultural Perspectives." *Ecology of Food and Nutrition* 46:281–312.

Willerslev, R., P. Vitebsky, and A. Alekseyev. 2014. "Sacrifice as the Ideal Hunt: A Cosmological Explanation for the Origin of Reindeer Domestication." *Journal of the Royal Anthropological Association.* n.s. 21:1–23.

Wilson, P. 1988. *The Domestication of the Human Species.* New Haven: Yale University Press.

Wilson, W. 1951a. *Dietary Survey of Aboriginals in the Northern Territory.* Canberra: Commonwealth Department of Health.

Wilson, W. 1951b. *Dietary Survey of Aboriginals in Western Australia, 1951.* Canberra: Commonwealth Department of Health.

Woodburn, J. 1982. "Egalitarian Societies." *Man.* n.s. 17:431–451.

Wrangham, R., J. Jones, G. Laden, D. Pilbeam, and N. Conklin-Brittain. 1999. "The Raw and the Stolen: Cooking and the Ecology of Human Origins." *Current Anthropology* 40:567–594.

Wright, W., and S. Muzzatti. 2007. "Not in My Port: The 'Death Ship' of Sheep and Crimes of Agri-Food Globalization." *Agriculture and Human Values* 24:133–145.

Wroe, S., J. Field, M. Archer, D. Grayson, G. Price, J. Louys, J. Faith, G. Webb, I. Davidson, and S. Mooney. 2013. "Climate Change Frames Debate over the Extinction of Megafauna in Sahul (Pleistocene Australia–New Guinea)." *Proceedings of the National Academy of Sciences USA* 110:8777–8781.

Wurgaft, B. 2019. *Meat Planet: Artificial Flesh and the Futures of Food.* Berkeley: University of California Press.

Wurz, S. 2013. "Technological Trends in the Middle Stone Age of South Africa between MIS 7 and MIS 3." *Current Anthropology* 54:S305–S319.

Wynn, T., and F. Coolidge. 2010. "Beyond Symbolism and Language." *Current Anthropology* 51:S5–S16.

Xie, R., C. Sabel, X. Lu, W. Zhu, H. Kan, C. Nielsen, and H. Wang. 2016. "Long-Term Trend and Spatial Pattern of $PM_{2.5}$ Induced Premature Mortality in China." *Environment International* 97:180–186.

Xu, X., L. Han, and X. Lu. 2016. "Household Carbon Inequality in Urban China, Its Sources and Determinants." *Ecological Economics* 128:77–86.

Yang, J., and M. Qiu. 2016. "The Impact of Education on Income Inequality and Intergenerational Mobility." *China Economic Review* 37:110–125.

Yang, P. 2016. "The History of the Shanghai Containerized Freight Index (SCFI)." *Flexport Blog*. www.flexport.com/blog/shanghai-containerized-freight-index-scfi-history/.

Yao, S., D. Luo, and J. Wang. 2014. "Housing Development and Urbanization in China." *World Economy* 37:481–500.

Yuan, H. 2016. "China Eats So Much Pork These Feed Producers Became Billionaires." *Bloomberg News*, May 11. www.bloomberg.com/news/articles/2016-05-11/china-eats-so-much-pork-these-feed-producers-became-billionaires.

Zappia, N. 2016. "Revolutions in the Grass: Energy and Food Systems in Continental North America, 1763–1848." *Environmental History* 21:30–53.

Zeder, M. 2012. "The Domestication of Animals." *Journal of Anthropological Research* 68:161–190.

Zeder, M. 2016. "Domestication as a Model System for Niche Construction Theory." *Evolutionary Ecology* 30:325–348.

Zezza, A., and L. Tasciotti. 2010. "Urban Agriculture, Poverty, and Food Security: Empirical Evidence from a Sample of Developing Countries." *Food Policy* 35:265–273.

Zhang, C. 2015. "Income Inequality and Access to Housing: Evidence from China." *China Economic Review* 36:261–271.

Zhang, J., G. Harbottle, C. Wang, and Z. Kong. 1999. "Oldest Playable Musical Instruments Found at Jiahu Early Neolithic Site in China." *Nature* 401:366–368.

Zhang, Z., and X. Wu. 2017. "Occupational Segregation and Earnings Inequality: Rural Migrants and Local Workers in China." *Social Science Research* 61:57–74.

Zhuang, Y. 2015. "Neolithisation in North China: Landscape and Geoarchaeological Perspectives." *Environmental Archaeology* 20:251–264.

Zilio, C. 2014. "Moving toward Sustainability in Refrigeration Applications for Refrigerated Warehouses." *HVAC&R Research* 20:1–2.

Index

Page numbers in italic refer to tables.